SOUTHERN STEAM
JANUARY – JULY 1967

SOUTHERN STEAM JANUARY – JULY 1967

Countdown to Extinction

Alan J Goodwin

PEN & SWORD
TRANSPORT

First published in Great Britain in 2018 by
PEN & SWORD TRANSPORT
An imprint of
Pen & Sword Books Ltd
Yorkshire - Philadelphia

ISBN 978 1 47389 113 5

Typeset in Aura Technology and Software Services, India.
Printed and bound in China by Imago Publishing Ltd.

Pen & Sword Books Ltd incorporates the Imprints of Aviation, Atlas, Family History, Fiction, Maritime, Military, Discovery, Politics, History, Archaeology, Select, Wharncliffe Local History, Wharncliffe True Crime, Military Classics, Wharncliffe Transport, Leo Cooper, The Praetorian Press, Remember When, Seaforth Publishing and Frontline Publishing.

For a complete list of Pen & Sword titles please contact

PEN & SWORD BOOKS LTD
47 Church Street, Barnsley, South Yorkshire, S70 2AS, England
E-mail: enquiries@pen-and-sword.co.uk
Website: www.pen-and-sword.co.uk

Or
PEN AND SWORD BOOKS
1950 Lawrence Rd, Havertown, PA 19083, USA
E-mail: Uspen-and-sword@casematepublishers.com
Website: www.penandswordbooks.com

Contents

Introduction

I have to confess to a strong bias towards Southern steam. I was born in Dover in 1951, about as far on the Southern from any other region as you can get. I grew up in a world with an array of different locomotive types: 'P', 'C' and 'O1' 0-6-0s; pre-grouping 4-4-0s; Brighton built Fairburn tanks; 'N' Class 2-6-0s; 'King Arthurs'; 'Schools'; 4-4-0s and of course Bulleid 'Pacifics'.

My father was an old school friend of one of the running foreman at Dover loco shed. In what must have been the autumn of 1957 we visited the depot and I was given a footplate ride from the shed to the turntable and back on the newly rebuilt *Barnstaple*. I think that from that moment onwards I was hooked. At around that time the rest of the first fifteen rebuilt 'West Countries' started to appear, with names like *Okehampton*, *Clovelly* and *Budleigh Salterton* that sounded impossibly exotic to a six year old.

Fast forward to the beginning of 1966 when, with a group of friends, I started travelling to London to see what remained of steam; at first just to Waterloo and then further afield when I had the money from the usual schoolboy paper round. Unfortunately, owing to cost and distance, we still only managed a dozen or so trips between then and early May 1967.

Why stop in May? At first there was the small matter of 'O' levels to negotiate, and after these had finished in mid-June I was convinced that nothing much would be happening in the last few weeks – little did I know!

On Monday, 5 August 1968, the day after regular steam on British Railways ended, I joined the railway as a Traction Trainee and qualified as a train driver in 1975. I retired in 2011, spending all except five of those forty-three years on the Southern region. Did I happen to mention that I had a leaning towards the Southern?

The year 1967 was just one in a decade of great change. By New Year's Eve we had seen alterations to:

International boundaries – At the end of the Six Day War, the Israelis had annexed the Golan Heights and the West Bank, a dispute that rumbles on to this day.

Morality (legally at least) – The British Parliament voted to decriminalise male homosexuality between consenting adults, and later in the year to allow abortion in certain circumstances.

The way we listen to music - On Monday 14 August the Marine etc. Broadcasting (Offences) act came into force, making pirate radio stations illegal and paving the way for the introduction of BBC Radio One at the end of September. I can vividly recall siting in my friend's front room listening to the final hour of 'Wonderful Radio London' and casting aspersions on the government of the day. As the final note of The Beatles' *A Day in the Life* sounded just before three in the afternoon another era came to an end.

Talking of the Beatles, *Sergeant Pepper's Lonely Hearts Club Band*, with its heavy use of strings and sound effects, probably caused a change in the direction of music and paved the way for the progressive rock of the following years.

Deference – The 'Summer of Love' hastened the decline in deference to authority and our elders.

Bank Holidays – The August Bank Holiday was moved from the first to the last Monday of the month and renamed the Late Summer Bank Holiday.

The pound in our pockets – As a result of the widening trade gap, low UK productivity and a sharp rise in unemployment, on 19 November the government devalued the pound by 14%, changing the conversion rate from £1 = $2.8 to $2.4.

And finally, of course, the withdrawal of the last steam locomotives on the Southern Region main line.

A lot has already been written about the final years of Southern steam and indeed there have been other books on the subject this past year. This book is meant to be an accompaniment to the others by contributing detailed information of the final workings. Inevitably there will be some old ground covered, but by concentrating on the final months I hope to keep this to a minimum.

I started this exercise in 1992 to try to complete the matrix of the final week in John Bird's 'Waterloo Sunset' supplement in *Steam Railway* magazine. Later on I thought that it might be interesting to expand that to the four weeks of the interim timetable, and then finally to include what would have been the final week (5 to 11 June), especially as there was so much steam activity on Saturday 10 June: truly steam's last weekend fling. I find it interesting now to look back and see just how the railway managed to keep the last steam locomotives going in those final weeks.

So now I have to state that absolutely everything recorded in this book concerning the last five weeks is the result of observations by other people who have kindly given me access to their records. I have cross checked everything as far as possible, but where there are gaps in the workings any mistakes in the detective work are purely mine. As there are still some gaps in the records my research is an ongoing process. If any reader can add or amend any observations please feel free to contact me via the publisher.

Also, I have endeavoured to obtain permission to use or obtain copyright for all the photographs in this book. However, for some of those credited to *Author's collection – photographer unknown* this has not been possible. If anyone's pictures have been reproduced without acknowledgement please contact me via the publisher to arrange reimbursement of copyright fee.

CHAPTER ONE

January to March 1967

On Monday 2 January 1967, new locomotive diagrams were issued by the South-Western division of the Southern region (a 'diagram' being the work allocated to a particular locomotive for a day). The 'Brush Type 4' diesel locomotives gained much more work, including the *Bournemouth Belle*, and steam was reduced to thirteen diagrammed departures from Waterloo on weekdays, three of which were on the early morning paper trains. All this was unknown to my friends and I however, as we set out from home on that day for a trip to Southampton and Eastleigh shed. As it turned out, we had all the elements of the next six months in one day.

Our intention was to take the 10.30 to Southampton, and we arrived at Waterloo to find a filthy rebuilt 'Light Pacific' 34104 *Bere Alston* at the head of the train. The locomotive just managed to keep time to Hampton Court Junction, but soon after that it became apparent that something was not right. By Woking, passed four minutes late, we were down to 45 miles per hour. A full six minutes were taken from there to pass Brookwood, where speed was only 35 mph, and the inevitable happened when the train came to a halt on the down main line at Farnborough.

The driver used the signal post telephone, we guessed to request a replacement locomotive at Basingstoke. The three minute stop was

'Merchant Navy Pacific' 35028 *Clan Line* waits to leave Waterloo with the 13.30 train to Weymouth. Thursday 26 January 1967. (*Jim Blake*)

Rebuilt 'West Country' 34047 *Callington* stands on the repair road at Bournemouth shed. The locomotive would be out of action for the next four weeks. Sunday 12 February 1967. (*Dick Manton*)

Standard Class '4' 2-6-0 No. 76011 also appears to be receiving attention inside Bournemouth shed. Sunday 12 February 1967. (*Dick Manton*)

Moving to the right we can see that 'Merchant Navy' 35013 *Blue Funnel* is stabled on the next road to 76011. Sunday 12 February 1967. (*Dick Manton*)

Moving outside Bournemouth shed, Standard Class '5' 4-6-0 No. 73155 stands on the 'back road'. The locomotive is sporting its red Ron Cover 'soup tin' number plate and a painted shed code plate. Sunday 12 February 1967. (*Dick Manton*)

Standard Class '4' 2-6-0 No. 76006 calls at Weybridge with the 11.05 vans from Waterloo to Basingstoke. Tuesday 14 February 1967. (*Keith Lawrence*)

enough to allow the boiler pressure to recover a little, and we eventually arrived at Basingstoke an hour and twenty minutes from Waterloo. *Bere Alston* was uncoupled from the train, but it was not finished yet! After moving forward it stopped again for a couple of minutes, right on the points and blocked the replacement locomotive from reaching the train.

Leaving Basingstoke half an hour after we should have passed through, now behind a respectable looking Standard '5' 4-6-0 No. 73110

Standard Class '4' 2-6-4T No. 80145 carriage shunting at Waterloo. Thursday 16 February 1967. (*Jim Blake*)

'Battle of Britain Pacific' *34077 603 Squadron* rests at Waterloo having arrived with the 09.24 from Bournemouth. The driver appears to be checking a lubricator and the fact that a safety valve is lifting was probably mentioned in dispatches! Tuesday 21 February 1967. (*Jim Blake*)

The Red Knight, it was full regulator wherever possible. After touching 80 mph at Popham Down tunnels, the brakes were slammed on for a long 20 mphr permanent way speed restriction just south of Micheldever station. There was time for speed to recover into the 70s again before the slow approach to Southampton, and despite the speed restriction the locomotive had only lost a further four minutes – it had been a magical run.

34104	2 January 1967		Load 10 = c.350t	
Distance (miles)			Time (mins/secs)	Speed (mph)
0.00	WATERLOO	dep	00.00	
1.35	VAUXHALL		04.10	34
2.65	QUEENS ROAD		06.07	48
3.90	CLAPHAM JUNCTION		07.50	40
7.20	WIMBLEDON		12.05	51
8.65	RAYNES PARK		13.40	55
9.75	NEW MALDEN		14.58	58
11.00	BERRYLANDS		16.11	62
12.05	SURBITON		17.25	55
14.40	ESHER		20.05	52
15.90	HERSHAM		21.50	54
17.05	WALTON-on-THAMES		23.05	56
19.15	WEYBRIDGE		25.35	47
20.40	BYFLEET AND NEW HAW		27.14	48

34104	2 January 1967		Load 10 = c.350t	
Distance (miles)			Time (mins/secs)	Speed (mph)
21.65	WEST BYFLEET		28.50	46
24.35	WOKING		32.28	45
28.00	BROOKWOOD		38.27	35
33.25	FARNBOROUGH (Three minute stop)	arr	47.35	
33.25	FARNBOROUGH	dep	50.35	
36.50	FLEET		56.20	50
39.85	WINCHFIELD		60.15	53
42.20	HOOK		63.25	42
47.80	BASINGSTOKE	arr	71.35	
73110				
Distance (miles)			Time (mins/secs)	Speed (mph)
00.00	BASINGSTOKE	dep	00.00	
08.45	Roundwood Signal Box		13.06	55/80
10.30	MICHELDEVER (20 mph PWS for one mile after station)		15.20	40 20
14.00	Wallers Ash		21.30	50
18.80	WINCHESTER		25.40	75
21.90	SHAWFORD		28.18	68
25.75	EASTLEIGH		31.43	66
27.20	SO'TON AIRPORT P'WAY		33.05	60
28.00	SWAYTHLING		33.58	57
29.45	ST. DENYS		35.28	58
30.40	Northam Junction.		36.45	25
31.45	SOUTHAMPTON CENTRAL	arr	39.50	

After visiting Eastleigh depot a discussion ensued as to whether we should go back to Southampton to catch the fast to Waterloo or take the 12.59 semi-fast from Bournemouth back to London. As the latter train had frequently produced an original Bulleid 'Pacific' in the past it was decided to catch that one. Of course, it was hauled by a Brush diesel – my only recollection of the journey was leaning out of a front carriage window as we rounded the curves after Vauxhall, only to find half a can of cold tea heading towards me from the cab window!

There is a postscript to this tale. Whereas *Bere Alston* lasted until late May and put in some fine performances, *The Red Knight* succumbed after only three more weeks in traffic. It shows how unpredictable things were becoming in those last months of Southern steam.

Following this trip we turned our attention to the delightful Lymington branch, managing to visit three times before steam haulage finished forever. We travelled behind both Ivatt and Standard tanks, and the sprightly run across the New Forest, followed by the short

Standard Class '5' 4-6-0 No. 73117 *Vivien* leaves Salisbury, probably with the 14.36 to Waterloo. 'Warship' diesel–hydraulic 'Type 4' D830 *Majestic* stands in the loop with a freight. Tuesday 21 February. (*Dave Mant*)

'Battle of Britain Pacific' 34087 *145 Squadron* leaves Waterloo with the 13.30 to Weymouth. Friday 24 February 1967. (*Jim Blake*)

crawl across Lymington harbour to the pier station is something that lives long in the memory.

On one of these visits, I had walked to the head shunt at Lymington pier to take a photograph and was more than a little put out to see that my two friends had been granted a ride in the cab while the locomotive was running round the train. I was at the other end waiting for them and as they got out of the cab I asked the driver if I could come in. The reply was: 'You can have a cab ride up the branch if you like Son.' Bliss!

Also, on another of these trips, I had my best run behind steam from Southampton to Waterloo. After a slow start, 'West Country Pacific' 34093 *Saunton,* with a load of ten coaches, was handled with consummate skill to convert a fifteen minute late departure into an almost on-time arrival at Waterloo, without exceeding eighty miles per hour anywhere and scrupulously adhering to all speed restrictions.

34093	18 February 1967	Load 10 = 370t		
Distance (miles)		Time (mins/secs)	Speed (mph)	
0.00	SOUTHAMPTON CENT dep	00.00		
1.05	Northam Junction	03.45	15	
2.10	ST DENYS	06.20	32	
3.50	SWAYTHLING	09.00	35	
4.40	SOUTHAMPTON AIRPORT	10.25	35	
5.85	EASTLEIGH	12.20	45	
6.70	Allbrook Junction	13.20	52	
9.65	SHAWFORD	16.30	56	
12.80	WINCHESTER	19.40	60	
14.70	Winchester Junction	21.46	62	
17.50	Wallers Ash	24.17	64	
21.20	MICHELDEVER	27.53	60	
23.50	Roundwood signal box	30.00	62	
26.70	Wooton	33.01	70	
29.00	Worting Junction	35.13	60	
31.50	BASINGSTOKE	37.45	65	
37.10	HOOK	42.36	74	
39.45	WINCHFIELD	44.40	70	
42.80	FLEET	47.22	77	

34093	18 February 1967	Load 10 = 370t		
Distance (miles)		Time (mins/secs)	Speed (mph)	
46.05	FARNBOROUGH	50.05	72	
48.30	MP 31(Summit)	51.57	70	
51.30	BROOKWOOD	54.24	73	
54.95	WOKING	57.50	70	
57.65	WEST BYFLEET	60.02	78	
58.90	BYFLEET & NEW HAW	61.00	80	
60.15	WEYBRIDGE	62.05	78	
62.15	WALTON-on-THAMES	63.45	75	
63.30	HERSHAM	64.38	78	
64.80	ESHER	65.55	72	
66.00	Hampton Court Junction	66.48	72	
67.25	SURBITON	67.55	70	
68.30	BERRYLANDS	69.43	30	PWS
69.55	NEW MALDEN	71.08	55	
70.65	RAYNES PARK	72.22	57	
72.10	WIMBLEDON	73.50	60	
73.75	EARLSFIELD	75.35	60	
75.40	CLAPHAM JUNCTION	77.35	40/50	
77.95	VAUXHALL	81.20	45	
79.25	WATERLOO arr	83.50		

On all of these days out, like a lot of other enthusiasts, what we really wanted to see were the remaining original Bulleid 'Pacifics'. Sightings were becoming rare given that there were only seven left at the beginning of 1967, and when we did see one it was usually standing spare or on a special boat train.

As far as I can ascertain, this is what happened to those that fell by the wayside in the first three months of the year:

34002 – Withdrawn at the end of March, *Salisbury* actually only just made it into 1967, its last recorded working being the 07.05 Basingstoke to Waterloo on Wednesday 4 January. It was then kept at Nine Elms for repairs to the trailing driving axle but never worked again.

Nearing journey's end, 'Battle-of-Britain Pacific' 34087 *145 Squadron* attracts plenty of attention as it rounds the curve at Clapham Junction. A Standard Class '4' 2-6-4T, possibly 80012, stands at the exit from the sidings. Saturday 25 February. (*Ernie's Railway Archive*)

34019 – Withdrawn week ending 19 March, the last recorded working for *Bideford* was Nine Elms 136 diagram on Wednesday 22 February: the 08.35 Waterloo to Weymouth and the 15.50 return. On arrival at Nine Elms it was taken out of service with a condemned firebox. This loco seems to have led a somewhat charmed life towards the end. Its availability from the beginning of 1967 was certainly poor, seventeen days out of a possible fifty-two, and six of those were standing spare!

Standard Class '4' 2-6-0 No. 76067 rests on Salisbury shed. The loco was a regular on the weekday Salisbury to Portsmouth van train at the time. Sunday 26 February 1967. (*Jim Blake*)

34006 – Also withdrawn week ending 19 March, there was a premier job for *Bude* on its last day, Friday 24 February. It worked the down *Bournemouth Belle*, part of a 'Brush Type 4' diagram, and was then changed over to the second part of Salisbury 461 duty. This involved working the 17.42 from Bournemouth to Eastleigh, a local freight to Southampton Docks, then setting out with the 00.54 Eastleigh to Weymouth the following day. Unfortunately the loco failed at Brockenhurst, and on being replaced returned to Eastleigh light engine. On Saturday 4 March it was sent light engine from there to its home shed, Salisbury, for further repairs, but did not work again.

A regular performer on the main line until the end of October 1966, *Bude* seems to have been kept on light duties for most of the time after that. Perhaps it was the effort of working the *Bournemouth Belle* that finished it off.

Of the three remaining unmodified locomotives, only two, *Biggin Hill* and *Lapford*, were in regular use during the first three months of the year. There was little to be seen of *Blackmore Vale*, as it spent most of the time at Guildford shed undergoing repairs and examination.

The interloper! Standard Class '3' 2-6-0 No. 77014 hauls the breakdown train back towards Guildford and home. Sunday 26 February 1967. (*Keith Lawrence*)

Standard Class '5' 4-6-0 No. 73119 *Elaine*, backs out of Waterloo after arriving with the 08.46 from Bournemouth. The large BR1F tender dominates the photograph. Tuesday 28 February 1967. (*Jim Blake*)

Two Class '5' 4-6-0 Standard locomotives stand on shed at Basingstoke. They are 73020 and 73117. Photo taken during March 1967. (*Keith Lawrence*)

Rebuilt 'West Country' 34104 *Bere Alston* stands on the disposal pit at Nine Elms. The locomotive has just arrived after working the 11.07 train from Bournemouth to Waterloo. In the background is LNER 'K4' 2-6-0 No. 3442 *The Great Marquess*, being made ready for rail tour duty the following day. Saturday 11 March 1967. (*Dick Manton*)

Another view of *Bere Alston* at Nine Elms. This angle also gives a fine, uninterrupted view of the coaling stage. Saturday 11 March 1967. (*Dick Manton*)

Rebuilt 'West Country' 34018 *Axminster*, by now, like so many others, nameless, stands in the gloom of Nine Elms shed. A shaft of sunlight picking out the two figures on the left adds interest to the picture. Saturday 11 March 1967. (*Dick Manton*)

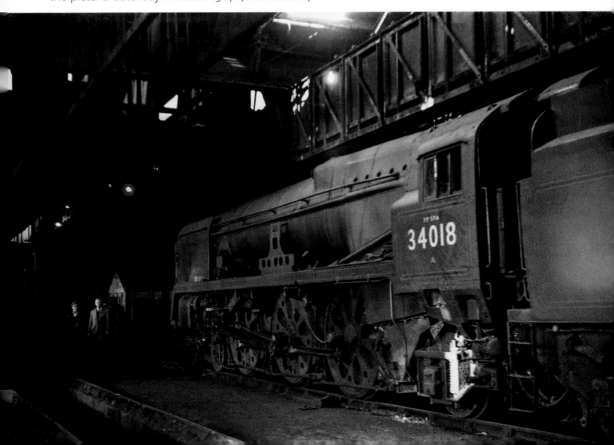

Standard Class '4' 4-6-0 No. 75075 stands inside the shed at Nine Elms. Saturday 11 March 1967. (*Dick Manton*)

Moving further in, one of the last two remaining Standard Class '3' 2-6-2 tanks, No. 82019, stands inside the shed at Nine Elms on the same day, Saturday 11 March 1967. (*Dick Manton*)

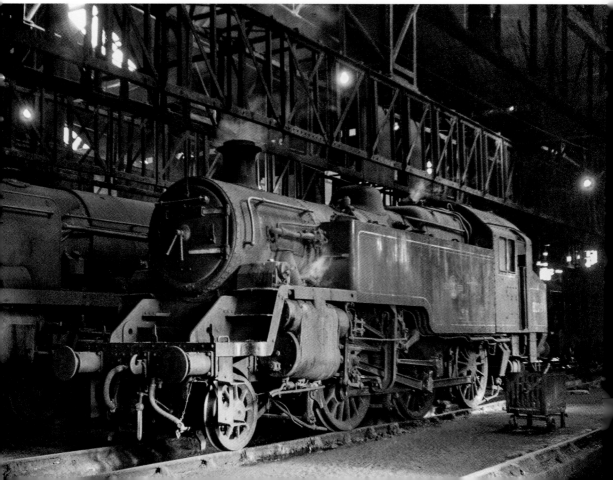

The other 'stars of the show' were, of course, the 'Merchant Navies'. Of the ten that remained at the start of the year, two were withdrawn during this period:

35026 – Although not withdrawn until the week ending 26 March, *Lamport & Holt Line* did not make it into 1967 at all. It was out of use at Weymouth from Thursday 29 December 1966 with a fractured driving wheel. Its last working is not known.

Standards Class '4' 2-6-4T No. 80154 and Class '5' 4-6-0 No. 73093 stand on one of the stores roads outside Nine Elms shed. The tank loco appears to be carrying an Exmouth Junction duty number, but this probably refers to the Nine Elms driver's duty. Saturday 11 March 1967. (*Dick Manton*)

'Merchant Navy Pacific' 35003 *Royal Mail*, substituting for a 'Brush Type 4' diesel, about to leave Waterloo with the 12.30 to Bournemouth, the all-Pullman *Bournemouth Belle*. Monday 13 March 1967. (*Jim Blake*)

Pacific 35014
Nederland Line approaches Weybridge station with the lightly loaded 06.56 Bournemouth to Waterloo, an easy job for a 'Merchant Navy Class' locomotive. Tuesday 14 March 1967. (*Keith Lawrence*)

Careworn 'Battle of Britain Pacific' 34090 *Sir Eustace Missenden – Southern Railway* rests quietly at Waterloo after arriving with the 09.24 from Bournemouth. Thursday 16 March 1967. (*Jim Blake*)

35014 – Also withdrawn week ending 26 March, *Nederland Line* was by far the most used 'Merchant Navy' for its time in traffic, working a total sixty-three days out of a possible eighty-one. The loco was last recorded as working the 15.20 relief passenger train from Waterloo to Weymouth on Thursday, 23 March, and it was withdrawn immediately.

There was a minor revision of the diagrams at the beginning of March, resulting in the loss of the 15.35 departure from Waterloo to steam haulage. It was during this month that it was realised delivery of the 'REP' electric tractor units would be late, so a decision was made to put the changeover to electric traction back to Monday 10 July.

Out in the real world, Alf Ramsey was awarded a knighthood and Bobby Moore the OBE in the New Year's honours list for their parts in England's World Cup victory the previous year. Just four days into the New Year came the tragic death of Donald Campbell on Coniston Water, while attempting to set a new world speed record on water. Who can forget the appalling sight of his boat "Bluebird" turning almost a complete somersault before plunging back into the lake, and his poignant final words, "I'm going."

On 23 January Milton Keynes was formally designated a new town, eventually swallowing up Bletchley, Wolverton, Stony Stratford and no less than fifteen smaller villages in the process.

March was notable for two contrasting pieces of energy news. On the 4th, the first North Sea gas was pumped ashore at Easington, North Yorkshire; but just two weeks later the super tanker *Torrey Canyon* ran aground on Seven Stones reef, between Land's End and the Scilly Isles. The massive oil slick that ensued spread along the south coast of England and the Normandy shore, leaving sludge in places up to a foot deep and contaminating an estimated 20,000 seabirds. The wreck was bombed by the RAF for two days until it finally sank on 30 March, and the oil slick was eventually dispersed by favourable weather.

Three Bulleid 'Pacifics' raise steam on Bournemouth shed. Left is 'Merchant Navy' 35007 *Aberdeen Commonwealth*, sporting a head code that denotes light engine to Eastleigh shed. Next is 'West Country' 34104 *Bere Alston*, and on the right is 'Merchant Navy' 35028 *Clan Line*. Photo taken during March 1967. (*Alan Hayes*)

Unmodified Bulleid 'West Country Pacific' 34015 *Exmouth* purrs through Weybridge with the 11.30 Waterloo to Bournemouth, part of Salisbury 461 diagram that would see the loco cover just over 300 miles in a day. Thursday 16 March 1967. (*Keith Lawrence*)

Rebuilt Bulleid 'Light Pacific' 34108 *Wincanton* stands at Selsdon with the 'Southern Rambler' railtour on Sunday 19 March 1967. This was the last steam hauled train to Brighton and Eastbourne, and the locomotive was the third choice to haul the train – sisters 34056 *Croydon* and 34089 *602 Squadron* being unavailable. (*Christopher Yapp*)

'Battle of Britain Pacific' 34071 *601 Squadron* waits to back on to a train at the end of the platform at Waterloo. The locomotive is carrying the head code for a boat train to Southampton Eastern Docks. Monday 20 March 1967. (*Jim Blake*)

Standard Class '3' 2-6-2 tank 82019 passes Vauxhall with empty coaches from Waterloo to Clapham Junction. Saturday 25 March 1967. (*Ernie's Railway Archive*)

A journey along the Lymington branch on Saturday 25 March 1967.

The two coach train, headed by Standard Class '4' 2-6-4 tank 80134, awaits departure from Brockenhurst with the 12.07 to Lymington Pier on Saturday 25 March 1967. The driver looks impatient to be off and with just a week of steam operation remaining on the branch perhaps he is contemplating his imminent retirement. (*David Harvey*)

The fireman of Standard Class '4' 2-6-4T No. 80134 picks up the token at Lymington Junction for the single line section to Lymington Town. The train is the 12.07 from Brockenhurst. (*David Harvey*)

A view from the carriage window as 80134 crosses the causeway between Lymington Town and Pier stations. (*David Harvey*)

No. 80134 runs round its train at Lymington Pier. (*David Harvey*)

Having run round, 80134 prepares to shunt the train into the bay platform to await the arrival of the 'Hants and Dorset Branch Flyer' rail tour, arranged by the Manchester Rail Travel Society. (*David Harvey*)

The special train approaches Lymington Pier behind sister locomotive 80151. This tour had already taken in the Fawley branch with USA 0-6-0 tank 30064, and would later go to Blandford Forum and Swanage hauled by Ivatt 2-6-2 tank 41320. (*David Harvey*)

Viewed from the bay platform, 80151 arrives at Lymington Pier. (*David Harvey*)

After the arrival of the rail tour, 80134 pulls onto the causeway with the 13.15 from Lymington Pier to Brockenhurst. (*David Harvey*)

Further up the line, the train runs through the New Forest on the way to Brockenhurst. (*David Harvey*)

Admiring looks from train spotters as 'Merchant Navy Pacific' 35028 *Clan Line* waits at Waterloo with the 13.30 train to Weymouth. Saturday 25 March 1967. (*Jim Blake*)

The author (extreme left) and friend contemplate one last trip to Lymington Pier behind Standard Class '4' 2-6-4T No. 80134. Saturday 25 March 1967. (*Dave Lennon*)

Rebuilt 'West Country' 34040 *Crewkerne* has been removed from the 10.30 Waterloo to Weymouth at Basingstoke with a hot box on the tender. The replacement loco, Standard '4' 4-6-0 No. 75077, waits in front. Easter Monday 27 March 1967. (*Alan Hayes*)

CHAPTER TWO

April and May 1967

By the end of March, sufficient electric stock had been delivered to make a large impact on the stock workings, such that a revision of the diagrams on Monday 3 April would see just seven regular steam departures from Waterloo – eight when the Channel Islands Boat Train commenced running on the 10th – with nothing at all after the

Another steam substitute on the *Bournemouth Belle*. This time it is 'West Country Pacific' 34037 *'Clovelly.'* Tuesday 4 April 1967. *(Jim Blake)*

'Battle of Britain Pacific' 34090 *Sir Eustace Missenden – Southern Railway*, backs out of Waterloo while 'West Country Pacific' 34100 *Appledore* waits to leave with the 12.43 boat train for the liner *Achille Lauro* at Southampton Eastern Docks. Wednesday 5 April 1967. *(Jim Blake)*

A Standard Class '4' 2-6-0 has run round the 17.02 Bournemouth to Wareham at the latter station, and prepares to take the empty stock back to Poole. Saturday 8 April 1967. (*Alan Hayes*)

Leaking steam from just about everywhere, 'Battle of Britain Pacific' 34090 *Sir Eustace Missenden – Southern Railway* leaves Waterloo with the *Bournemouth Belle*. At the same time, 'Warship' diesel hydraulic D815 *Druid* waits with the 13.00 to Exeter. Friday 14 April 1967. (*Jim Blake*)

08.35 Weymouth until the 17.09 to Basingstoke and Salisbury. Only the steam hauled boat trains to Southampton Docks and the tank engines on empty stock workings would break the monotony at Waterloo during the day.

It was on Monday 10 April that two of us set out from Dover with the intention of catching the 10.30 Waterloo to Southampton service. The joy of actually getting to Waterloo in time soon turned to disappointment when we saw that the service was now formed of '4-REP' No. 3003 and eight 'TC' (Trailer Control) carriages. Never mind, innocents that we were, we decided to wait for the 11.30 departure. This time it was an electro-diesel locomotive and 'TC' stock, but not wanting to waste any

'Battle of Britain Pacific' 34089 *602 Squadron*, having worked the 08.46 from Bournemouth, reverses out of Waterloo. The 4,500 gallon tender is shown to good effect. Friday 14 April 1967. (*Jim Blake*)

Standard Class '4' 2-6-0 No. 76007 basks in the spring sunshine outside Salisbury depot. Sunday 16 April 1967. (*Dave Mant*)

Standard Class '5' 4-6-0 No. 73065 stands at Bournemouth after arriving with the 11.18 from Weymouth. The train will go forward as the 12.34 to Waterloo with a different locomotive. Tuesday 18 April 1967. (*Professor Stefan Buczacki*)

more time we took it to Winchester and then a 'DEMU' to Eastleigh. At least on the way we were rewarded with a sighting of Guildford's Standard Class '3' 2-6-0 No. 77014 at Woking, the first time we had caught sight of it since April the previous year.

Standard Class '4' 4-6-0 No. 75074 with a permanent way train at Waterloo. Tuesday 18 April 1967. (*Jim Blake*)

'Merchant Navy Pacific' 35007 *Aberdeen Commonwealth* waits to work empty stock out of Waterloo. This loco was to be the last in service fitted with a second series 5,100 gallon tender, acquired from 35017 *Belgian Marine* after that loco was withdrawn. Wednesday 19 April 1967. (*Jim Blake*)

After a quick walk to Eastleigh depot we asked to visit the shed but for the first time were refused admittance. I did manage to take a couple of photographs beside the coaling stage, one of which was of Standard 2-6-4 tank 80151, beautifully clean after its rail tour duty the day before.

So then it was a short hop to Southampton Central to take our usual 15.14 to Waterloo. Oh dear, 'REP' 3003 and 'TC' stock again! It had been a very frustrating day.

One person admires 'West Country Pacific' 34001 *Exeter* as it waits to back out of Waterloo, but the others seem to be van spotters! Friday 21 April 1967. (*Jim Blake*)

'Merchant Navy Pacific' 35003 *Royal Mail* arrives at the construction site that is Southampton Central with the 11.30 from Waterloo. Sunday 23 April 1967. (*Jim Blake*)

BR Standard Class '4' 2-6-0 No. 76011 receives attention to a wheelset under the hoist at Weymouth shed. The 'Mogul' would be put back into service and play a large part during the last five weeks of steam working. Sunday April 23 1967. (*Andrew Southwell*)

Our next, and what would be my last outing, was on 6 May. Being a Saturday we were able to buy a cheap day ticket and be at Waterloo in time for the 08.35 departure to Weymouth. Joy of joys – the 08.30 fast to Weymouth was steam hauled as well, and by a 'Merchant Navy' loco at that. My friend decided to go no further than Southampton, but I just had to take it all the way, and 35008 *Orient Line* did not disappoint. With twelve well-filled coaches totalling four hundred tons behind

Rebuilt 'Battle of Britain Pacific' 34060 *25 Squadron* shunts a single wagon across the main lines at Walton-on-Thames. (*Keith Lawrence*)

Having deposited the wagon in the down goods yard, 34060 runs back towards the ground signal and the next part of Special 27 duty. Both pictures: Saturday 29 April 1967. (*Keith Lawrence*)

'West Country Pacific' 34044 *Woolacombe* makes a smoky departure from Waterloo with a special train to Bournemouth. Monday 1 May 1967. (*Jim Blake*)

On a bright sunny spring afternoon, Standard Class '4' 2-6-4 tank 80152 approaches Hinton Admiral with the 16.28 Bournemouth to Eastleigh service. Saturday 6 May 1967. (*Author's collection – photographer unknown*)

the tender, we encountered three 20 mph speed restrictions and three signal checks. Had it not been for a four minute signal stop at Northam Junction we would have arrived at Southampton just three minutes late. Although the schedules were extended to allow for engineering works at this time, it was also a fine example of the recovery powers of the Class '8' Pacific.

35008	6 May 1967		Load 12 = 420t		
Distance (miles)			Time (mins/secs)	Speed (mph)	
0.00	WATERLOO	dep	00.00		
1.35	VAUXHALL		03.55	37	
2.65	QUEENS ROAD		05.55	45	
3.90	CLAPHAM JUNCTION		07.40	40	PWS (20)
5.55	EARLSFIELD		11.38	25	
7.20	WIMBLEDON		13.53	50	
8.65	RAYNES PARK		15.23	55	
9.75	NEW MALDEN		16.35	60	
11.00	BERRYLANDS		17.45	53	
12.05	SURBITON		18.55	52	Sigs
13.30	Hampton Court Junction		20.15	60	
14.40	ESHER		21.15	65	
15.90	HERSHAM		22.45	62	
17.05	WALTON-on-THAMES		23.53	60	
19.15	WEYBRIDGE		25.50	63	
20.40	BYFLEET AND NEW HAW		27.05	62	
21.65	WEST BYFLEET		28.23	57	Sigs
24.35	WOKING		31.05	59	
28.00	BROOKWOOD		34.40	65	
31.00	MP 31(Summit)		37.38	60	
33.25	FARNBOROUGH		40.05	45	PWS (20)
36.50	FLEET		45.00	55	
39.85	WINCHFIELD		48.10	65	
42.20	HOOK		50.25	62	
47.80	BASINGSTOKE		55.58	60	
50.30	Worting Junction		59.25	35	Sigs

35008	6 May 1967	Load 12 = 420t		
Distance (miles)		Time (mins/secs)	Speed (mph)	
56.25	Roundwood Signal Box	68.35	55	Sigs
58.10	MICHELDEVER	70.35	65	
61.80	Wallers Ash	73.52	69	
64.70	Winchester Junction	76.08	80	
66.60	WINCHESTER	78.00	55	
69.70	SHAWFORD	84.10	25	PWS (20)
73.55	EASTLEIGH	88.55	63	
75.00	SOUTHAMPTON AIRPORT	90.15	66	
75.80	SWAYTHLING	91.05	58	
77.25	ST DENYS	92.33	59	
78.20	Northam Junction (Signal stop for 3 mins 45 secs)	94.10	20	
79.25	SOUTHAMPTON CENT arr	101.45		

'West Country Pacific' 34037 *Clovelly* is about to leave Waterloo with the 07.18 to Salisbury. Saturday 6 May 1967. (*Jim Blake*)

The fine running continued for the rest of the journey to Weymouth, and after lunch I decided to take a ride to Dorchester in time to catch the 13.08 train from Bournemouth back to Weymouth. Rebuilt 'West Country' 34036 *Westward Ho* turned up, and I do not think I have heard such an off-beat locomotive before or since. In fact, one beat per revolution seemed to be missing altogether! No-one was more surprised than I when I found out that this loco survived well into the last week of steam, even hauling the *Bournemouth Belle* on Wednesday, 5 July.

This time at Weymouth I visited the shed, and after taking the 16.46 departure to Dorchester South – *Westward Ho* again – I settled down to await the 17.30 Weymouth to Waterloo, hauled by 'West Country Pacific' 34024 *Tamar Valley*. Another fine run completed my day, taking exactly eighty-five minutes from Southampton to Waterloo, with a speed of 65 mph at Roundwood summit, a maximum of 85 mph near Fleet and a clear run to Waterloo, with a time of just under twenty-four minutes from Woking. The day had more than made up for the disappointments of 10 April and provided a high note on which to say my goodbye to Southern steam.

Rebuit 'West Country Pacific' 34021 *Dartmoor* has a water stop at Fareham while working the first leg of the 'Dorset Coast Express' railtour. The loco will hand over to unmodified sister 34023 *Blackmore Vale*. Sunday 7 May 1967. (*Ernie's Railway Archive*)

34024	6 May 1967	Load 10 = c.350t	
Distance (miles)		**Time** (mins/secs)	**Speed** (mph)
0.00	SOUTHAMPTON CENTRAL dep	00.00	
1.05	Northam Junction	03.23	20
2.10	ST DENYS	05.18	39
3.50	SWAYTHLING	07.08	50
4.40	SOUTHAMPTON AIRPORT	08.05	54
5.85	EASTLEIGH	09.35	60
6.70	Allbrook Junction	10.25	62	PWS
9.65	SHAWFORD	17.30	38
12.80	WINCHESTER	21.30	50
14.70	Winchester Junction	23.50	52
17.50	Wallers Ash	26.35	60
21.20	MICHELDEVER	30.05	62
23.50	Roundwood signal box	31.52	65
26.70	Wooton	35.15	68
29.00	Worting Junction	37.15	65
31.50	BASINGSTOKE	39.40	70
37.10	HOOK	44.20	75
39.45	WINCHFIELD	46.08	82
42.80	FLEET	48.33	85
46.05	FARNBOROUGH	52.05	25	PWS
48.30	MP 31 (Summit)	55.15	53
51.30	BROOKWOOD	58.02	75
54.95	WOKING	61.02	58	Sigs
57.65	WEST BYFLEET	63.15	75
58.90	BYFLEET & NEW HAW	64.13	80
60.15	WEYBRIDGE	65.13	80
62.15	WALTON-on-THAMES	66.48	77
63.30	HERSHAM	67.40	80
64.80	ESHER	68.50	80
66.00	Hampton Court Junction	69.40	72

34024	6 May 1967		Load 10 = c.350t	
Distance (miles)		Time (mins/secs)	Speed (mph)	
67.25	SURBITON	70.48	67	
68.30	BERRYLANDS	71.45	70	
69.55	NEW MALDEN	72.47	71	
70.65	RAYNES PARK	73.45	57	Sigs
72.10	WIMBLEDON	75.10	60	
73.75	EARLSFIELD	76.51	45/55	
75.40	CLAPHAM JUNCTION	78.45	40	
77.95	VAUXHALL	82.10		
79.30	WATERLOO arr	85.00		

Two more original 'Light Pacifics' and one 'Merchant Navy' were withdrawn during these two months. In order of final trips they were:

34015 – Withdrawn week ending 16 April, *Exmouth* is last recorded as working the first part of Weymouth 432 diagram on Tuesday 28 March. This was the 08.27 Weymouth to Bournemouth, followed by the 10.31 Bournemouth to Waterloo. The locomotive had suffered problems with the tender since the beginning of the year, and it was a tender bearing that caused its demise.

35012 – Withdrawn week ending 23 April, the last known work for *United States Lines* was the Channel Islands Boat Train on Monday 17 April: the 08.10 Waterloo to Weymouth Quay and the 16.00 return. On arrival at Nine Elms it was found to have a broken expansion joint bracket and a leaking regulator valve and was withdrawn straight away.

34057 – Withdrawn from Salisbury shed during week ending 7 May. Like 34006 on its last day, *Biggin Hill* was given the down *Bournemouth Belle* to work on Thursday 4 May (34023 *Blackmore Vale* hauled the return service – what a day for that train!). No. 34057 returned to London somehow, possibly on the 17.42 stopping service from Bournemouth to Eastleigh and then the 20.40 vans to Clapham Junction. At Nine Elms it was found to have a cracked inside cylinder and leaking thermic syphons and was immediately laid aside.

This left just two unmodified 'Light Pacifics' and seven 'Merchant Navies' to see out the end of steam, and all played a large part in the last weeks.

Rebuilt 'West Country Pacific' 34021 *Dartmoor* takes water at Fareham while working the first leg of the 'Dorset Coast Express' rail tour. Sunday 7 May 1967. (*Keith Widdowson*)

Half an hour later, the 'Dorset Coast Express' takes the 15 mph curve at Northam Junction and heads west. Sunday 7 May 1967. (*Ernie's Railway Archive*)

Having taken over from 34021, unmodified sister 34023 *Blackmore Vale* makes a photographic stop at Corfe Castle. Sunday 7 May 1967. (*Keith Widdowson*)

'West Country Pacific' 34036 *Westward Ho* runs off the main line at Byfleet and New Haw and heads for Feltham with the Ford carflat train. Tuesday 9 May 1967. (*Keith Lawrence*)

Standard Class '5' 73085 *Melisande* makes a lovely study in light and shade as it waits to back out of Waterloo. The loco has just worked the 08.46 from Bournemouth. Thursday 10 May 1967. (*Jim Blake*)

'Warship' Type 4 diesel–hydraulic D801 *Vanguard* calls at Basingstoke with the 13.00 Waterloo to Exeter. These locos were the mainstay of the Exeter service at the time but the writing was on the wall. Withdrawals commenced with this locomotive in August 1968, and the entire class was gone by the end of 1972. Wednesday 10 May 1967. (*Rail-Online photos*)

A grubby Standard Class '5' No. 73043 waits at Waterloo with the 07.18 to Salisbury. The loco number has been chalked on the front at least three times in case of uncertainty! Saturday 13 May 1967. (*Jim Blake*)

Standard Class '4' 2-6-0 No. 76031 rests on Basingstoke shed. The loco was the last remaining example of a small number fitted with a tablet catcher for working over the Somerset and Dorset line. Saturday 13 May 1967. (*Jim Blake*)

Events away from the railway included the UK winning the Eurovision song contest for the first time on Saturday 8 April, with Sandie Shaw performing *Puppet on a String*. In the same month the initial M-o-T test for cars was reduced from ten years old to three, and the first ever 'Big Mac' burger was served in Uniontown, Pennsylvania.

Original Bulleid
'Light Pacific' 34023
Blackmore Vale
prepares to leave
Nine Elms depot to
work the 18.00 boat
train from Waterloo
to Southampton
Western Docks,
for the P&O liner
Oriana. Saturday 13
May 1967. (*Author's
collection*)

On Saturday 6 May, Manchester United won the first division title, and on the 25th Celtic became the first team from the United Kingdom to win the European cup final by coming from behind to beat Inter-Milan 2-1.

**'West Country
Pacific'** 34001 *Exeter*
wreathed in steam
at Waterloo at
the head of the
12.20 boat train
to Southampton
Eastern Docks for
the Sitmar Line
vessel *Fair Star*.
Wednesday 17 May
1967. (*Jim Blake*)

With many inspection covers missing, original Bulleid 'West Country Pacific' 34102 *Lapford* departs from Waterloo with the 17.09 to Basingstoke. After a layover of nearly forty-five minutes this train departed Basingstoke at 19.11 for Salisbury. Note the large 5,500 gallon tender that *Lapford* kept for its whole life. Thursday 18 May 1967. (*Jim Blake*)

Lacking the same inspection covers, original Bulleid 'West Country Pacific' 34023 *Blackmore Vale* drifts towards Woking with the 08.46 from Bournemouth to Waterloo. The smaller 4,500 gallon tender compares nicely to that of *Lapford* in the previous photograph. Saturday 20 May 1967. (*Jim Blake*)

Taken from above the entrance to Fisherton tunnel, 'Merchant Navy Pacific' 35003 *Royal Mail* lifts a ballast train out of Salisbury. Saturday 20 May 1967. (*Dave Mant*)

Finally, on Sunday 28 May, nine months and a day after setting off, Francis Chichester arrived back in Plymouth on his yacht *Gypsy Moth IV*, becoming the first person to complete a true single-handed circumnavigation of the globe from west to east via the Capes. A few weeks later he was knighted by the Queen, using the same sword that Queen Elizabeth I used to knight Sir Francis Drake after his round the world voyage.

Rebuilt 'West Country' 34037 *Clovelly* heads towards Weybridge with a long welded-rail train. This was probably the regular 06.10 working from Redbridge Engineers Yard to Wimbledon. Photo taken during May 1967. (*Keith Lawrence*)

Looking reasonably clean, 'Battle of Britain Pacific' 34090 *Sir Eustace Missenden – Southern Railway* arrives at Waterloo with the 08.46 from Bournemouth. Tuesday 23 May 1967. (*Jim Blake*)

Rebuilt 'West Country Pacific' 34036 *Westward Ho* stands at Woking with the 07.18 from Waterloo to Salisbury and creates its own smoke screen. Saturday 27 May 1967. (*Jim Blake*)

Standard Class '5' No. 73020 stands at Waterloo with an engineer's train. Saturday 27 May 1967. (*Jim Blake*)

**'Merchant Navy
Pacific' 35013** *Blue Funnel* running light engine towards Southampton at St Denys. Saturday 27 May 1967. (*Gerald T. Robinson*)

**'West Country
Pacific' 34024** *Tamar Valley* stands in the down slow platform at Basingstoke after arrival with the 12.39 from Waterloo. The headcode 8C on the 'Crompton' Type 3 diesel–electric in the down main Platform identifies the train as the 11.20 freight from Banbury to Basingstoke West Yard. Saturday 27 May 1967. (*Christopher Yapp*)

Standard Class '4' 2-6-4T No. 80145, 'West Country Pacific' No. 34036 *Westward Ho* and Ivatt Class '2' 2-6-2T No. 41312 stand at the end of adjacent platforms at Waterloo. The Pacific had arrived at 12.10 with the 08.46 from Bournemouth. Friday 2 June 1967. (*Jim Blake*)

Standard Class '5' No. 73093 waits to leave Waterloo with the 07.18 to Salisbury. It is currently displaying the wrong head code: that for trains terminating at Basingstoke. Saturday 3 June 1967. (*Jim Blake*)

'Merchant Navy
Class Pacific'
35007 *Aberdeen
Commonwealth* in
Pirbright cutting on
Saturday 3 June 1967.
After working the
04.40 from Waterloo
to Salisbury, it was
booked to return
light engine to
Nine Elms. Later
in the day it was
commandeered
to work the return
'Dorset Limited' rail
tour to Weymouth
after the failure of
sister locomotive
35030 *Elder–
Dempster Lines.*
(*Keith Lawrence*)

Standard Class
'5' 4-6-0 No.
73037 approaches
Battledown with
empty banana vans
to Southampton
Docks. Saturday
3 June 1967.
(*Gerald T. Robinson*)

A lovely study of Standard Class '5' 4-6-0 No. 73020 at
Basingstoke shed. Saturday 3 June 1967. (*Gerald T. Robinson*)

'Merchant Navy Pacific' 35008 *Orient Line* climbs steadily through
Micheldever station with the 16.00 Weymouth Quay to Waterloo
Channel Islands Boat Train on Saturday 3 June 1967. (*David Harvey*)

Standard Class '4' 2-6-0 No. 76063 stands between two rebuilt 'Light Pacifics' in the scrap line at Eastleigh shed on Sunday 4 June 1967. The locomotive was withdrawn at the beginning of May and was one of the last to leave Eastleigh after the end of steam. It was cut up at Buttigieg's yard, Newport, towards the end of the year. (*Jim Blake*)

Standard Class '4' 2-6-0 No. 76066, also at Eastleigh on the 4 June and in contrast to the previous locomotive, still had plenty of life in it. Covering much of the South Western system on a variety of work, it lasted until the penultimate day, Saturday 8 July. (*Jim Blake*)

A squire and two knights perhaps? Standard Class '4' 2-6-0 No. 76069 and 'Battle of Britain' locomotive 34090 *Sir Eustace Missenden – Southern Railway* stand in the shed yard at Weymouth on the day of the A4 rail tour. The tour locomotive, preserved 'A4 Pacific' 4498 *Sir Nigel Gresley* can be seen on the left of the picture. No. 76069 would not work again, but *Sir Eustace* would have nearly another four weeks left in service. Sunday 4 June 1967. (*Keith Lawrence*)

Another view of 76069 at Weymouth depot on Sunday 4 June 1967. Towards the end of its life it acquired a large BR1F tender from one of the Class '5' Standard 'Arthurs.'(*Jim Blake*)

Rebuilt 'West Country Pacific' 34024 *Tamar Valley* gets a thorough cleaning at Eastleigh depot. I wonder what the discussion was about? Sunday 4 June 1967. (*George Woods*)

CHAPTER THREE

5 to 11 June

Before reviewing events that happened during the last five weeks of Southern Region main line steam, mention must be made of the Beatles' LP, *Sergeant Pepper's Lonely Hearts Club Band*, as it had been released worldwide on Thursday 1 June. It entered the UK charts at number one and stayed there for fifteen weeks, selling some quarter of a million copies during the first week alone. Although not without its critics in later years, the album contained many innovative features and remains one of the soundtracks to the 'Summer of Love'.

On the morning of Monday 5 June, after around three weeks of escalating tension and threats by the Arab states, principally Egypt, Syria and Jordan, the state of Israel launched pre-emptive air strikes on Egyptian airfields and ground force attacks in Sinai and Gaza.

One of the first consequences of this was closure of the Suez Canal by Egypt on 6 June, and as a result fifteen cargo vessels were trapped in the canal for eight years until it was re-opened in 1975.

As a result of this closure, the Sitmar Line migrant ship *Castel Felice*, homeward bound from Australia and in the vicinity of Aden, had to turn about and return to the United Kingdom via the Cape of Good Hope, adding approximately twelve days to the journey. The next

Rebuilt 'West Country Pacific' 34008 *Padstow* accelerates through Eastleigh with the 16.20 Southampton Western Docks to Nine Elms 'H' Shed banana train. Monday 5 June 1967. (*Bill Wright*)

'**West Country** Pacific' 34102 *Lapford* trundles through Eastleigh station with the 17.43 special freight from Southampton East Docks to Basingstoke. Wednesday 7 June 1967. (*David Harvey*)

Sitmar owned ship in the approximately fourteen-day rotation was the *Fairsky*, which was routed via the Panama Canal and so was unaffected by the troubles. It arrived as scheduled on Tuesday 4 July, one day before the *Castel Felice*!

The above of course had an effect on the boat train arrangements for this ship, with three scheduled for later in June having to be cancelled and rearranged for the first week of July.

The closure of the canal also had an effect on the Chandris Line vessel *Australis*, which had just entered the Mediterranean Sea outbound for Australia, having left Southampton on 2 June with no less than 1,225 assisted migrants entailing two boat trains. It also had to turn about and complete its journey via the Cape.

Standard Class '5' 4-6-0 No. 73043 runs through Wimbledon with the 16.20 freight from Southampton West Docks to Nine Elms goods yard. The locomotive has not yet acquired its Ron Cover 'Soup Tin' number plate. Friday 9 June 1967. (*Ernie's Railway Archive*)

Standard Class '4' 4-6-0 passes Nine Elms Junction with empty stock from Clapham Junction to Waterloo, prior to working the 10.35 relief passenger train to Bournemouth. Saturday 10 June 1967. (*Author's collection – photographer unknown*)

On 7 June, 'West Country' Class 34001 *Exeter* became derailed at the entrance to Bournemouth locomotive depot causing some disruption, and unmodified sister 34102 *Lapford* reappeared after spending a fortnight in Eastleigh shed having a tender bearing repaired.

That same Wednesday, the American writer, critic and satirist Dorothy Parker died of a heart attack, aged seventy-three. She was famous for her sharp wit, examples of which are "Katharine Hepburn delivered a striking performance that ran the gamut of emotions, from A to B." and "I require three things in a man: he must be handsome, ruthless and stupid."

'Merchant Navy Pacific' 35030 *Elder–Dempster Lines* stands on Weymouth depot after working the 10.24 relief passenger train from Waterloo. Saturday 10 June 1967. (*Author's collection – photographer unknown*)

The 14.36 from Salisbury has just arrived in the adjacent platform, and, substituting for a 'Warship' diesel locomotive, rebuilt 'West Country Pacific' 34108 *Wincanton* is about to shunt over to attach to the stock to form the 5.00pm to Exeter, which it worked as far as Salisbury. (*Jim Blake*)

Wincanton **has** now moved over, and it looks like someone is in between it and the train, 'coupling up'. Both pictures: Saturday 10 June 1967. (*Jim Blake*)

On Thursday 8th, the first Test Match between England and India began play at Headingley, Leeds. England won by six wickets, and in their first innings Geoff Boycott made his highest test score of 246 not out. Also on the 8th, Standard Class '4' 2-6-0 No. 76066 began four days of deputising for Pacifics, so it was probably in good health. On the following day, the larger Class '5' 4-6-0 No. 73093 also commenced four days standing in for larger locos, racking up a fair number of miles in the process.

Now let us indulge ourselves a little. If you could have a 'one shot, one day' time machine that would transport your railway enthusiast self to June or July 1967, when and where would you go? Would you go back to relive your best haulage of the period, try for something new or aim for one place to see what was happening there?

My choice would be Bournemouth Central station on Saturday 10 June. This was the last busy Saturday for steam and also the last

Rebuilt 'West Country' 34021 *Dartmoor* arrives at Andover Junction with the 18.38 Salisbury to Waterloo. Saturday 10 June 1967. (*Alan Hayes*)

time that all seven surviving 'Merchant Navies' could be seen working on the same day, though you would have to be at Bournemouth from around 07.30 in the morning until 9.30 in the evening to see then all. Cue lots of cheese and pickle sandwiches, pork pies and cups of British Rail buffet tea! In total, twenty-eight working examples of all remaining classes, except Standard '3s' 77014 and 82019/29 could be seen at work, as long as one arrived in time to see the Bournemouth West Pilot leave the shed at 05.15.

Other interesting workings on this day were 34108 *Wincanton* deputising for a failed 'Warship' diesel on the 12.36 Salisbury to Waterloo and 17.00 return. In the morning Standard '4' 2-6-4 tank No. 80145 was turned out for the 07.18 from Waterloo to Salisbury. This train had originally been booked for Class '4' No. 76026, which had failed, the tank obviously being the best loco remaining for the job. The only other loco spare at Nine Elms was Standard '5'

Original Bulleid 'Pacific' 34023 *Blackmore Vale* leaves Salisbury with the final steam hauled leg of the Warwickshire Railway Society's 'Farewell to Steam on the L.S.W.R.' rail tour. Sunday 11 June 1967. (*Dave Mant*)

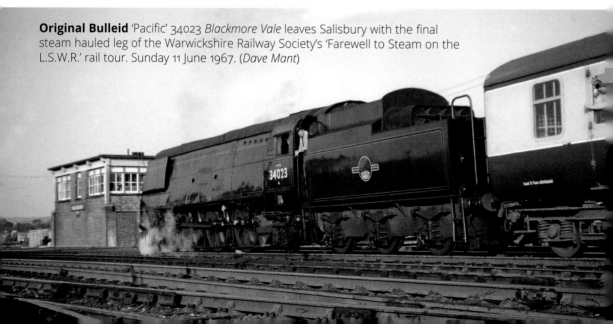

No. 73085 *Melisande*, but it was required for the rail tour the following day and Nine Elms would not have wanted to lose it. The tank had a very eventful week, not returning to London until Friday 16 June, even working all the way down to Weymouth in the process.

For two rebuilt 'West Country Pacifics' however, 10 June was their last day in service. 34008 *Padstow* and 34100 *Appledore* were both stopped at Nine Elms after working trains up from Weymouth. As there would be a reduction of two main line diagrams from the following Monday, presumably repairs were not deemed cost effective or necessary.

On a more sombre note, the Holywood actor Spencer Tracy died aged sixty-seven. He was nominated for nine Oscars for best actor, winning two in consecutive years, for his roles in *Captains Courageous* and *Boys Town*. He had completed his final film, *Guess who's coming to dinner*, just seventeen days earlier, on May 24.

Also, by the evening of the 10th, Syrian resistance on the Golan Heights had collapsed, and with the Israeli army in control, what became known as The Six Day War was effectively over.

Lastly for this week, on Sunday 11th, a rail tour was promoted by the Warwickshire Railway Society. The train ran from Birmingham to Weymouth, with steam haulage taking over from an electric loco at Mitre Bridge Junction. Six different locos were involved, including the aforementioned *Melisande*, with the train running via Swanage on the way down and Salisbury on the way back. It had originally been planned to run the tour down to Lymington as well, but due to single line working between Winchfield and Basingstoke there was insufficient time.

'Merchant Navy Pacific' 35023 *Holland–Afrika Line* has reversed the 11.30 Waterloo to Bournemouth onto the up main line at Winchfield, in preparation for single line working to Basingstoke. A group of enthusiasts take the opportunity to get their feet on the disused main line platform and chat to the driver! Sunday 11 June 1967. (*Alan Hayes*)

CHAPTER FOUR

12 to 18 June

On Monday 12 June two loco changes took place on up passenger trains. On both occasions Standard '5' 4-6-0s replacing the smaller Class '4' 2-6-0s. Firstly, 73037 took over from 76031 on the 08.46 Bournemouth to Waterloo, probably at Eastleigh, and in the evening 73092 replaced 76064 at Basingstoke on the 18.51 Bournemouth to Woking. Looking at where all four locos were based, it is quite possible that the changeovers were to get the locos back on their home shed duties rather than any problems with the smaller Standards.

On the same day the former boxer 'Bombardier' Billy Wells died. He had been British and Empire Heavyweight champion from 1911 to 1919, and became the first heavyweight to be awarded the Lonsdale belt. In later life he took over as the third man to be seen striking the gong at the beginning of all J. Arthur Rank films.

The evening of the 12th saw the world premiere in Leicester Square of the fifth Bond film, *You Only Live Twice*. It was extremely successful, grossing well over 100 million dollars at the box office.

On Wednesday 14 June the spacecraft *Mariner 5* was launched from Cape Kennedy. Its mission to collect data about the atmosphere, radiation and magnetic field of the planet Venus was completed in early December 1967.

Original Bulleid
'Light Pacific' 34102 *Lapford* makes ready to leave Wareham with the 11.18 Weymouth to Waterloo. The locomotive will hand over to rebuilt sister 34021 *Dartmoor* at Bournemouth. Tuesday 13 June 1967. (*John Knight*)

Standard Class '5' 4-6-0 No. 73020 takes the route south from Tunnel Junction with the 19.20 Salisbury to Northam vans. Tuesday 13 June 1967. (*Dave Mant*)

Standard Class '5' 4-6-0 No. 73093, with a few glands leaking, crawls through Poole station with a ballast train. This is probably the 07.08 from Brockenhurst to Wool on Wednesday 14 June 1967. (*Author's collection – photographer unknown*)

Rebuilt 'West Country Pacific' 34024 *Tamar Valley* rests on the stops at Waterloo after arrival with the 08.46 from Bournemouth. The two duty numbers on the discs, 280 above the buffer beam and 135 on the left hand side of the smokebox, bear no relation to the train worked, actually part of 138 diagram. Thursday 15 June 1967. (*Jim Blake*)

During the evening of the same day the 17.23 Boat train for the Holland–Amerika liner *Statendam*, hauled by rebuilt 'West Country' *Axminster*, was turned into a relief for the 5.30pm Waterloo to Bournemouth. Ordinary passengers for Basingstoke, Winchester and Eastleigh were carried, no doubt a pleasant surprise for some.

Later still that evening a treat was in store for Alan Hayes, John Tyler and others aboard the 18.38 Salisbury to Waterloo. Original Bulleid 'Pacific' 34102 *Lapford*, with seven coaches, provided a delightful cameo, running from Basingstoke to Woking in 21 minutes 37 seconds start to stop, including a 50 mph temporary speed restriction at Sturt Lane. I have detailed in the table the run as timed by Alan Hayes, and for comparison a run with rebuilt sister 34104 *Bere Alston* with the same train on Friday May 19. This was also timed by Alan Hayes, and shows what a 'Light Pacific' could do with eleven coaches and an unchecked run (see opposite page).

As mentioned in the previous chapter, Nine Elms Standard 2-6-4T No. 80145 recommenced its wanderings. Having spent the first part of the week at Salisbury, it was turned out for the 15.55 to Basingstoke and stayed on the Eastleigh diagram circuit until it returned to London on the Friday evening.

On Thursday 15th, 'Merchant Navy Pacific' 35028 *Clan Line* became the last recorded member of its class to work a boat train to Southampton Docks. After arriving at Waterloo at 09.16 with the morning commuter train from Salisbury, it was turned round quickly to work the 11.20 train with passengers for the Italian liner *Achille Lauro*.

Just over an hour later, original 'West Country Pacific' 34023 *Blackmore Vale* was turned out to work the *Bournemouth Belle* down and back.

Distance (miles)		34102		34104	
		14 June 1967		19 May 1967	
		Load 7 = 230 gross		Load 11 = c.380 gross	
		Time (mins/secs)	Speed (mph)	Time (mins/secs)	Speed (mph)
0.00	BASINGSTOKE dep	00.00		00.00	
4.10	Newnham Siding	05.22	75		
5.60	HOOK	06.30	82	06.43	73
7.95	WINCHFIELD	08.08	92	08.34	81/86
11.30	FLEET	10.13	98/100	10.55	83/86
14.55	FARNBOROUGH	12.38	62.5	13.19	78.5
	Sturt Lane (50 mph PWS for 34102 only)	13.42	58/52		
16.75	MP 31(Summit)	14.58	60.5	15.01	76.5
18.15	Pirbright Junction	16.04	75		
19.75	BROOKWOOD	17.22	88	17.11	86.5
23.40	WOKING arr	21.37		21.00	

As it arrived at Waterloo in the evening the only other unmodified loco of the class remaining in service, 34102 *Lapford,* was waiting to depart with the 18.54 to Salisbury.

The *Bournemouth Belle* also enjoyed steam haulage in both directions on the following day; this time rebuilt 'West Country' No. 34024 *Tamar Valley*' doing the honours.

Also on Friday 16, Guildford shed's Standard Class '5' No. 73018 worked a parcels train to Redhill in place of a 'Type 3' diesel. It then hauled the 16.34 passenger train from Redhill to Reading, thus becoming the last steam locomotive to work a passenger train over this route. Its work for the day was not done however, as on arrival back at Guildford that evening it was immediately put out on a ballast train.

The Monterey Pop Festival, regarded as one of the main events of 'The Summer of Love,' started on the evening of the 16th. Artists appearing over the three days included Eric Burdon and the Animals, Simon and Garfunkel, The Byrds, Otis Redding, The Grateful Dead, The Who and Jimmy Hendrix. It was estimated that the number of people that turned up would have filled the 7,000 approved capacity of the performance area many times over!

On the morning of Saturday 17th, although this would have actually happened before the Monterey festival started, China carried out its first Hydrogen bomb test. In so doing it became the fourth nation behind the United States, Russia and the United Kingdom to possess Thermo-nuclear weapons.

In brilliant evening sunshine, original Bulleid 'West Country Pacific' 34102 *Lapford* reverses into Waterloo to work the 18.54 to Salisbury. (*Jim Blake*)

A few moments later, *Lapford* is on the train and appears to be impatient to leave. A 'Warship' diesel waits on the left with the 19.00 to Exeter. Both pictures: Thursday 15 June 1967. (*Jim Blake*)

Turning now to Sunday 18th, we come to what was the last privately sponsored rail tour. This was the Railway Correspondence and Travel Society's 'Farewell to Southern Steam', and what a finale it would have been if not for the last three weeks of the interim timetable. If only such a tour could have been recreated for the 50th anniversary.

Six different locomotives were involved – seven if you count Ivatt tank 41298 bringing the empty stock into Waterloo – and fourteen sets of men from six different depots. Even Feltham got a look in, though this was only to relieve on 'Merchant Navy' *Blue Funnel* in the evening, work empty stock to Clapham Junction and dispose of the loco at Nine Elms. Add in the amount of light engine running and it is plain to see that this was not a cheap tour to operate.

All the locomotives for the tour were requested – even 41298 – but in the event three did not make it. Salisbury engines 34013 *Okehampton* and 34052 *Lord Dowding* were inked in to work, but *Okehampton* was being used elsewhere and *Lord Dowding* was under repair at its home shed, so Salisbury sent its other two 'Light Pacifics', No. 34089 *602 Squadron* and No. 34108 *Wincanton*, instead. Likewise, nominated 'Merchant Navy Pacific' 35030 *Elder-Dempster Lines* was under repair so 35013 *Blue Funnel* was used for the last leg of the tour.

A metaphor for the demise of steam? Original Bulleid 'West Country Pacific' 34023 *Blackmore Vale* runs from light into shade into Waterloo with the up *Bournemouth Belle*, the 16.37 from Bournemouth. Thursday 15 June 1967. (*Jim Blake*)

Standard Class '5' 4-6-0 No. 73093 arrives at Bournemouth Central with the 12.12 from Weymouth, while 'Merchant Navy Pacific' 35023 waits to leave the depot to work the 15.01 to Weymouth. Friday 16 June 1967. (*J. A. Sheridan*)

Rebuilt 'West Country Pacific' 34037 *Clovelly* runs into Bournemouth Central station with empty stock. Did it carry on empty or form the 16.28 to Eastleigh? Friday 16 June 1967. (*J. A. Sheridan*)

Three different Standard locomotives at Guildford. From the right: Class '4' 4-6-0 No. 75074, Class '4' 2-6-0 No. 76031 and under the coal stage, Class '5' 4-6-0 No. 73118. Probably Saturday 17 June 1967. (*Author's collection*)

CHAPTER FIVE

19 to 25 June

'West Country Pacific' 34034 *Honiton,* which had been under repair at Nine Elms for over a week needing attention to its inside big end, was turned out on Monday 19 June to work the 04.40 Waterloo to Salisbury and 18.38 return. To the annoyance of shed staff no doubt, it limped home with a problem to the pony truck bearing and did not work again, being withdrawn on 2 July.

Also on that day, an interesting working occurred when five WD coaches and a brake van were taken from the Longmoor Military railway to Cricklewood for a 20th Century Fox filming contract. Although booked to be hauled by a Guildford Standard '5', in the event the train was worked by Type 3 'Crompton' D6578.

Train running was not always of a high standard in the last weeks of Southern steam; on the evening of the 19th Keith Widdowson had an abysmal run with 'Merchant Navy Pacific' 35028 *Clan Line* on the 17.30 Weymouth to Waterloo. Having already lost four minutes between Bournemouth and Southampton Central due to two temporary speed restrictions, the train took three minutes over two hours for the non-stop run from there to Waterloo. There does not appear to be anything wrong with the locomotive however, as it was able to reach 91 mph between Fleet and Farnborough, and after yet another severe signal check at Woking, achieved another maximum of 78 mph at Hersham.

35028	19 June 1967	Load 10 + van		
Distance (miles)		Time (mins/secs)	Speed (mph)	
0.00	SOUTHAMPTON CENT dep	00.00		
1.05	Northam Junction	03.58	20	
2.10	ST DENYS	05.56	37	
3.50	SWAYTHLING	07.53	47	
4.40	SOUTHAMPTON. AIRPORT	08.53	50/52	Sigs
5.85	EASTLEIGH	13.05	26	
6.70	Allbrook Junction	14.28	39	
9.65	SHAWFORD	18.09	54	
12.80	WINCHESTER	21.22	60.5	
14.70	Winchester Junction	24.32	17	PWS
17.50	Wallers Ash	30.22	42	

35028	19 June 1967	Load 10 + van		
Distance (miles)		Time (mins/secs)	Speed (mph)	
18.90	Weston	32.07	53/56	Sigs
21.20	MICHELDEVER	34.24	40	
23.50	Roundwood signal box	39.59	18.5/22	Sigs
26.70	Wooton	58.27	18	Sigs
29.00	Worting Junction	65.17	52.5	
31.50	BASINGSTOKE	67.30	75	
37.10	HOOK	71.32	86/83	
39.45	WINCHFIELD	73.15	85/90	
42.80	FLEET	75.30	89/91	
46.05	FARNBOROUGH	77.33	87/56.5	PWS
48.30	MP 31(Summit)	79.48	60.5/78.5	
51.30	BROOKWOOD	82.17	75/5	Sigs
54.95	WOKING	91.26	16	
57.65	WEST BYFLEET	95.18	63	
58.90	BYFLEET & NEW HAW	96.40	70	Sigs
60.15	WEYBRIDGE	97.41	61	
62.15	WALTON-on-THAMES	99.36	73	
63.30	HERSHAM	100.27	78	
64.80	ESHER	101.40	76	
66.00	Hampton Court Junction	102.30	74.5	
67.25	SURBITON	103.38	67	
68.30	BERRYLANDS	104.42	65	
69.55	NEW MALDEN	105.40	66.5	
70.65	RAYNES PARK	106.50	69	
72.10	WIMBLEDON	108.06	62.5/64	Sigs
73.75	EARLSFIELD	110.13	21/15.5	PWS
75.40	CLAPHAM JUNCTION	115.32	37.5/57.5	Sigs
77.95	VAUXHALL	119.07	25	Sigs
79.25	WATERLOO arr	122.49		

Once again substituting for a failed 'Warship' diesel, 'West Country Pacific' 34108 *Wincanton* is made ready to haul the 13.00 Waterloo to Exeter, which it worked as far as Salisbury. Wednesday 21 June 1967. (*Jim Blake*)

'Merchant Navy Pacific' 35003 *Royal Mail* pauses at Poole, with probably the 17.41 Weymouth to Bournemouth on Thursday 22 June 1967. (*Author's collection – photographer unknown*)

On that same evening, following on from an interview published in *Life* magazine, Beatle Paul McCartney admitted on Independent Television News that he had taken LSD. The use of the drug was widely asserted to have influenced the music of *Sergeant Pepper.*

Tuesday 20th saw the birth of Australian actress Nicole Kidman in Honolulu, Hawaii, and the boxer Muhammad Ali was convicted of refusing to be drafted into the United States army. He was sentenced to five years in prison, fined $10,000 dollars and banned from boxing for three years, but on appeal the prison sentence was quashed.

Rebuilt 'West Country Pacific' 34095 *Brentor* had a grand day out on Wednesday 21st, when it worked a railway officer's inspection train from Bournemouth West to Waterloo via Weymouth, Yeovil and Salisbury.

The second Test Match between England and India started on Thursday 22 June at Lord's cricket ground. This time India were defeated by an innings and 124 runs, and in the second innings Ray Illingworth recorded his best test match bowling figures of six wickets for 29 runs. England went on to win the three match series three-nil.

The day after, Friday 23, saw Standard Class '3' 2-6-2T No. 82019 take a break from its regular empty stock duties and go light engine to Marylebone for filming, presumably for the same contract as the coaches from Longmoor previously described. Standard Class '4' 2-6-0 No. 76026 deputised for it on the non- *Kenny Belle* parts of 105 and 106 empty coaching stock diagrams.

Rebuilt 'West Country Pacific' 34034 *Honiton* stands amid the remains of the Old Shed at Nine Elms on Friday 23 June 1967. Officially under repair, the locomotive did not work again and was withdrawn week ending 2 July. *(Jim Blake)*

Rebuilt 'West Country Pacific' 34004 *Yeovil* stands outside the New Shed at Nine Elms. Friday 23 June 1967. (*Jim Blake*)

Standard Class '5' 4-6-0 No. 73037 puts in a spot of extra shunting at Bournemouth, believed to be in June 1967. (*Author's collection – photographer unknown*)

Two Standard Class '5' 4-6-0 tender locos, No. 73093 nearest the camera and No. 73037 behind, keep company with Class '4' 2-6-4T No. 80011 on Bournemouth depot. Sunday 25 June 1967. (*Author's collection – photographer unknown*)

'Merchant Navy Pacific' 35003 *Royal Mail* arrives at Weymouth towing three withdrawn locomotives from Bournemouth. They are Standard Class '4' 2-6-0 No. 76008 and two Ivatt 2-6-2 tanks, numbers 41230 and 41295. Sunday 25 June 1967. (*Author's collection – photographer unknown*)

On Saturday 24 there was not a great deal of steam activity during the day, but after working the 22.07 vans from Basingstoke to Waterloo, unmodified Bulleid 'Light Pacific' 34023 *Blackmore Vale* was retired, leaving just 34102 *Lapford* to carry the torch for the original locomotives into the final week. It has been reported that this was to save *Blackmore Vale* from developing any serious faults as it had been earmarked for preservation. This would not be surprising as it had racked up something like 1,150 miles in six days that week, and around 1,275 in just five days the week before.

Also late that same evening Standard '5' No. 73029 may have been the last steam loco to reach Alton, on the 22.47 ballast train from Woking. After running round, 73029 worked under Engineer's instruction back to Bentley, and for the record, the train consisted of four wagons loaded with Building Department materials and two brake vans.

On the morning of Sunday 25, one of the spare engines at Weymouth, 'Merchant Navy Pacific' 35003 *Royal Mail*, was sent to Bournemouth shed to bring three condemned locomotives back to the depot.

At 1.30pm, after Sunday dinner, thousands of adolescent schoolboys, myself included, sat down to listen to the final episode of the third series of *Round the Horne* – required listening as it would be practically the sole topic of conversation at school the following day. The musings of Rambling Sid Rumpo, J. Peasmold Gruntfuttock, Julian and Sandy *et al* were all in the best possible taste. It must have been funny as my Father always found plenty in the programme to laugh about too!

That evening – UK time – while 'Merchant Navy' 35030 *Elder–Dempster Lines* was working the regularly steam hauled 7.36pm train from Bournemouth to Waterloo, an estimated four hundred to seven hundred million people were watching *Our World*, the first live international satellite television broadcast. Fourteen countries took part, and while many contributions concerned the latest technological innovations, the programme is probably best remembered today for the live recording of the Beatles' *All you need is Love*.

CHAPTER SIX

26 June to 2 July

On the morning of Monday 26 June, ailing 'Light Pacific' 34090 *Sir Eustace Missenden – Southern Railway* set off from Waterloo with the 08.35 to Weymouth. It was suffering injector trouble, so arrangements were made for a replacement locomotive at Eastleigh. Standard Class '4' 4-6-0 No. 75076 took over the train, and although it kept reasonable time, the effort appeared to be too much for it. The loco did not work another passenger train and was taken out of service almost immediately.

Class mate 75068 also fell by the wayside this week, leaving just three Standard '4' 4-6-0s to see out the end of steam, with one of those, 75077, appearing to be confined to non-passenger duties. Another of the class, 75074, had its moment of glory at the end of the week when it deputised for a 'Light Pacific' on the Friday night excursion from Colne to Portsmouth Harbour. Later on the morning of Saturday 1, No. 75074 also worked a Bolton bound train from Portsmouth as far as Willesden Junction.

The evening of the 26th saw the sparks flying on the lightly loaded 18.15 from Weymouth to Waterloo, when Driver Burridge and

Ivatt Class '2' 2-6-2T 41298 on the empty coaches of the 08.46 from Bournemouth at Waterloo. The locomotive is fitted with a non-standard, narrower chimney. Monday 26 June 1967. (*Jim Blake*)

Rebuilt 'West Country Pacific' 34024 *Tamar Valley*, having worked the 08.46 from Bournemouth, follows 41298 and the empty coaches towards the end of the platform at Waterloo. The pacific will also work empty coaches to Clapham Junction before retiring to Nine Elms for servicing. Both photographs: Monday 26 June 1967. (*Jim Blake*)

'Merchant Navy Pacific' 35003 *Royal Mail* achieved 106 mph between Winchfield and Fleet. This was no fluke as the same loco was worked up to 105 mph with the same train at the same location two nights later.

The first Automatic Teller Machine (ATM) in the UK was installed at the Enfield branch of Barclay's bank on Tuesday, 27 June. The actor/comedian Reg Varney had the honour of withdrawing the first wad of cash from it.

A shortage of tank locomotives at Nine Elms this week saw two tender engines drafted in to work empty stock on Tuesday: Standard '4' 4-6-0 No. 75074 and 'Light Pacific' 34024 *Tamar Valley*. No. 75074 was also in use on a special empty stock diagram the following day, as was Class '4' 2-6-0 No. 76064 on Thursday 29th.

In the early hours of Wednesday 28th, Salisbury's rebuilt 'West Country Pacific' 34108 *Wincanton* worked home with the 00.35 freight from Basingstoke, three days after its official withdrawal date! It had worked the same diagram, Salisbury 462, on Monday night/Tuesday morning as well.

After working the 17.30 from Weymouth to Waterloo on Wednesday 28 June, 'Merchant Navy Pacific' 35013 *Blue Funnel Certum Pete Finem*, to give it its full name, was found to have leaking boiler tubes – enough to cause its immediate withdrawal. It looks as though Standard Class '5' 4-6-0 No. 73020 was released from Guildford, its home shed, to work in place of *Blue Funnel*.

Ivatt Class '2' 2-6-2T No. 41319 leaves platform seventeen at Clapham Junction with the *Kenny Belle* for Kensington Olympia. Tuesday 27 June 1967. (*Christopher Yapp*)

Later that morning, 41319 performs a spot of carriage shunting at Clapham Junction. The locomotive appears to have been given some sort of pre-TOPS numbering system! Tuesday 27 June 1967. (*Christopher Yapp*)

Standard Class '5' 4-6-0 No. 73020 rumbles through Woking with a freight for Feltham Yard. Tuesday 27 June 1967. (*Author's collection – photographer unknown*)

A rarely photographed light engine movement. Original Bulleid 'Light Pacific' No. 34102 *Lapford*, returns to Bournemouth after shunting at Brockenhurst. Photographed on Sway bank, probably on Tuesday 27 June 1967. (*Author's collection – photographer unknown*)

Standard Class '4' 4-6-0 No. 75074 stands at Waterloo while deputising for one of the Nine Elms tank engines on 101 duty. Tuesday 27 June 1967. (*Jim Blake*)

Another view of 75074 on 27 June. Ivatt tank 41298 is part hidden on the right. (*Jim Blake*)

A Ministry of Defence 0-4-0 diesel shunting loco WD 8212, had been standing since the 15 June in one of the sidings at Brockenhurst, having got no further on a transfer from Bicester to West Moors. It completed its journey by being towed away to West Moors on Thursday 29 June, the most likely locomotive for the job being Standard Class '4' tank 80011. I would guess that the diesel was limited to 15 mph, as the journey of approximately thirty-three miles was scheduled to take no less than seven hours, with layovers at Bournemouth Goods Yard and Poole.

'West Country Pacific' 34018 *Axminster* has brought the 08.46 from Bournemouth into Waterloo and now awaits a path to Nine Elms. Tuesday 27 June 1967. (*Jim Blake*)

Standard Class '4' 2-6-0 No. 76064 stands at the buffer stops in Waterloo after bringing in empty stock to form the 13.20 boat train to Southampton Eastern Docks for the *Queen Elizabeth*. Two wonderful advertisements hang from the roof: a fortnight in the Bahamas for £159 anyone? Thursday 29 June 1967. (*Jim Blake*)

That evening, 'Battle of Britain Pacific' 34060 *25 Squadron* was failed at Nine Elms, and the running foreman could find nothing larger than Standard Class '4' 4-6-0 No. 75075 to work the 18.54 from Waterloo to Salisbury.

On this same Thursday the Rolling Stones guitarist Keith Richards was given a prison sentence of a year by Chichester Crown Court for allowing cannabis to be smoked in his home. At the same time his band mate Mick Jagger was sentenced to three months in jail for possession of amphetamines. In August however, both sentences were quashed on appeal as they were considered harsh for first offences.

Also on the 29th, in the early hours of the morning, the American actress Jayne Mansfield was killed in a car crash in Louisiana. She was on her way to appear in a television show, and was just thirty-four years old.

Friday 30 June was the busiest day for boat train traffic during the last five weeks of Southern main line steam. There were no less than seven trains, three down and four up, hauled by six different 'Light Pacifics'. The last working unmodified example, 34102 *Lapford*, was the one locomotive to work in both directions.

Into July now, and on the morning of Saturday 1, rebuilt 'Light Pacific' 34025 *Whimple* provided cover for electric multiple units on the 09.24 Bournemouth to Waterloo. On the same morning sister locomotive 34024 *Tamar Valley* failed at Nine Elms while being prepared to work the 08.54 boat train for the P&O cruise liner *Iberia*.

'West Country Pacific' 34036 *Westward Ho* reverses out of Eastleigh station towards the shed, after working the 13.52 Bournemouth to Southampton. To say that the locomotive looks a little careworn would be an understatement! Thursday 29 June 1967. (*Bill Wright*)

In the early morning sunshine, Ivatt Class '2' 2-6-2T No. 41312 stands outside Waterloo. Next to it, 'Merchant Navy Pacific' 35023 *Holland–Africa Line*, is about to set back onto the 08.35 Waterloo to Weymouth. Friday 30 June 1967. (*Ernie's Railway Archive*)

The only locomotive available to work the train was Standard Class '4' 2-6-0 No. 76064, which was unable to keep to time and caused delays to other traffic as it proceeded west.

While returning to London that evening with the Channel Islands Boat Train, 'West Country Pacific' 34018 *Axminster* suffered a hot axle box and was removed from the train at Woking, and was replaced by an electro-diesel locomotive. The Pacific retired to Guildford shed, and after repairs was confined to light duties.

Away from the railway, there were many items of news on Saturday 1 July. The actress Pamela Anderson was born in Ladysmith, British Columbia, Canada, and it was also the day that the European Economic Community was formally created, two years after the Brussels treaty was signed.

On television, it was the day of the first colour television broadcast in the United Kingdom. The honour fell to a singles tennis match at Wimbledon; home favourite Roger Taylor and American Cliff Drysdale were the participants. That evening, the first episode of the popular game show *The Golden Shot* was aired, quickly giving rise to the catch phrase 'Bernie – the bolt!'

The main event however, was the final episode of *The Forsyte Saga*, the twenty-six part serialisation of John Galsworthy's novels. The series was originally broadcast on BBC2 on Saturdays, but when it was repeated in 1968 on the more widely available BBC1 it was so popular that the nation practically shut down on Sunday evenings and there are stories of church services being rescheduled earlier in the evening so that worshippers could be home in time for the start of the programme.

On Sunday 2 July British Railways ran their own 'Farewell to Southern Steam' tours. Four tours were planned, but in the event only two ran due to poor ticket sales. One of those cancelled was booked for steam in one direction only, so it was no surprise that there was little interest.

The first tour was a Waterloo to Weymouth return and the second just to Bournemouth and back – not very imaginative when compared with the tours that had preceded them on 11 and 18 June. The two designated 'Merchant Navy' locomotives, 35008 *Orient Line*, and 35028 *Clan Line*, had been held at Nine Elms for days in preparation for the tours. Their external condition on that day – highly polished and nameplates restored – was a credit to everyone involved. Internally, the two 'Merchants' must have been in fine fettle too, as running of both trains was of a high standard throughout.

Ivatt Class '2' 2-6-2T No. 41319 carriage shunting at Waterloo. Friday 30 June 1967. (*Jim Blake*)

The fireman of rebuilt 'West Country Pacific' 34093 *Saunton* keeps an eye on the water as the tender gets a top up in the short dock at Waterloo. The locomotive is between working the 12.10 arrival from Bournemouth and the 13.15 special empties to Clapham Junction. Standard Class '3' 2-6-2T No. 82019 stands further along the dock. Note also the LNER standard van on the left. Friday 30 June 1967. (*Jim Blake*)

Later the same day *Saunton* makes ready to leave Waterloo with the Fridays-only 18.22 to Bournemouth. Both pictures: Friday 30 June 1967. (*Jim Blake*)

'Merchant Navy Class Pacific' 35030 *Elder–Dempster Line'* reverses at Waterloo onto the 09.15 from to Bournemouth. This was a special train for members of the House of Commons on Saturday 1 July 1967. (*Author's collection – photographer unknown*)

Later that morning, *Elder–Dempster Lines* departs from Southampton Central with the same train. The party returned to London in the evening, departing from Bournemouth at 18.30. Saturday 1 July 1967. (*Author's collection – photographer unknown*)

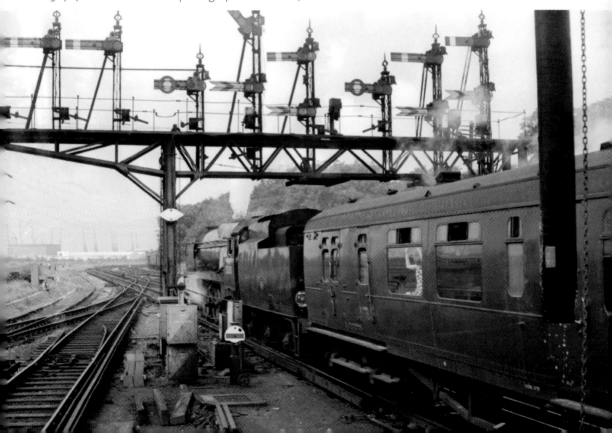

Having arrived at Bournemouth, *Elder–Dempster Lines* is turned on the shed turntable, while 'West Country' 34021 *Dartmoor* waits its turn amid a variety of steam shed clutter. Saturday 1 July 1967. (*Jonathan Greenwood*)

'USA' Class 0-6-0 No. 30067 shunts an assortment of freight wagons in the down loop platform at Eastleigh. Saturday 1 July 1967. (*Author's collection*)

Standard Class '5' 4-6-0 No. 73037 enters the up main platform at Eastleigh, with a train comprised mostly of 'Grampus' wagons, probably bound for the ballast sidings. Saturday 1 July 1967. (*Author's collection*)

Standard Class '4' 2-6-0 No. 76064 takes the down through line at Eastleigh with the 08.54 boat train from Waterloo to Southampton Eastern Docks, carrying passengers for the P&O cruise liner *Iberia*. Saturday 1 July 1967. (*Author's collection – photographer unknown*)

Standard Class '5' 4-6-0 No. 73093 calls at Southampton Central with the 12.35 Waterloo to Weymouth. Saturday 1 July 1967. (*Author's collection*)

'West Country Pacific' No. 34095 *Brentor* awaits its next duty on Guildford shed. Saturday 1 July 1967. (*Christopher Yapp*)

Rebuilt 'West Country Pacific' 34095 *Brentor* passes Walton-on Thames with a ballast train bound for Woking down yard. Sunday 2 July 1967. (*Keith Lawrence*)

Standard Class'5' 4-6-0s No. 73029 and No. 73043, along with Class '4' 2-6-0 No. 76031 and a 'Hymek' diesel-hydraulic, stand on Basingstoke shed. The photograph was taken from the returning 'End of Southern Steam' special from Weymouth, hauled by 'Merchant Navy Pacific' 35008 *Orient Line*. Sunday 2 July 1967. (*Author's collection*)

CHAPTER SEVEN

3 to 9 July 1967

Observers out of bed early in the Weymouth area on Monday 3 July may have been treated to the second rare pairing of 'Merchant Navy Pacifics' on the same train on consecutive days, when 35023 *Holland–Afrika Line* was booked to give rear end assistance to classmate 35007 *Aberdeen Commonwealth* on Bincombe bank with the 06.20 special empty coaches to Christchurch. The previous day, as is well documented, 35007 piloted 35008 *Orient Line* out of Weymouth on the 'Farewell to Southern Steam' rail tour.

During the first three days of this week 'Brush Type 4' diesel availability appears to have been at a low ebb, and many trains diagrammed to them were covered by steam locomotives. On Monday, 'West Country Pacific' 34025 *Whimple* worked the whole of 'Brush Type 4' diagram 91. This comprised two round trips from Waterloo to Bournemouth, including the *Bournemouth Belle* both ways, and ending with the 22.35 Waterloo to Weymouth 'Mails' as far as Eastleigh. The locomotive stayed on the train however and worked through to Weymouth, thereby covering some 580 miles in a little over twenty-four hours. Not bad for an engine entering its last week of service!

'Battle-of-Britain Pacific' 34060 *25 Squadron* leaves Weybridge with the 11.38 van train from Waterloo to Basingstoke. Monday 3 July 1967. (*Keith Lawrence*)

This was the last time that a steam locomotive worked the down 'Mails'. By coincidence, that same night the up 'Mails', the 22.13 from Weymouth to Waterloo, was also hauled by steam for the last time, when 'Battle of Britain Pacific' No. 34087 *145 Squadron* replaced failed 'Brush Type 4' D1926 on the train at Southampton.

Also at Weymouth, Standard Class '4' 2-6-0 No. 76006 reappeared after around seven weeks under repair to replace sister locomotive 76009 on Bournemouth 411 duty. Further east, it would seem that Standard Class '5' 4-6-0 No. 73092 was released from Guildford to replace hot-box casualty 34018 *Axminster* on main line duties, the latter locomotive working out of Guildford shed on ballast trains for the rest of the week.

On that same evening, ITN began a trial thirteen-week run of *News at Ten*, with head newscasters, Alastair Burnet, Andrew Gardner and George Ffitch reading the news.

Alan Hayes was lucky enough to be on the 17.30 Weymouth to Waterloo from Southampton, and the following day on the 11.18 Weymouth to Waterloo, also from Southampton. The two locomotives concerned, 'Merchant Navy Pacific' 35007 *Aberdeen Commonwealth* and 'West Country' 34021 *Dartmoor*, gave superb performances.

On 4 July, 'West Country Pacific' 34095 *Brentor* became the last Southern Region steam locomotive in 1967 to work into Reading, when it deputised for a 'Brush Type 4' on the 09.40 cross country service from Poole to Manchester. It later returned to Poole with the 16.03 from Reading (*ex* Newcastle) and may have failed there, not returning to

Original Bulleid 'Light Pacific' 34102 *Lapford* calls at Brockenhurst, thought to be with the 08.46 Bournemouth to Waterloo on Monday 3 July 1967. (*Author's collection – photographer unknown*)

		35007			34021		
		3 July 1967			4 July 1967		
		Load 10 + van = c.370t			Load 11 = c.380t		
Distance (miles)		Time (mins/secs)	Speed (mph)		Time (mins/secs)	Speed (mph)	
0.00	SOUTHAMPTON CENTRAL dep	00.00			00.00		
1.05	Northam Junction	03.44	23		03.22	24	
2.10	ST DENYS	05.27	38		05.13	39.5	
3.50	SWAYTHLING	07.16	50.5		06.56	53	
4.40	SOUTHAMPTON AIRPORT	08.12	55		07.52	60	
5.85	EASTLEIGH	09.42	59.5		09.14	63.5	
6.70	Allbrook Junction	10.31	61		10.02	64.5/67	
9.65	SHAWFORD	13.26	61	PWS	12.41	65	
11.50	St Cross	15.17	56.5		14.25	63	
12.80	WINCHESTER	16.39	59/60.5		15.38	61.5	
14.70	Winchester Junction	18.48	56/32	PWS	17.52	47/35	PWS
17.50	Wallers Ash	22.42	47		22.15	41	
18.90	Weston	24.20	56		24.08	50	
21.20	MICHELDEVER	26.27	61.5		26.33	55	
23.50	Roundwood signal box	28.15	62.5/70.5		28.37	53.5/64	
26.70	Wooton	31.32	68.5/33	Sigs	32.19	57/55	
29.00	Worting Junction	34.24	49.5		34.48	58.5	
31.50	BASINGSTOKE	36.48	75.5/82		37.14	68.5	
37.10	HOOK	40.56	83		41.39	79	
39.45	WINCHFIELD	42.35	89/94		43.28	80.5/78	
42.80	FLEET	44.45	93/96		45.55	82	
46.05	FARNBOROUGH	46.53	87		48.22	c.75/57	
48.30	MP 31(Summit)	48.35	78		50.23	59/65	PWS
51.30	BROOKWOOD	50.45	87/89		53.12	63.5	

		35007			34021		
		3 July 1967			**4 July 1967**		
		Load 10 + van = c.370t			**Load 11 = c.380t**		
Distance (miles)		Time (mins/secs)	Speed (mph)		Time (mins/secs)	Speed (mph)	
54.95	WOKING	53.19	80/84		56.45	65.5	
57.65	WEST BYFLEET	55.14	82.5/84		59.03	73	
58.90	BYFLEET & NEW HAW	56.08	82		60.01	78/79	
60.15	WEYBRIDGE	57.04	80/78.5		61.00	78.5/77	
62.15	WALTON-on-THAMES	58.37	81.5		62.33	82.5	
63.30	HERSHAM	59.26	80		63.23	84.5	
64.80	ESHER	60.36	82		64.29	83	
66.00	Hampton Court Junction	61.25	76		65.18	73	
67.25	SURBITON	62.28	75.5		66.24	70.5	
68.30	BERRYLANDS	63.20	73		67.21	69	
69.55	NEW MALDEN	64.18	74		68.21	68.5	
70.65	RAYNES PARK	65.14	72		69.26	67.5	
72.10	WIMBLEDON	66.24	67.5		70.49	63.5	
73.75	EARLSFIELD	67.54	64.5		72.22	64	
75.40	CLAPHAM JUNCTION	69.44	40		74.06	38	
76.65	QUEENS ROAD	71.21	53.5			54	
77.95	VAUXHALL	73.11	34		77.25	39	
79.30	WATERLOO arr	76.16			80.22		

Bournemouth shed until 20.30, coupled to 76026. Certainly it spent the next two days under repair.

That same day, Parliament voted to partially decriminalise male homosexuality in England and Wales. When the bill, known as The Sexual Offences Act 1967, received Royal assent later the same month, homosexual acts between consenting males over the age of twenty-one would become legal, as long as no-one else was present.

Standard Class '5' No. 73065 propels the weed killing train towards Weybridge junction. (*Keith Lawrence*)

Having propelled the train as far as Wimbledon, 73065 runs the 'weed killer' back through Weybridge towards Woking. Both pictures: Monday 3 July 1967. (*Keith Lawrence*)

Rebuilt Bulleid 'Pacific' 34060 *25 Squadron* at Locke King bridge, Weybridge, with the 08.46 train from Bournemouth to Waterloo. It was due into the capital at 12.10, and it seems incredible now that a train could take nearly three and a half hours for a 108 mile journey. (*Keith Lawrence*)

Just behind 34060, sister locomotive 34093 *Saunton* is at Locke King bridge with the Waterloo-bound boat train from Southampton East Docks carrying passengers from the Holland–America liner *Rotterdam.* Both pictures: Tuesday 4 July 1967. (*Keith Lawrence*)

The entrance to Nine Elms depot at the end of Brooklands Road. What wonders await us inside? The loco nearest the camera appears to be Standard Class '5' 4-6-0 No. 73092, with the 'Queen Mary' and 'Cunarder' chalk inscriptions on the smokebox that it carried during the last week. Tuesday 4 July 1967. (*George Woods*)

On the following day, Wednesday 5 July, the *Bournemouth Belle* was steam hauled for the last time. Rebuilt 'West Country Pacifics' shared the honours, with 34024 *Tamar Valley* working down to Bournemouth and 34036 *Westward Ho* taking the train back to Waterloo.

For 'Merchant Navy Pacific' 35028 *Clan Line* it was the last day in traffic. Sadly, it was no sparkling run on the 12.34 from Bournemouth to the capital, as the train took six minutes longer than the generous ninety-eight minutes scheduled, with four signal checks, three permanent way speed restrictions and a signal failure at Basingstoke to contend with.

It was also the final day in service for last remaining unmodified Bulleid 'Pacific', 34102 *Lapford*. Having worked the 06.49 commuter train up from Salisbury and back to Basingstoke with the 11.38 vans from Waterloo, it was last seen later in the day running light engine to Eastleigh.

Now a little mystery: pictured on page 108 is Standard Class '5' 4-6-0 No. 73065 on a train at Surbiton. The only information is that the photograph was taken in July 1967, so if the caption is correct, which day was it? The locomotive is in the same condition as other photos of it at the end of Southern steam, and the clock on the tower reads 07.35. The shadows prove that it is morning, so this is exactly the right time for the 06.29 from Basingstoke to Waterloo.

I believe that this also took place on Wednesday 5, as the 06.29 from Basingstoke was the first part of Brush diagram 92, the loco having run light from Eastleigh to work the train. As D1926, having worked a boat train to London the evening before, was probably left spare at Waterloo, it seems logical to me that the spare steam loco at Basingstoke – in this case 73065 – would have started the day off from there. The 'Type 4' would then have slotted into the diagram commencing with the 08.30 from Waterloo to Bournemouth.

The follow up question is of course, how did 73065 get back to Basingstoke? If any reader can shed any light on either of these workings I would be most grateful.

On Thursday 6 July, 'Merchant Navy Class' 35007 *Aberdeen Commonwealth* suffered a blown cylinder gland on the driver's side near Brookwood while working the 17.30 from Weymouth to Waterloo. The run is well known but a few facts deserve repeating. Having passed Roundwood summit at 70½ mph with eleven coaches and achieved the Holy Grail of reaching Worting Junction in under thirty minutes from Southampton Central, 'Merchant Seven' was worked up to 98 mph near Fleet before the gland blew out. The driver was still able to coax the loco up to 75 mph at Walton-on-Thames and arrive at Waterloo in eighty-four minutes from Southampton. On inspection it was found that the driver's side big end was now red hot, and at this stage either damage would have been enough to cause immediate withdrawal.

Standard Class '3' 2-6-2T No. 82029 and the last surviving unmodified 'West Country Pacific' 34102 *Lapford* at rest outside Nine Elms shed. Standard Class '5' 4-6-0 No. 73092 is in the background. Tuesday 4 July 1967. (*George Woods*)

Standard Class '5' 4-6-0 No. 73065 waits at Surbiton with what appears to be the 06.29 Basingstoke to Waterloo. July 1967. (*Rail-Online photos*)

Rebuilt 'West Country Pacific' 34024 *Tamar Valley* accelerates the last steam hauled down 'Bournemouth Belle' west of Wimbledon. Wednesday 5 July 1967. (Author's collection)

On Friday 7, 'Battle of Britain Pacific' 34052 *Lord Dowding* worked its first passenger train in many weeks when it was pressed into service for the 06.49 Salisbury to Waterloo. It stayed on Nine Elms 147 diagram, eventually working to Weymouth and becoming the last working 'Battle of Britain' when it hauled the 14.20 special freight to Westbury.

Later on Friday, Standard Class '5' 4-6-0 No. 73029, having arrived with the 16.51 from Basingstoke, was turned round at Salisbury in a remarkable thirty-five minutes to work the 18.38 to Waterloo. Its replacement on Guildford 165 diagram was none other than Standard Class '3' 2-6-0 No. 77014. This loco had worked down to Salisbury light engine earlier and was given two days extra life starting with the 19.20 vans to Northam and becoming the last working main line steam locomotive on the Southern Region when it hauled the 21.20 vans from Bournemouth to Weymouth on Sunday evening.

Friday and Saturday saw the last amateur finals at Wimbledon. Australian John Newcombe was the victor in the men's singles on Friday, beating the German Willhelm 'Billy' Bungert in straight sets. American Billie Jean King won the Ladies final the following day by defeating Britain's Ann Haydon-Jones, also in straight sets. Mrs Jones would get her revenge two years later, becoming champion by beating Mrs King in three sets.

On that Saturday, the actress Vivien Leigh died aged fifty-three. She was most famous for her role as Scarlett O'Hara in *Gone with the Wind*, and had been in London to begin rehearsals for a play when she fell seriously ill with tuberculosis.

Standard Class '5' 4-6-0 No. 73093 leaves Basingstoke with the 09.02 special freight to Feltham yard. Thursday 6 July 1967. (*Alan Hayes*)

And so to the last rites: over the final weekend the remaining locomotives were worked where possible to the holding areas of Salisbury and Weymouth depots. Some, like 'West Country Pacific' 34037 *Clovelly* had a very busy day on Saturday 8 (see roster) before running light engine to Salisbury, while many others were just sent light engine from the other sheds as there was no more work for them.

There was still time for a few more 'treats', however. On Saturday morning, 34095 *Brentor* reached a maximum of 94 mph near Wallers Ash with the 02.45 paper train from Waterloo to Bournemouth. Later, 'Merchant Navy Pacific' 35023 *Holland–Afrika Line*, with eleven coaches on the 08.30 from Waterloo, ran from Southampton to Bournemouth unchecked in one second under thirty minutes, as timed by Keith Widdowson.

35023		**Load 11 = c.380t**	
Distance (miles)		**Time** (mins/secs)	**Speeds** (mph)
0.00	SOUTHAMPTON CENT. dep	00.00	
0.95	MILLBROOK	02.56	34.5
2.65	REDBRIDGE	05.20	51.5
3.30	TOTTON	06.03	53
6.20	LYNDHURST ROAD	09.10	58
8.85	BEAULIEU ROAD	11.43	63/74.5
13.60	BROCKENHURST	15.42	68
14.55	Lymington Jcn.	16.37	63/60
16.05	SWAY	18.24	64.5/73
19.05	NEW MILTON	20.54	71
21.55	HINTON ADMIRAL	22.53	83/88.5
24.85	CHRISTCHURCH	25.17	63/64
26.80	POKESDOWN	27.17	50
27.30	Boscombe	28.02	45.5
28.55	BOURNEMOUTH arr	29.59	

Standard Class '5' 4-6-0 No. 73018 takes water at Yeovil Pen Mill while working the 14.45 tomato vans from Weymouth to Westbury. Thursday 6 July 1967. (*George Woods*)

'Merchant Navy Pacific' 35008 *Orient Line* passes the closed Wishing Well Halt with the 17.41 Weymouth to Bournemouth. Thursday 6 July 1967. (*George Woods*)

During the previous week, one of the clerks at the Wimbledon Divisional Manager's Office had produced a pair of steam diagrams for the *Bournemouth Belle* in each direction on Sunday 9 July. Intending that day to take the last opportunity to travel on the *Belle*, Keith Widdowson and friend Mike Hudson, both also diagram clerks, turned up at Waterloo fully expecting to see a steam locomotive on the front, only to find 'Brush Type 4' diesel D1924 instead. They were unaware that top management had vetoed steam haulage for the last day late on Friday after they had left work.

Mike quickly calculated that due to the diagram alterations a 'Type 4' would not be available to work the 14.07 from Weymouth to Waterloo, so they took a train via Alton to Southampton Central and waited. Mike was right: at a quarter past four, after some well recounted confusion at Bournemouth as to whether the loco would be detached or not, 'Merchant Navy Pacific' 35030 *Elder–Dempster Lines* duly ran in. The last 'Merchant Navy' on the last steam hauled train into London produced a good run with a ten minute early arrival – what a finale!

Incidentally, it was a consequence of the diagram alterations that Standard Class '3' 2-6-0 No. 77014 worked the 21.20 vans from Bournemouth to Weymouth. That train had originally been booked for the locomotive that would have hauled the down *Bournemouth Belle*.

Let the last word go to Richard Peirce and three friends who were determined to be at Waterloo on the last day:

Taken from the 07.18 Waterloo to Salisbury arriving at Fleet, rebuilt 'Battle of Britain Pacific' 34052 *Lord Dowding* leaves with the last steam-hauled 06.49 from Salisbury. This was the first time since at least the beginning of June she had worked a passenger train. Friday 7 July 1967. (*Jim Blake*)

The locomotive of the 07.18 Waterloo to Salisbury, 'West Country Pacific' 34024 *Tamar Valley*, waits for time at Andover Junction. Friday 7 July 1967. (*Jim Blake*)

'On a lovely summers morning we arrived to find the steam station pilots had finished the day before and the station was strangely silent. Sadly, the rumours that little would be running were all too true.

'We decided to visit Nine Elms. On arrival we found the gatehouse unmanned and a number of people were walking round the shed. To our surprise 'Merchant Navy Pacific' 35023 Holland–Afrika Line still had whispers of steam after its run to Weymouth and back the previous day, and in addition Standard Class '4' 4-6-0 No. 75075 was in light steam for the Nine Elms breakdown train. They were the only

A week after its last known working, 'Battle of Britain Pacific' 34090 *Sir Eustace Missenden – Southern Railway* stands inside Salisbury shed. Friday 7 July 1967. (*Jim Blake*)

engines among many that seemed to be in steam and left a lasting impression, being just visible in front of the deeper gloom of the shed.

'In the 'Old' shed area stood a number of other engines, notably Standard Class '4' 2-6-0 No. 76064, set aside after working the *Iberia* Waterloo–Southampton Boat train on 1 July. It was clean and looked ready to go out again. Nearby, on its own, was Ivatt 2-6-2T No. 41284 (withdrawn in March), minus its chimney which had been donated to preserved sister 41298. The latter resided in the 'New' shed near others earmarked for preservation: *Clan Line* and *Blackmore Vale*.

'The completion of our visit coincided with the authorities appearing and ushering everyone out on the basis that an engine was expected. With this in mind we hurried back to Vauxhall and ran up the steps to get a train back to Waterloo, just missing the last down *Bournemouth Belle* hauled by 'Brush Type 4' D1924. We did manage to catch the 12.37 to Waterloo, and were just leaving the station when to our left we saw 'West Country Pacific' 34021 *Dartmoor* on the Southampton–Waterloo Boat train catching us up.

'From Vauxhall we maintained an even pace with it; a superb and unforgettable couple of minutes seeing the engine working

'Merchant Navy Pacific' 35008 *Orient Line* prepares to leave Bournemouth shed to take over the 11.18 Weymouth to Waterloo, departing from Bournemouth at 12.34. The locomotive made a stunning climb to Roundwood, with a running time of just under 25 minutes from Southampton that included a 40 mph temporary speed restriction near Winchester Junction. Friday 7 July 1967. (*Author's collection*)

alongside us. It remains one of my best memories of Southern steam and is caught in the photograph on page 123 – taken by someone else on our train. As we approached Waterloo we could see an 'Electro-Diesel' locomotive standing outside the station – the driver was balanced on the buffer beam taking a picture!

'All too soon, our train was stopped at the Waterloo home signal and we watched as 34021 disappeared into the depths of the station on platform 14. On our arrival, we rushed across to see Dartmoor, but the platform had been closed to all but a small number of railway staff.

'About 13.17, once the pilot had removed the empty stock, the engine ran quickly out of the station and off to Nine Elms to turn and then Salisbury. With no further steam action likely, we decided to go to Kings Cross in the hope of seeing some 'Deltics'.

'At the end of the afternoon, we went back to Waterloo and were told that unexpectedly 35030 *Elder–Dempster Lines* was due to arrive at 17.56 with the 14.07 Weymouth to Waterloo. There followed a rush to the country end of platform 11, just in time to watch the train run in to platform 13 ten minutes early. We retraced our steps to join a small but appreciative crowd beside the still hot 'Merchant' at the buffer stops.

'The crew changed and Driver Jim Evans and Fireman John Cottee took over to take it to Nine Elms. In the heat, only about a dozen of us had returned to the end of platform 11 to watch the locomotive back out. It departed into the evening light and the echo of its whistle could be heard as it ran down to Vauxhall. It was a very moving moment and a real '*Waterloo Sunset*' to round off a very sad day.'

Ivatt Class
'2' 2-6-2T No. 41319 arrives at Kensington Olympia with the empties from Clapham Junction to form the 16.36 service back. Friday 7 July 1967. (*Alan Hayes*)

Standard Class '5' 4-6-0 No. 73029 pause at Eastleigh with the 10.15 Fratton to Basingstoke vans. Friday 7 July 1967. (*G. W. Sharpe*)

One of the Nine Elms depot staff, possibly Doug Richards, contemplates the artist David Shepherd's work. The three identifiable locomotives in the picture are Standard '4' 2-6-0 No. 76064, 'West Country' No. 34008 *Padstow* and 'Merchant Navy Pacific' No. 35007 *Aberdeen Commonwealth*. The sketch though, appears to be of the tank engine on the right. All four locomotives are already out of use. Friday 7 July 1967. (*Jim Blake*)

With a wealth of railway interest as a backdrop, 'West Country Pacific' 34025 *Whimple* leaves the turntable at Nine Elms and heads for the shed. Friday 7 July 1967. (*Jim Blake*)

Having been serviced, 'West Country Pacific' 34025 *Whimple* stands ready at Nine Elms for its last working, the 18.54 Waterloo to Salisbury. Friday 7 July 1967. (*Jim Blake*)

'Battle of Britain Pacific' 34052 *Lord Dowding* pauses at Winchester City with the 19.06 Basingstoke to Eastleigh. Friday 7 July 1967. (*G. W. Sharpe*)

'Merchant Navy' 35023 *Holland–Afrika Line,* working the 08.30 Waterloo to Weymouth, arrives at Winchester city for its first scheduled stop. The train had previously made an unscheduled call at Woking to pick up a group of enthusiasts who had missed their connection to Waterloo. Saturday 8 July 1967. (*Alan Hayes*)

A weary-looking Standard Class '4' 2-6-0 No. 76006 runs through the building site that is Southampton Central station with the 10.42 engineer train from Bournemouth Central goods yard to Eastleigh. This is almost the last working for this locomotive. Saturday 8 July 1967. (*Author's collection – photographer unknown*)

Standard Class '5' 4-6-0 No. 73020 waits at Bournemouth shed prior to working empty stock to Weymouth. Saturday 8 July 1967. (*Alan Hayes*)

Standard Class '5' 4-6-0 No. 73020 leaves Bournemouth shed for the last time, in readiness to work the 17.21 empty coaches to Weymouth. Sister loco 73092 in the background will work the 21.20 to Eastleigh later that evening. Saturday 8 July 1967. (*Author's collection*)

Rebuilt 'West Country Pacific' 34037 *Clovelly* passes Durnsford Road with the 18.20 boat train from Waterloo to Southampton Eastern Docks, for the Holland–America liner *Rotterdam*. Saturday 8 July 1967. (*Author's Collection*)

Standard Class '5' No. 73029 pauses at Guildford with the 09.47 special empties from Fratton to Clapham Junction on Sunday 9 July 1967. (*Keith Lawrence*)

Standard Class '4' 2-6-4T No. 80139 is being made ready to run from Basingstoke to Salisbury with Class '5' tender loco 73093. It appears that the tank has been awarded the CDM, after an advertisement at the time for a well-known chocolate bar! Sunday 9 July 1967. (*Keith Lawrence*)

Guildford's shunting loco, USA 0-6-0 tank 30072, prepares to leave its home depot and run light to Salisbury via Fareham. Sunday 9 July 1967. (*Keith Lawrence*)

A large crowd, many disappointed I suspect, watch 'Brush Type 4' D1924 as it departs from Waterloo with the last down *Bournemouth Belle*. Sunday 9 July 1967. (*Author's collection – photographer unknown*)

Rebuilt 'West Country Pacific' 34021 *Dartmoor* cuts through the heat haze at Surbiton with the last steam hauled boat train from Southampton Docks to Waterloo. Passengers aboard are off the Chandris Line ship *Ellinis*. Sunday 9 July 1967. (*Author's collection – photographer unknown*)

Nearing journey's end, *Dartmoor* coasts into Waterloo, again with the last steam hauled boat train from Southampton Docks. Sunday 9 July 1967. (*Author's collection – photographer unknown*)

Having run light engine from Nine Elms, *Dartmoor* reverses off the Salisbury turntable to join the other disposed locomotives in the shed. Sunday 9 July 1967. (*Dave Mant*)

Suitably inscribed 'USA' 0-6-0 tank 30072 is the last steam locomotive to arrive at Salisbury. The tank had run light engine from Guildford via Fareham, and was so short of steam on arrival it had to be moved on to a shed road by the diesel shunter. Sunday 9 July 1967. (*Dave Mant*)

A very nostalgic photograph, and not a loco or train in sight! Five friends walk along Wandsworth Road, heading towards Nine Elms depot for a final visit. Sunday 9 July 1967. (*Alan Hayes*)

Last rites – Nine Elms driver Jim Evans poses beside the last steam locomotive to bring a passenger train into Waterloo, 'Merchant Navy Pacific' 35030 *Elder–Dempster Lines,* after bringing the locomotive light engine from the terminus. His fireman Colin Cottey looks on from the cab. Sunday 9 July 1967, at approximately 18.30. (*Alan Hayes*)

Standard Class '4' 4-6-0 No. 75075 stands out of use inside the shed at Nine Elms, flanked by two 'Merchant Navy' locomotives, 35008 *Orient Line*'on the left and 35030 *Elder–Dempster Lines* on the right. Saturday 15 July 1967. (*Dick Manton*)

The photographer swings to the right to capture a full view of *Elder–Dempster Lines*. Both it and 75075 retain the chalked "Farewell to Steam" inscriptions on the front of the locomotives. Saturday 15 July 1967. (*Dick Manton*)

Epilogue

So that was it – no further reprieves, no strategic reserve in case of new traction failures or the completely new timetable going wrong. Naturally both these things happened and it took the rest of the year for the service to settle down. Water columns were quickly removed and sheds demolished over the next year or so. During the next few months, dead steam engines were hauled by diesel locomotives from Nine Elms and Eastleigh to the collecting point at Salisbury. From there and the other dump at Weymouth they were moved in twos and threes to the scrapyards in South Wales, the last not leaving Salisbury until March 1968.

I do not intend to end on such a downbeat though. When steam was completely eliminated from the national system in August 1968, British Rail instituted a steam ban. We all thought that was the very end – but no, in 1972 the ban was repealed. Starting with a small number of permitted locomotives allowed over a small number of routes, the steam rail tour programme has burgeoned into what we see today. It would be remiss of me not to express thanks to the dedicated groups of volunteers and donors that keep our locomotives fit for main line running, and also the powers that be that allow these wonderful machines to do what they were designed for.

And so it was that on Monday 9 July 2012 a group of us joined the *Cathedrals Express* at Waterloo to mark the 45th anniversary of the end of Southern steam. Hauled by 'Merchant Navy Pacific' 35028 *Clan Line*, this was originally routed from Waterloo to Yeovil Junction, down to Weymouth and direct back to Waterloo. However, owing to flooding near Yetminster, the return route was expected to be via Salisbury and Southampton, but a little while after leaving London it was announced that the original plan would be followed after all.

We had some smart running in places on the way down, but what I really wanted was a good run from Eastleigh back to Waterloo. Back in 1966/67, I had never travelled behind a 'Merchant' IN to London, so I was hoping to experience what I knew one could do. And did it! After allowing a cross-country service to pass us at Shawford Junction, *Clan Line* was eased out onto the main line and opened up as soon as Driver Don Clarke saw a green signal near St Cross. What followed had us buzzing for days afterwards. Not one caution signal was seen until Earlsfield, and after surmounting Roundwood at 68 mph, *Clan Line* reeled off the fifty miles to Wimbledon in forty minutes. Speeds were in the 71 to 76½ mph range the whole time – a tribute to the loco crew's skill and the planners who worked out the path.

35028	9 July 2012	Load 11 = c.425t gross		
Distance (miles)		**Time** (mins/secs)	**Speed** (mph)	
0.00	SIGNAL STOP dep	00.00		
0.30	Shawford Junction	02.45	30	Slow line to up line
0.60	SHAWFORD	03.15	35	Allowing preceding train to clear.
3.45	ST CROSS	(06.25)	38	
4.75	WINCHESTER	08.10	47.5	c. 2000edhp?
6.65	Winchester Junction	10.40	55	(Full regulator and 30-35% cut off from St Cross to summit.
10.85	Weston	14.53	61	
13.15	MICHELDEVER	17.00	64.5	
15.45	Litchfield Tunnel(Summit)	19.05	68	
17.25	Steventon	20.40	71	
18.65	Wooton	21.50	71.5/74	
20.95	Worting Junction	23.40	75	
23.45	BASINGSTOKE	25.45	71.5/76	
27.55	Newnham Siding	29.05	73.5	
29.05	HOOK	30.20	75/76	
31.40	WINCHFIELD	32.12	75.5/76.5	
34.75	FLEET	34.53	74.5/75	
38.00	FARNBOROUGH	37.30	74.5	
40.25	MP 31(Summit)	39.15	72.5/76	
43.25	BROOKWOOD	41.40	76.5	
46.90	WOKING	44.37	76	
49.60	WEST BYFLEET	46.45	75	
50.85	BYFLEET & NEW HAW	47.45	75	
52.10	WEYBRIDGE	48.45	71	
54.10	WALTON-on-THAMES	50.30	75/76	
55.25	HERSHAM	51.25	75	
56.75	ESHER	52.40	73.5	
57.95	Hampton Court Junction	53.35	72	
59.20	SURBITON	54.37	71	
60.25	BERRYLANDS	55.33	72	
61.50	NEW MALDEN	56.30	73.5	
62.60	RAYNES PARK	57.25	73	
64.05	WIMBLEDON	58.40	69	
65.70	EARLSFIELD	60.10	55/15	Signal check
67.35	CLAPHAM JUNCTION	64.30	32/36	Sig stop. To Reversible line
69.90	VAUXHALL	74.28	32	2 Sig stops before W'loo
71.20	WATERLOO arr	81.35		

Standard Class '4' 2-6-4T No. 80146 heads a line of ten locomotives at Salisbury awaiting their journey to the scrapyard. Others identifiable are Standard Class '4' 4-6-0 No. 75075, next in line, and at the far end, two 'Merchant Navy Pacifics', No. 35003 *Royal Mail* and No. 35008 *Orient Line*. Sunday 1 October 1967. (*Derek Jones*)

This would have been the equivalent of an unchecked Southampton to Waterloo run in approximately seventy six minutes, without once exceeding 76½ mph.

It is pleasing to report that "Clan Line", back after a two year overhaul just in time for the fiftieth anniversary, was performing as well as ever. Hopefully we will see it doing what it was designed for many years into the future.

Still looking ready for service, original Bulleid 'Pacific' 34102 *Lapford* waits to be towed away from Salisbury shed. Friday 10 November 1967. (*Dave Mant*)

The inside connecting rod of a Bulleid 'Pacific' is removed to enable easier movement to the scrapyard. Salisbury shed, Friday 10 November 1967. (*Dave Mant*)

Shafts of sunlight beam down on withdrawn locomotives inside Salisbury shed. They are, from the left, Standard Class '5' 4-6-0s No. 73043, No. 73065, No. 73093, No. 73029 and 'West Country Pacific' No. 34037 *Clovelly*. Christmas Eve, Sunday 24 December 1967. (*Dave Mant*)

Still at Salisbury on Saturday 16 March 1968, 'Merchant Navy Pacifics' No. 35008 *Orient Line* and No. 35023 *Holland–Afrika Line* await their turn to be towed away. They will be in the last group to leave at the end of the month. (*Dave Mant*)

Preserved 'Merchant Navy Pacific' No. 35028 *Clan Line* rests at Waterloo after its exhilarating run back to the capital on Monday 9 July 2012. (*Al Kennett*)

KEY TO ROSTERS

Depot diagrams:

101 – 149	Nine Elms (A)
161 – 177	Guildford (C)
254 – 325	Eastleigh (D)
394 – 412	Bournemouth (F)
461 – 463	Salisbury (E)

For reasons of space, depots are indicated by the letter of their shed code on the roster, as shown in brackets above. If a daily special diagram is known to be allocated to a particular depot it is indicated thus:

AS1 = Nine Elms Special 1   DS8 = Eastleigh Special 8 etc.

If the depot the daily special diagram was allocated to is unknown, or the work was arranged at the last minute, it is written as Spl.

NB: Diagrams 171 – 177 were Guildford special diagrams that were published on the weekly alteration sheet, and consequently it is possible in some cases that the work content was altered on a daily basis.

If a locomotive arrived at Guildford shed much earlier or later than booked time, the actual time of arrival is written in brackets at the end of the duty.

Also, for reasons of space, many place names are abbreviated. Hopefully they are self-explanatory or the full name is written elsewhere in the day's work.

Standard abbreviations are used after the departure time to indicate the type of train (other than a timetable passenger service). They are:

sp – special passenger train, e or ecs – empty coaching stock, se – special empties.

f or ft – freight train or sf – special freight. v – van train or sv – special vans, o/r – on rear

F & CS – Freight and Carriage Shunting, dep – departmental, M P Crane – Motive Power crane

bst – ballast train, engrs – engineers train, mats – materials train, lwr – long welded rail train.

le – light engine, ebv – engine and brake van. WAO – Work as Ordered.

Locomotive daily workings:

Diagram in bold and underlined (eg **145**) – known to have worked all or part of diagram.

Diagram number and text in normal script – probably worked diagram shown.

Text in *italics* – possibly worked diagram shown (No evidence found - author's best guess).

Rosters, 5 – 11 June

	MONDAY 5/6	TUESDAY 6/6	WEDNESDAY 7/6	THURSDAY 8/6	FRIDAY 9/6	SATURDAY 10/6	SUNDAY 11/6
34001 (A)	Bournemouth-Repairs	**407** 05.44 Bo'mouth-Eastleigh 08.29 Eastleigh-Bo'mouth 10.51 Bo'mouth-Weymth 17.00v Weymth-Bo'mouth 21.05e Bomo-Branksome 21.20le to Bovurnemouth	**FS10** Not Known and not worked - *DERAILED ON LOCO OUTLET*	Bournemouth-Repairs	Bournemouth-Repairs	Bournemouth-Repairs	Bournemouth-Repairs
34004 (F)	**462 (1)** 04.40 Wloo-Woking 06.30 Woking-Salisbury	**461** 06.49 Salisbury-Wloo 17.09 Wloo-Basingstoke 19.11 Basing-Salisbury	**ES8** 15.15le to Soton East Dks 16.50sf Soton East Dks-Westbury 19.20le to Salisbury	**467/136(2)** 10.00le Salis-Warm(F.S) 12.00le Warminster-Salis/ xx.xxle Salisbury-Eleigh 19.50 Eastleigh-Bo'mouth 22.05e Bo'mouth-Poole 22.40le to Weymouth	**137** 05.30f Weymouth-Poole 09.08f Poole-Wareham-Wool-Wareham-Furzebrook-Poole 17.42 Bo'mouth- 20.50f Eastleigh-Soton East Docks	**137(fri)/138** 00.54 Eleigh-Weymouth/ 06.43 Weymth-Bo'mouth 08.46 Bournemouth-Wloo	**ES14(railtour)** 09.35sp Mitre Bridge-Woking (D/H 73085) 10.50sp Woking-Wareham 14.00sp Wareham-Swanage -Wareham (T/T80146) 15.16sp Wareham-Weymth
34008 (A)	**140** 10.30sf Nine Elms Goods-Soton East Docks 16.20sf Soton West Docks-Nine Elms "H" Shed	**145** 08.35 Wloo-Weymouth 17.41 Weymth-Bo'mouth 21.00 Bo'mouth-Weymth	**147(1)** 07.49 Weymth-Bo'mouth	**411** 07.51 Bo'mouth-Weymth 11.18 Weymth-Bo'mouth	**411** As Thursday	**ES17** 05.15v Bo'mouth-Weymth 09.00sp Weymouth-Wloo	*OUT OF SERVICE (SUPERHEATER ELEMENTS)* (Withdrawn w/e 25th June)
34013 (E)	**145** 08.35 Wloo-Weymouth 17.41 Weymth-Bo'mouth 21.00 Bo'mouth-Weymth	**138** 06.43 Weymth-Bo'mouth 08.46 Bournemouth-Wloo	**461(2)** 17.09 Wloo-Basingstoke 19.11 Basing-Salisbury	**461** 06.49 Salisbury-Wloo 17.09 Wloo-Basingstoke 19.11 Basing-Salisbury	**461** As Thursday	**461** 07.35 Salisbury-Wloo	**136** 03.35 Wloo-Ports & S'sea 07.20le to Eastleigh 17.44 Soton West Docks-Waterloo (B32 - "Achille Lauro")
34018 (A)	Salisbury-Repairs *HOT BOX*	Salisbury-Repairs	Salisbury-Repairs	**Spl** 20.42sf Salisbury-Northam Yard 22.10le to Eastleigh	*DS16* 13.05le Eleigh-Soton Dks 14.00sf Soton East Dks-Feltham 16.50le to Eastleigh	Eastleigh-No Diagram	*Eastleigh-No Diagram*

	MONDAY 5/6	TUESDAY 6/6	WEDNESDAY 7/6	THURSDAY 8/6	FRIDAY 9/6	SATURDAY 10/6	SUNDAY 11/6
34021 (A)	136 02.30 Wloo-Ports. Harb 07.30 Port & S'sea-Eleigh 19.50 Eastleigh-Bo'mouth 22.05e Bo'mouth-Poole 22.40le to Weymouth	137 05.30f Weymouth-Poole 09.08f Poole-Broadstone-Poole-Wareham-Furzebrook-Poole 17.42 Bo'mouth-Eastleigh 20.50f Eleigh-Soton. E. Dock	137(tues)/138 00.54 Eleigh-Weymouth/ 06.43 Weymth-Bo'mouth 08.46 Bournemouth-Wloo	DS10 xx.xxsf or ecs Nine Elms or Clap Jcn-Elgh or Soton Dks	DS11? 18.40 Soton West Docks-Waterloo (B28 "Caronia")	AS3 10.00sp Wloo-Salisbury 18.38 Salisbury-Wloo	Nine Elms-Repairs *BOILER TUBES*
34023 (A)	AS1 08.50se Clapham Jcn.-Farnborough-Salisbury 10.30p Farnborough-Salisbury (To Okehampton)	113(2) 18.38 Salisbury-Wloo	395/149 02.45 Wloo-Bournemouth 07.08 Bo'mouth-Weymth/ 17.30 Weymouth-Wloo	Nine Elms-Exams	AS2 18.43 Wloo-Sot West Dks (B26 - "Iberia") xx.xxle Soton Docks-Wloo or Nine Elms-No Diagram	113 04.40 Wloo-Woking 06.30 Woking-Salisbury	AS5(railtour) 19.15sp Salis-Basingstoke (single loco) 19.59sp Basingstoke-Willesden Jcn. 21.40le to Nine Elms (D/H 73085)
34024 (F)	AS3 14.00 Waterloo-Southampton East Dks (B13 - Andes")	137(Mon)/Spl. 00.54 Eleigh-Weymouth/ xx.xxsf Weymth-Nine Elms	136(1)/165(2) 02.30 Wloo-Ports. Harb/ 10.15v Fratton-Basingstoke 16.51 Basing-Salisbury 19.20v Salisbury-Northam 21.22f Soton W Dks-Eleigh 23.10v Northam-Ports& S.	165(cont)/AS1/147(2) 01.30v Port & S-Fratton 02.10le to Eastleigh/ 05.10le Eleigh-Redbridge 06.10tvr Rbdge-Wimbledon c10.50le to Nine Elms/ 18.54 Wloo-Basingstoke	148 07.05 Basingstoke-Wloo 11.05v Wloo-Basingstoke 19.06 Basing-Soton Cent 21.18e Soton-Brockenhurst 22.00le Brock'hst-Weymth	134(2) 16.36 Weymth Jcn-Wloo (16.15 Ex Quay)	AS4 17.30 Waterloo-Southampton West Dks (B30 - "Ellinis")
34025 (F)	394(1)/396(2) 06.45 Poole-Bo'mouth 08.00se Hamworthy Jcn-Christchurch 08.08 Christchurch-Brock F & C.S. 09.00-09.50/ 16.03 Brockhst-Christ'ch 16.59le Christ'ch-Brockhst c&va shunt 18.45-19.45	394(1)/396(2) alt? 06.45 Poole-Bo'mouth 08.08 Christchurch-Brock F & C.S. 09.00-09.50/ 16.03 Brockhst-Christ'ch 16.59le Christ'ch-Brockhst c19.45sf Brock-Weymouth?	146 14.45sf Weymth-Westbury 17.30le to Weymouth	138 06.43 Weymth-Bo'mouth 08.46 Bournemouth-Wloo	136(1)/DS10(1)/254(2) 02.30 Wloo-Ports. Harb 07.30 Port & S'sea-Eleigh/ 10.51 Sot East Dks-Wloo 18.22 Wloo-Bournemouth 23.55le to Eastleigh	136(2) 14.20le Eastleigh-Soton C. (C.S. 15.00-16.15) 16.20 Soton C.-Bo'mouth 20.25v Bomo-Bevois Pk. xx.xxle to Eastleigh	138 09.55le Eastleigh-Soton C. 11.00v Soton C.-Bo'mouth (09.25 Ex Basingstoke) 19.59 Bournemouth-Wloo
34034 (A)	395 02.45 Wloo-Bournemouth 07.08 Bo'mouth-Weymth	149 17.30 Weymouth-Wloo	Nine Elms-Repairs	DS9 09.20 Waterloo-Southampton West Dks (B23 - "United States") 14.00sf East Dks-Feltham 17.00le to Nine Elms	254(1) 08.54 Wloo-Southampton East Docks (B25 - "Queen Mary") 13.05le Eastleigh-Nine Elms	Nine Elms-Repairs	Nine Elms-Repairs
34036 (A)	Weymouth-Repairs	146 14.45sf Weymth-Westbury 17.30le to Weymouth	137(1) 05.30f Weymouth-Poole 09.08f Poole-Wareham-Wool-Wareham-Furzebrook-Poole 17.42 Bo'mouth-Eastleigh 20.50f Elgh-Soton East Dks	137 Weds (cont) 00.54 Eleigh-Weymouth	Weymouth-Repairs *BRAKE GEAR*	Weymouth-Repairs	Weymouth-Repairs

34037 (D)	**254/147(2)** 11.27 Soton West Docks -Waterloo (B14-"Edinburgh Castle")/ 18.54 Wloo-Basingstoke	**148** 07.05 Basingstoke-Wloo 11.05v Wloo-Basingstoke 19.06 Bas-Southampton 21.18e Soton C.-Brockhst 22.00le Brock-Bo'mouth?	**394** 06.45 Poole-Bo'mouth 08.08 Christ'ch-Brock'hst F & C.S. 09.00-09.50 09.50le to Bournemouth 15.01 Bo'mouth-Weymth 18.15 Weymouth-Wloo	**395/146** 02.45 Wloo-Bournemouth 07.08 Bo'mouth-Weymth/ 14.45sf Weymth-Westbury 17.30le to Weymouth	**149** 17.30 Weymouth-Wloo	**136(1)** 02.30 Wloo-Ports Harbour 06.00e Ports Harb-Fratton 06.50le to Eastleigh	Eastleigh-No Diagram
34052 (E)	**ES10** xx.xxle to Chilmark Sidings 16.15sf Chilmark- Salisbury (possibly ran approx. 3 hours later)	Salisbury-Repairs	Salisbury-Repairs	Salisbury-No Diagram	**467** 10.00le Sal-Warminster F. S. 10.50 - 12.00 12.00le Warm-Salis 00.10sf(sat) Salis-Fratton 03.00le to Salisbury	**ES25** 05.30le Salis-Basingstoke 08.36sf Basing-Andover 09.30le to Salisbury	Salisbury-No Diagram
34060 (D)	Basingstoke - Repair *(INJECTOR)*	**283** 11.29v Basingstoke- Soton West Docks 16.20 Soton C.-Bo'mouth E. C. S. Bo'mouth Area 17.30 - 23.00	**280(1)** 05.15v Bo'mouth-Weymth 10.13 Weymth-Bo'mouth *(poss 396(2) vice 76009)*	**ESpl** *20.00le Bo'mouth-Wareham 21.05sf Wareham-Basing 01.20le to Eastleigh*	Eastleigh-Wash Out	Eastleigh-No Diagram	**145** 10.48 Soton East Docks -Waterloo (B31-"Ellinis") 17.54 Wloo-Salisbury
34087 (D)	**137(1)** 05.30f Weymouth-Poole 09.08f Poole-Wareham- Wool-Wareham- Furzebrook-Poole 17.42 Bo'mouth-Eastleigh 20.50f Elgh-Soton East Dks	Eastleigh-Wash Out	Eastleigh-Repairs	Eastleigh-Repairs	Eastleigh-Repairs	Eastleigh-Repairs	Eastleigh-Repairs
34089 (E)	**461** 06.49 Salisbury-Wloo 17.09 Wloo-Basingstoke 19.11 Basing-Salisbury	**462** 21.00f Salis-Basingstoke 00.35f Basing-Salisbury	Salisbury-Repairs *LEAKING TUBES*	Salisbury-No Diagram	Salisbury-No Diagram	Salisbury-Boiler inspection	Salisbury-No Diagram
34090 (D)	**138** 06.43 Weymth-Bo'mouth 08.46 Bournemouth-Wloo 13.44se Wloo-Clapham Jcn.	Nine Elms-No Diagram	**AS2** 08.34 Wloo-Sot E Dks (B19 - 'Nieuw Amsterdam') 14.00sf East Dks - Feltham 17.00le to Nine Elms	**136(1)/DSpl?** 02.30 Wloo-Ports Harb 07.30 Port & S-Eleigh/ 12.37sf Sot E Dks-Basing 14.50le to Eastleigh	Eastleigh-Wash Out	Eastleigh-Repairs	*140 2100le Eastleigh-Basing 22.02v Basingstoke-Wloo*

	MONDAY 5/6	TUESDAY 6/6	WEDNESDAY 7/6	THURSDAY 8/6	FRIDAY 9/6	SATURDAY 10/6	SUNDAY 11/6
34093 (D)	*145(Sun)/146* *00.54 Eleigh-Weymouth/* *Weymouth-Spare*	**147** 07.49 Weymth-Bo'mouth 12.34 Burne'mouth-Wloo 18.54 Wloo-Basingstoke	**148** 07.05 Basingstoke-Wloo 11.05v Wloo-Basingstoke 19.06 Bas-Southampton 21.18e Soton C-Brockhst 22.00le Brockhst-Weymth	**149** 17.30 Weymouth-Wloo	**134** 17.23 Waterloo- Bournemouth 20.15e Bournemouth- Hamworthy Junction C. S. 20.35 - 21.55 21.58le to Bournemouth	**FS19** 10.45le Bournemouth- Hamworthy Junction 11.57se Ham. Jcn-Poole 12.05sp Poole-Wloo	**FS15** 09.33 Wloo-Bournemouth (via Alton - Piloted by D6501) ECS Bo'mouth area to 14.30
34095 (D)	**DSpl?** 18.37 Soton West Dks- Waterloo (B15 - "United States")	**136(1)/165(2)** 02.30 Wloo-Ports. Harb/ 10.15v Fratton-Basing 16.51 Basing-Salisbury 19.20v Salisbury- Northam 21.22f Sot. W Dks-Eleigh 23.10v Northam-Ports & S.	**165(tues)cont/DS6** 01.30v Ports & S'sea -Fratton 02.10le to Eastleigh/ 10.55 Soton. East Docks -Waterloo (B22 - "Aragon")	**DS11** xx.xx(am)sf Nine Elms Goods- Soton East Docks	**DS13** c.12.40le Eastleigh- *Andover* 14.15sf Andover- *Feltham* xx.xxle to Nine Elms	**134(1)** 07.58 Wloo-Weymth Jcn. (to Wey Quay)	Weymouth- Repairs
34100 (E)	**467/462(2)** 10.00le Salis-Warminster F. S. 10.50 - 12.00 12.00le Warm-Salisbury/ 21.00f Salis-Basingstoke 00.35f Basing-Salisbury	**467/Spl** 10.00le Salis-Warminster F. S. 10.50 - 12.00 12.00le Warm-Salisbury/ 20.42sf Salisbury- Northam Yard 22.10le to Salisbury	**467/113(2)** 10.00le Salis-Warminster F. S. 10.50 - 12.00 12.00le Warm-Salisbury/ 18.38 Salisbury-Wloo	Nine Elms-No Diagram	**145** 08.35 Wloo-Weymouth 17.41 Weymth- Bo'mouth 21.00 Bo'mouth-Weymth	**147/149** 09.30sv Weymouth-Eleigh 13.00le to Weymouth/ 18.15 Weymouth-Wloo (Piloted by D6510? to Dorchester South?)	*OUT OF SERVICE* *(TENDER BEARING)* *(Withdrawn w/e 2nd* *July)*
34102 (D)	Eastleigh- Repairs *HOT BOX*	Eastleigh- Repairs *Poss. test trip l. e. to* *Basingstoke and return*	**DS7** 12.37sf Soton East Docks- Basingstoke 14.40le to Eastleigh 17.43sf Soton East Docks- Basingstoke 20.00le to Eastleigh	**DS4** 05.13sf Eleigh-Weymouth 10.00sv Weymouth- Clapham Jcn. (banked to Bincombe by 76007) 16.00se Clapham Jcn- Eastleigh	**DS8/136(2)** 06.10(materials) Redbridge-Wimbledon 14.40se Stewarts Lane- Eastleigh/ 19.50 Eastleigh- Bo'mouth 22.05e Bo'mouth-Poole 22.40le to Weymouth	**146/FS20** 15.40se Weymouth- Hamworthy Jcn 16.45le to Bo'mouth(Turn)/ *18.08 Bo'mouth-Weymth*	**139/Dsl?** 06.23 Weymth. Jcn-Wloo (06.00 Ex Quay- via Netley & Cobham) 12.42e Waterloo- Clapham Jcn/ *18.30 Wloo-Bournemouth*
34108 (E)	**463** 08.31v Salis-Basingstoke 10.45v Basing- Port & S'sea C. S. 13.20 - 15.00 16.00v Port & S-Fratton 19.06v Port & S-Salisbury	**463** As Monday	**463** As Monday	**463** As Monday	**463** As Monday	**Dsl.** 12.36 Salisbury-Wloo 17.00 Wloo-Salisbury (or possibly Exeter!)	Salisbury-No Diagram

35003 (A)	**281** 07.18 Wloo-Salisbury C.S. 13.30 - 14.15 15.55 Salis-Basingstoke	**282** Basingstoke - Spare	**283** 11.29v Basingstoke- Southampton West Dks 16.20 Soton C-Bo'mouth E.C.S. Bo'mouth Area 17.30 - 23.00	**280(1)/394(2)** 05.15v Bo'mouth- Weymth 10.13 Weymth-Bo'mouth/ 15.01 Bo'mouth-Weymth 18.15 Weymouth-Wloo	**396(1)/397(2)** 06.23 Weymth-Bincombe (bank 06.00 Ex Wey Quay) 06.46le to Weymouth 08.15 Wey-Dorch'ter Sth. 09.05se Dorch. South- Weymouth/ 20.15 Weymth-Bo'mouth	**395/146** 02.45 Waterloo- Bournemouth/ Weymth/ 07.08 Bo'mouth- Weymth/ 14.45f Weymth- Westbury 17.30le to Weymouth (or 34036)	*Bournemouth-* *No Diagram*
35007 (A)	**396(1)/394(2)** 08.27 Weymth-Bo'mouth 10.32f Bomo-Cent Goods 10.57f Cent Goods-Bomo/ 15.01 Bo'mouth-Weymth 18.15 Weymouth-Wloo	**395** 02.45 Wloo-Bournemouth 07.08 Bo'mouth-Weymth	**396(1)/147(2)** 08.27 Weymth-Bo'mouth 10.32f Bomo-Cent Goods 10.57f Cent Goods-Bomo/ 12.34 Bournemouth-Wloo 18.54 Wloo-Basingstoke	**283** 11.29v Basingstoke- Southampton West Dks 16.20 Soton Central- Bournemouth area 17.30 - 23.00	**412** 07.13e Bomo West- Branksome 09.20 Bo'mouth-Weymth 12.12 Weymth- Bo'mouth 13.52 Bo'mouth-Soton C. 18.30 Soton Central- Bournemouth 20.03e Bomo-Branksome	**411** 05.44 Bo'mouth-Eastleigh 08.29 Eastleigh-Bo'mouth 10.56e Bomo-Branksome 11.12le to Bournemouth	*FS13* *05.50 Bo'mouth-Eastleigh* *00.54(mon) Eastleigh-* *Weymouth*
35008 (A)	**135** 08.10 Wloo-Weymth. Jcn 16.23 Weymth. Jcn-Wloo (16.00 Ex Quay)	Nine Elms-Repairs	**135** As Tuesday	**135** As Tuesday	**135**	**397(1)/396(2)** 08.30 Wloo-Weymouth/ 17.00v Weymth-Bo'mouth	**394** 18.28le Bournemouth- Hamworthy Jcn. 19.05e Hamworthy Jcn- Bournemouth 19.36 Bournemouth-Wloo
35013 (A)	**135** 08.10 Wloo-Weymth. Jcn 16.23 Weymth. Jcn-Wloo (16.00 Ex Quay)	Nine Elms-Repairs	Nine Elms-Repairs	**145** 08.35 Wloo-Weymouth 17.41 Weymth-Bo'mouth 21.00 Bo'mouth-Weymth	**147(1)/138(2)** 07.49 Weymth-Bo'mouth 12.34 Bournemouth- Wloo/ 19.45 Wloo-Weymth Jcn. (to Weymouth Quay)	**139** 06.23 Weymth Jcn-Wloo (06.00 Ex Quay) 19.45 Wloo-Weymth Jcn (to Wey Quay)	**396** Pilot 08.20? Weymouth- Waterloo (D6512 + Rep + 8TC) to Dorchester South? xx.xxle to Weymouth (C.S. at Wey 09.30-16.10) Pilot 16.35sp to Dorch. Sth. xx.xxle to Weymouth (C.S. at Wey 17.00-22.20) 22.13bank Wey-Dorch Sth 22.35le to Weymouth
35023 (A)	**149** 17.30 Weymouth-Wloo	Nine Elms-Repairs *SUPERHATER ELEMENTS*	Nine Elms-Repairs	Nine Elms-Repairs	Nine Elms-Repairs	**AS2** 09.24sp Wloo-Weymouth 15.20se Wey-Clapham Jcn	**141** 11.30 Waterloo- Bournemouth E.C.S. Bo'mouth area 14.25 - 16.15 17.00v Bo'mouth-Weymth

	MONDAY 5/6	TUESDAY 6/6	WEDNESDAY 7/6	THURSDAY 8/6	FRIDAY 9/6	SATURDAY 10/6	SUNDAY 11/6
35028 (A)	**147(1)** 07.49 Weymnth-Bo'mouth 12.34 Bournemouth-Wloo	Nine Elms-Repairs	**145** 08.35 Wloo-Weymouth 17.41 Weymth-Bo'mouth 21.00 Bo'mouth-Weymth	**147(1)** 07.49 Weymth-Bo'mouth 12.34 Bournemouth-Wloo	Nine Elms-Repairs	**135** 08.10 Wloo-Weymth. Jcn 16.23 Weymth. Jcn-Wloo (16.00 Ex Quay) (Banked by 80011 Poole-Branksome)	Nine Elms-No Diagram
35030 (A)	Nine Elms-Repairs	**113(1)** 04.40 Wloo-Woking 06.30 Woking-Salisbury	**461(1)** 06.49 Salisbury-Wloo	Nine Elms-Repairs	Nine Elms-Repairs	**AS4** 10.24sp Wloo-Weymouth	**AS3(railtour)** 16.35sp Weymth-Salisbury 20.00le to Nine Elms
73018 (C)	**173** 19.55le Guildford-Woking Up Yard 20.38bst Woking-Surbiton 21.55bst Surb-Walton-o-T (WAO to West Byfleet) 06.10bst West Byfleet-Woking Up Yard 06.48le to Guildford	**172** 20.00le Guildford-Shalford 20.33bst Shalford-Surbiton 22.42bst Surb-Walton-o-T (WAO to W. Byfleet) 06.15bst West Byfleet-Woking Up Yard 07.18le to Guildfd (08.00)	**172** As Tuesday arr Guildfd 07.35 (07.00)	**172** As Tuesday arr Guild 07.35 (08.00)	**172** As Tuesday arr Guild 06.00	**CS9** 18.45le Guildford-Farnham 19.50bst Farn-Wok Up Yard 20.50bst Woking -Hook (WAO) 03.00bst Hook-Basingstoke 03.45bst Basingstoke-Woking Up Yard	**CS9(Sat) cont** 05.00le Woking-Guildford (C. S. 05.30-06.00) 06.00le to loco(06.35) SUN: *Guildfd- No diagram*
73020 (C)	**282** *Basingstoke-Spare* *xx.xxle to Nine Elms*	**AS1** 08.20 Waterloo-Southampton East Dks (B17 - "Sylvania") 14.00sf East Docks-Feltham xx.xxle to Nine Elms	**Spl/CS4** 07.25le Nine Elms-Guildfd (coupled to 76011) (arr 08.25)/ 23.25le Guildford-Surbiton 00.20bst Surbiton-Esher (WAO Viaduct insp unit to Walton-on Thames) 05.30bst Walton-o-T-Guildford Yard	**171(1)/Spl/CS3** 07.00le Guildford-Woking Up Yd 07.28bst Woking-Shalford 09.28bst *Shal-Wok Up Yard* 10.00le to Guildford / dep Guild 11.00 Shalford arr Guild 12.45/ Shunt? 23.05bst Guildford Yard-Aldershot 23.55bst Alders-Camberley (WAO Viaduct inspect unit to Ascot and berth) 05.45le to Guildford	**CS4/CS6** *10.45le Guildford-Woking Up Yard* 11.48bst Woking-Richmond *c13.10le to Guildfd(a14.35)/* 22.15le Guildford-Ascot 00.10bst Ascot-Bagshot (Viaduct inspection unit) 05.00bst Bagshot-Guildford (via Ascot - arr 06.40)	**CS8** 18.40le Guild-Wok Up Yd 19.23crane Woking-Fratton 08.30crane Fratton-Woking Up Yard 10.55 le to Guildfd(12.00)	*Guildford -No Diagram*
73029 (A)	**162** *09.02sf Basing-Feltham* *12.45sf Feltham-Eastleigh* *17.30le to Basingstoke*	*162* *09.02sf Basing-Feltham* *12.45sf Feltham-Eleigh* *17.30le to Basingstoke*	*282* *Basingstoke-Spare*	*282* *Basingstoke - Spare*	**283** *11.29v Basingstoke-Soton West Docks* 16.20 Soton Central-Bournemouth C&WE Shunt at Brockhurst 18.45-19.45 19.45le to Bournemouth	**280** 06.20le Bo'moth-Brockhst 07.25le Brock-Eastleigh 12.48 Eastleigh-Bo'mouth 16.28 Bo'mouth-Eastleigh 19.40e Eleigh-Soton Cent. 20.15 Soton C.-Bo'mouth	*280* *21.20v Bo'mouth-Weymth*

73037 (A)	**148** 07.05 Basingstoke-Wloo 11.05v Wloo-Basingstoke 19.06 Bas-Southampton 21.18e Soton C.-Brockhst 22.00le Brockhst-Weymth	396(1)/**394(2)** 08.27 Weymth-Bo'mouth/ 15.01 Bo'mouth-Weymth 18.15 Weymouth-Wloo	**113(1)**/281(2) 04.40 Wloo-Woking 06.30 Woking-Salisbury/ 15.55 Salis-Basingstoke	**162** 09.02sf Basing-Feltham 12.45sf Feltham-Eastleigh 17.45sf Soton East Docks-Basingstoke	282 Basingstoke - Spare	**282** 09.20le Basing-Nine Elms 12.39 Wloo-Basingstoke	Basingstoke - No Diagram
73043 (A)	Nine Elms-Repairs	Nine Elms-Repairs	Nine Elms-Repairs	**103** 06.20le Nine Elms- Clapham Jcn 07.22e Clapham Jcn- Waterloo 08.13le to Nine Elms	**140** 10.30sf Nine Elms Gds -Soton East Docks 16.20sf Soton West Dks -Nine Elms 'H' Shed	**AS1**/281 07.12se Clapham Jcn- Waterloo 08.22sp Waterloo- Bournemouth 10.43se Bournemouth- Hamworthy Jcn. 13.10se Bomo-Clapham J./ 23.40bst 9 Elms-Clap Jcn.	AS22(Sat) cont (WAO) 07.20bst Clapham Jcn- Wimbledon West Yd 07.58le to Nine Elms SUN: Nine Elms - Washout?
73065 (A)	280 10.13 Weymth-Bo'mouth 15.00le to Brockenhurst 16.15e Brockhst-Eastleigh 19.04l Northam-Eastleigh 20.40v Eleigh-Clapham Jcn	ASpl/28o(2) 15.06se Clapham Jcn- Micheldever 17.45le to Eastleigh 20.40v Eastleigh- Clapham Jcn	**281(1)**/462 07.18 Wloo-Salisbury C. S. 13.30 - 14.15/ 21.00f Salis-Basingstoke 00.35f Basing-Salisbury	462 14.00le Salis - Soton Dks 16.50f Soton East Dks- Westbury 19.20le to Salisbury 21.00f Salis-Basingstoke 00.35f Basing-Salisbury	462 As Thursday	ES26 05.55(dep) Salis East Yard- Micheldever 09.15(dep) Micheldever- Salisbury Carriage Sdgs.	Salisbury-Repairs
73085 (A)	**140** As Wednesday	**140** 10.30sf Nine Elms Goods- Soton East Docks 16.20sf Soton West Docks- Nine Elms "H" Shed	**140** As Wednesday	**140** As Wednesday	Nine Elms-No Diagram	Nine Elms-No Diagram	**AS1** 09.35sp Mitre Bdge- Woking (D/H 34004) 10.55le to Basingstoke 19.59sp Bas-Willesden Jcn (D/H 34023) 21.40le to Nine Elms
73092 (C)	Eastleigh - Repairs or No Diagram	**DS2** 11.27 Soton West Docks- Waterloo (B21 - "Begona")	ASpl? 07.40se Clapham Jcn- Waterloo 08.37le to Nine Elms	**281** 07.18 Wloo-Salisbury C. S. 13.30 - 14.15 15.55 Salis-Basingstoke	162 09.02sf Basing-Feltham 12.45sf Feltham-Eastleigh 17.30le to Basingstoke	283	Basingstoke - No Diagram

	MONDAY 5/6	TUESDAY 6/6	WEDNESDAY 7/6	THURSDAY 8/6	FRIDAY 9/6	SATURDAY 10/6	SUNDAY 11/6
73093 (C)	**113** 18.38 Salisbury-Wloo	**281** 07.18 Wloo-Salisbury C. S. 13.30 - 14.15 15. 55 Salis-Basingstoke	**DS5** 09.02f Basing-Feltham 12.45f Basing-Feltham 15.30sf Basing-Bramley xx.xxle to zBasing	**148** 07.05 Basingstoke-Wloo 11.05v Wloo-Basingstoke 19.06 Bas-Southampton 21.18e Soton C.-Brockhst 22.00le Brockhst-Weymth	396(1)/**394(2)** 08.27 Weymth-Bo'mouth 10.32f Bomo loco- Central Goods 10.57f Cent Gds- Bomo loco/ 15.01 Bo'mouth-Weymth 18.15 Weymouth-Wloo	**395** 02.45 Wloo-Bournemouth 07.08 Bo'mouth-Weymth 10.13 Weymth-Bo'mouth 17.02 Bo'mouth-Wareham 18.51e Wareham-Poole 21.00 Bo'mouth-Weymth	137/395 *11.20sf Weymth-Westbury (to Crewe) 14.00le to Weymouth/ 22.13 Weymth-Bo'mouth*
73118 (C)	**AS2** *c. 13.00se Clapham Jen- Waterloo 14.03le to Nine Elms*	**Spl 6** *xx.xx(am)sf Nine Elms Gds?- Soton East Docks 17.45sf Soton East Docks- Basingstoke*	**163/CS3** 14.05v Basing-Surbiton 14.59le to Guildford/ 21.40le Guildford Woking Up Yd 22.28bst Wok-Wokingham (WAO to Earley)	**CS3(weds)cont/171(2)** 03.35bst Earley- Woking Dn Yd c06.30le to Guildfd(08.15)/ 20.45le Guildford- Farnham 21.50bst Farm-West Byfleet (WAO to Walton-o-T)	**171(2)thurs cont** 06.00bst W-o-T - Surbiton 06.45bst Surbiton- Woking Dn Yd 07.35le to Guildfd(08.55) FRI: *Guildford - No diagram*	**CS6/CS11** 04.30le Guildford-Woking 05.20v Woking-Aldershot (CS and FS 05.45-10.45) 11.00le to Guildfd(12.30)/ 20.00le Guild-Wok Up Yd 20.38bst Wok-Walton o T	**CS11 (Sat) cont** (WAO) 09.45bst West Byfleet- Woking Up Yd 10.20le to Guildford SUN: *Guildford - No Diagram*
73155 (C)	*Guildford - No Diagram*	**171(1)/CS3** 08.00le Guildford-Shalford 09.28bst Shalfd-Wok Up Yd 11.10le Woking-Farnham 12.00le to Woking 12.40bst Woking-Farnham 13.30le to Guildford/ 23.00le to Guildford Yard 23.30bst Guiildfd Yd- Walton-on Thames (WAO Viaduct inspect unit to Esher) 05.30bst Esher-Surbiton 06.00le to Guildford	**171** 07.00le Guildford- Woking Up Yd 07.28bst Woking-Shalford 09.28bst Shalford- Woking Up Yd 11.10bst Woking-Farnham 12.00le to Guildford 20.45le Guildford- Farnham 21.50bst Farm-West Byfleet (WAO to Walton-o-T) 06.00bst W-o-T-Surbiton 06.45bst Surbiton- Woking Down Yd 07.35le to Guildfd (08.00)	*Guildford - No Diagram*	**171** 08.00le Guildford- Shalford 09.28bst Shalford- Woking Up Yd 11.10bst Woking- Farnham 12.00le to Woking 12.40bst Woking- Farnham 13.30le to Guildford 20.45le Guildford- Farnham 21.50bst Farnham- West Byfleet (WAO to Walton-o-T) 06.00bst W-o-T-Surbiton 06.45bst Surbiton- Woking Dn Yd 07.35le to Guildfd (08.00)	**CS24** 21.45le Guildford- Woking Up Yard 22.28bst Woking- Guildford(RR) 23.05bst Guildford- Wokingham (WAO) 07.30bst Earley- Guildford(RR) 09.00bst Guild-Wok Up Yd 09.50le to Guildfd(11.00)	*Guildford - No Diagram*
75068 (D)	*Bournemouth-No Diagram*	**FS11** 05.50le Bomo-Brockhst 07.08bsf Brockhst-Wool (WAO to Dorchester Sth) Turn loco at Weymouth 11.44bst Dorch Sth-Wool 12.46bst Wool-Brockhst 14.50le to Bournemouth	**404(1)** 07.52le Bo'mouth-Poole 08.30f Poole-Ringwood 12.10f Ringwood-Poole 15.35f Poole-Weymouth	396(1)/**407(2)** 08.27 Weymth-Bo'mouth/ 10.51 Bo'mouth-Weymth 17.00v Weymth-Bo'mouth 21.05e Bomo-Branksome 21.20le to Bournemouth	**407** 05.44 Bo'mouth-Eastleigh 08.29 Eastleigh-Bo'mouth 10.51 Bo'mouth-Weymth 17.00v Weymth-Bo'mouth 21.05e Bomo-Branksome 21.20le to Bournemouth	**410** 09.20 Bo'mouth-Weymth (05.30 Ex Wloo) 12.12 Weymth-Bo'mouth 13.52 Bo'mouth-Soton C. 18.30 Soton C.-Bo'mouth 20.15e Bo'mouth-Poole	*Bournemouth-No Diagram*

Duty							
75074 (D)	404(2) 22.13 Weymth-Bo'mouth (D/H D65xx)	**412** 07.13e Bomo West-Branks 09.20 Bo'mouth-Weymth 12.12 Weymth-Bo'mouth 13.52 Bo'mouth-Soton C 18.30 Soton C-Bo'mouth 20.15e Bomo-Branksome	**412** 07.13e Bomo West-Branks 09.20 Bo'mouth-Weymth 12.12 Weymth-Bo'mouth 13.52 Bo'mouth-Soton C 18.30 Soton C-Bo'mouth 20.15e Bomo-Branksome	404 07.52le Bo'mouth-Poole 08.30f Poole-Ringwood 12.10f Ringwood-Poole 15.35f Poole-Weymouth 22.13 Weymth-Bo'mouth (D/H D65xx)	**412** 05.00le Bo'mouth-Poole 06.45 Poole-Bo'mouth 07.51 Bo'mouth-Weymth 11.18 Weymth-Bo'mouth 17.42 Bo'mouth-Eastleigh 21.03e Soton C-Branksome		*Bournemouth-No Diagram*
75075 (D)	283 11.29v Basingstoke-Soton West Docks 16.20 Soton C.-Bo'mouth E.C.S. Bo'mouth Area 17.30 - 23.00	404 As Thursday	401 07.23e Branksome-Bomo 07.37 Bo'mouth-Eastleigh 14.02 Eastleigh-Bo'mouth 17.02 Bomo-Dorch South 18.22e Dorch South-Poole 19.30le to Bournemouth	404 07.52le Bo'mouth-Poole 08.30f Poole-Ringwood 12.10f Ringwood-Poole 15.35f Poole-Weymouth 22.13 Weymth-Bo'mouth (D/H D65xx)	280 05.15v Bo'mouth-Weymouth 10.13 Weymth-Bo'mouth 15.00le to Brockenhurst 16.15e Brockhst-Eastleigh 19.04f Northam-Eastleigh 20.40v Eastleigh-Clapham Jcn.	**DS15** 09.43se Clapham Jcn-Waterloo 10.35sp Waterloo-Bournemouth 14.25le to Eastleigh	DS10 07.05le Eleigh-Redbridge 08.20bst Redbdge-Eastleigh Marshalling Yard (W. A. O.) 14.10bst to Redbridge 15.20le to Eastleigh
75076 (D)	DSpl. xx.xxle Eleigh-Bomo 08.55ebv Bo'mouth-Wareham 10.08sf Wareham-Basingstoke	DSpl. 06.05sf Basing-Wareham 10.45le to Bournemouth (turn) xx.xxle to Eastleigh	166 10.15e Eleigh-Soton Cent 10.43 Soton C.-Bo'mouth 13.08 Bo'mouth-Weymth 16.46 Weymth-Bo'mouth 18.51 Bo'mouth-Woking 22.45le to Guildford	165 02.28le Guildford-Woking 03.18v Woking-Fratton 10.15v Fratton-Basing 16.51 Basing-Salisbury 19.20v Salisbury-Northam 21.22f Soton W Dks-Eleigh	**166** 10.15e Eleigh-Soton Cent 10.43 Soton C.-Bo'mouth 13.08 Bo'mouth-Weymth 16.46 Weymth-Bo'mouth 18.51 Bo'mouth-Woking 22.45le to Guildford	**165** 02.28le Guildford-Woking 03.18v Woking-Fratton 07.30 Ports & S'sea-Eleigh 22.20le Eleigh-Winchester 23.35bst Winchester-Shawford Jcn (WAO)	**Sat (165) cont** 08.00bst Albrook Junction-Eastleigh Marshalling Yd xx.xxle to loco
75077 (D)	**290** Local freights & vans Eleigh and Soton area 08.00 - 14.00 16.22 Eleigh-Soton Cent 17.16 Soton-Bomo & ecs 20.45le to Eastleigh Local freights 23.25 - 02.00	**290(Mon)cont/290** 04.40f Eleigh-Winchester 05.30le to Eastleigh As Monday	290 As Monday (To 14.00?)	**290** As Monday	290 As Monday	DS? 23.50le Eastleigh-Bevois Pk 00.48bst Bev Park-Millbrook (WAO to Redbridge & back) 06.30bst Millbrook-Bev. Pk 07.10le to Eastleigh	*Eastleigh-No Diagram*
76005 (F)	412 07.13e Bomo West-Branks 09.20 Bo'mouth-Weymth 12.12 Weymth-Bo'mouth 13.52 Bo'mouth-Soton C 18.30 Soton C-Bo'mouth 20.15e Bomo-Branksome	280(1)/400(2) 05.15v Bo'mouth-Weymth 10.13 Weymth-Bo'mouth 17.01bank CIBT to Branks 1735f Poole Yard-Bomo Cent Gds	407 05.44 Bo'mouth-Eastleigh 08.29 Eastleigh-Bo'mouth 10.51 Bo'mouth-Weymth 17.00v Weymth-Bo'mouth 21.05e Bomo-Branksome 21.20le to Bournemouth	407(1) 05.44 Bo'mouth-Eastleigh 08.29 Eastleigh-Bo'mouth	DS9 09.20le Bomo-Poole 10.25weedkiller Poole-Brockhst-Lymington Pier-Totton-Fawley-Redbridge-Romsey-Eastleigh c.19.45le to Bo'mouth	FS18 E.C.S. Bo'mouth area and C. S. at Hamworthy Jcn 08.15-18.55 (including banking 09.55, 16.25se and 18.20 Poole-Branksome)	

	MONDAY 5/6	TUESDAY 6/6	WEDNESDAY 7/6	THURSDAY 8/6	FRIDAY 9/6	SATURDAY 10/6	SUNDAY 11/6
76006 (F)	Weymouth -Repairs (From at least mid-May)	Weymouth - Repairs	Weymouth - Repairs	Weymouth -Repairs	Weymouth - Repairs	Weymouth - Repairs	Weymouth - Repairs
76007 (F)	**166** 10.15e Eleigh-Soton Cent 10.43 Soton C.-Bo'mouth 13.08 Bo'mouth-Weymth 16.46 Weymth-Bo'mouth 18.51 Bo'mouth-Woking 22.45le to Guildford	**165(1) / 136(2)** 02.28le Guildford-Woking 03.18v Woking-Fratton 07.30 Port & S'sea-Eleigh/ 19.50 Eastleigh-Bo'mouth 22.05e Bo'mouth-Poole 22.40le to Weymouth		**Spl./166(2)** 10.00sv(bank) Weymouth-Bincombe? (Spl4, 34102)/ 16.46 Weymth-Bo'mouth 18.51 Bo'mouth-Woking 22.45le to Guildford	**165** 02.28le Guildford-Woking 03.18v Woking-Fratton 10.15v Fratton-Basing 16.51 Basing-Salisbury 19.20v Salisbury-Northam 21.22f Sot W. Dks-Eleigh	**166** 10.15e Eleigh-Soton Cent 10.43 Soton C.-Bo'mouth 13.08 Bo'mouth-Weymth 16.46 Weymth-Bo'mouth 18.51 Bo'mouth-Woking 22.45le to Guildford	**CS6** 02.05le Guildford-Woking Up Yd 03.00bst Woking-Hook (WAO) 07.30bst Hook-Basing Yd 0800le to Guildfd (13.35)
76009 (F)	**407(1)** 05.44 Bo'mouth-Eastleigh/ *Eastleigh - Repairs*	**166(1)** 10.15e Eleigh-Soton Cent 10.43 Southampton Cent-Bournemouth	**411/396(2)** 07.51 Bo'mouth-Weymth 11.18 Weymth-Bo'mouth/ 14.32le Bo'mouth-Brockhst 16.03 Brock-Christchurch 17.00le C'ch-Brock(slunt) 19.45le to Bournemouth	**Spl?/28O(2)** xx.xxle Bo'mouth-Poole xxxxbank 10.00sv Poole -Branksome(34102)/ 16.15e Brockhst-Eastleigh 19.04 Northam-Eastleigh 20.40v Eastleigh- Clapham Jcn	**281** 07.18 Wloo-Salisbury C. S. 13.30 - 14.15 15. 55 Salis-Basingstoke	**162** 11.38v Basingstoke -Soton West Docks 13.45le to Eastleigh 15.15le (or A/O) Eastleigh-Basingstoke	*Basingstoke - No Diagram*
76011 (F)	**404(1)** 07.52le Bo'mouth-Poole 08.30f Poole-Ringwood 12.10f Ringwood-Poole 15.35f Poole-Weymouth	*Spl.(Dsl?)* *Passed through Bo'mouth with up vans c. 20.15 (Possibly the 18.25vans Weymouth-Eastleigh)*	*Spl.(Dsl?)* 00.10f or 02.00f Eastleigh-Feltham xx.xxle Feltham-Nine Elms 07.25le 9 Elms-Guildford (arr 08.25 – see 73020)	**161/163** 03.30le Guildford-Woking 04.32v Woking-Basing 06.50f Basing-Eastleigh 10.32v Bevoir Park-Basingstoke/ 14.05v Basing-Surbiton 14.59le to Guildford	**161/163** *As Thursday*	**161** 03.30le Guildford-Woking 04.32v Woking-Basing	*Basingstoke - No Diagram*
76026 (F)	**411** 07.51 Bo'mouth-Weymth 11.18 Weymth-Bo'mouth	**411/280(mid)** 07.51 Bo'mouth-Weymth 11.18 Weymth-Bo'mouth/ 15.00le to Brockenhurst 16.15e Brockhst-Eastleigh	**DSpl./280(2)** 10.27sf Eleigh Main Yd-Micheldever x.xxle to Eastleigh/ 20.40v Eastleigh-Clapham Jcn	**113** 04.40 Wloo-Woking 06.30 Woking-Salisbury 18.38 Salisbury-Wloo 21.15e Wloo-Clapham Jcn.	**113** *As Thursday*	**113** *Nine Elms - Repairs*	**108** 03.40 Wloo-Petersfield 06.50e Petersfield-Guildford C. S. 07.30 - 08.00 08.00le to Guildford loco 11.38e Guildford-Woking 12.25v Wok-Clapham Jcn

Loco	1	2	3	4	5	6	7
76031 (C)	**165(1)/163** 02.28le Guildford-Woking 03.18v Woking-Fratton 10.15v Fratton-Basing/ 14.05v Basing-Surbiton 14.59le to Guildford	**161/163/Spl/Dsl.** As 76011 Thurs./ Then: Dep Guild 17.10 (Work not known) Arr Guild 21.15/ c22.10v Guildford - Wloo xx.xxle to Guildfit(a02.45)	**161** 03.30le Guildford-Woking 04.32v Woking-Basing 06.50f Basing-Eastleigh 10.32v Bevoir Pk-Basing/	**166(1)** xx.xxle Basing-Eastleigh/ 10.15e Eleigh-Soton Cent 10.43 Soton C.-Bo'mouth 13.08 Bo'mouth-Weymth	*Weymouth-* *Repairs or Spare*	*Weymouth-* *Repairs or Spare*	*Weymouth-* *Repairs or Spare*
76064 (D)	**161/165(2)** 06.50f Basing-Eastleigh 10.32v Bevois Pk-Basing/ 16.51 Basing-Salisbury 19.20v Salisbury-Northam 21.22f Sot West Dks-Eleigh 23.10v Northam-Fratton	**165(Mon)cont/280(part)** 02.10le to Eastleigh/ 19.04f Northam-Eastleigh	**DSpl/290(2)** 08.35se Eleigh Carriage Wks-Walton-on-Thames 11.00le to Southampton West Docks/ 13.15f West Docks-Eleigh 16.22 Eleigh-Soton Cent 17.16 Soton Cent-Bomo 20.45le to Eastleigh Local freights 23.25-02.00 04.40f Eleigh-Winchester 05.30le to Eastleigh	**DSpl** 08.40le Eastleigh- Micheldever 10.30se Micheldever- Durnsford Road (Condemned stock) 13.15le to Eastleigh	**DSpl** c17.45le Eastleigh- Soton East Dks 18.45 East Docks-Central ("Stella Polaris" passengers - attach portion to 17.30 Weymouth-Waterloo) c19.30le to Eastleigh	*xx.xxle Eleigh-Basing* *Basingstoke-No Diagram*	*Basingstoke – No Diagram*
76066 (D)	**407(2)** 08.29 Eastleigh-Bo'mouth 10.51 Bo'mouth-Weymth 17.00v Weymth-Bo'mouth 21.05e Bomo-Branksome 21.20le to Bournemouth	**166(2)** 13.08 Bo'mouth-Weymth 16.46 Weymth-Bo'mouth 18.51 Bo'mouth-Woking 22.45le to Guildford	**165(1)/136(2)** 02.28le Guildford- Woking 03.18v Woking-Fratton/ 07.30 Ports&S'sea-Eleigh 19.50 Eleigh-Bo'mouth 22.05e Bo'mouth-Poole 22.40le to Weymouth	**137** 05.30f Weymouth-Poole 09.08f Poole-Broadstone- Poole-Wareham- Furzebrook-Poole 17.42 Bo'mouth-Eastleigh 20.50 Eleigh-Sot. East Dks	**137Thurs/138(1)/** **DS10(2)** 00.54 Eleigh-Weymouth/ 06.43 Weymth-Bo'mouth 08.46 Bournemouth-Wloo 13.15e Waterloo- Clapham Jcn./ xx.xxsf 9 Elms- Soton Docks xx.xxle to Nine Elms	**AS5** 11.24sp Waterloo- Bournemouth 14.00se Bomo-Branksome 14.20le to Bournemouth 16.30le to Branksome 17.17se Branks-Clapham J.	*Nine Elms-No Diagram*
76067 (F)	**343** (Diesel diag) Carriage shunting at Fratton Yd 06.30-23.00	**343** As Monday	**343** As Monday	**343** As Monday	**343** As Monday	*Fratton-Spare*	*Fratton-Spare*
76069 (C)	*Weymouth - Repairs* *(from 31st May?- last* *known working)*	*Weymouth - Repairs*	*Weymouth - Repairs*	*Weymouth - Repairs*	*Weymouth - Repairs*	*Weymouth - Repairs*	*Weymouth - Repairs*
77014 (C)	**173** 19.55le Guildflt-Wok Up Yd 20.38bst Woking-Surbiton 21.55bst Surb-Walton-o-T (WAO to West Byfleet) 06.10bst West Byfleet- Woking Up Yd 06.48le to Guildford(08.05)	**173** As Tuesday arr Guild 07.05 (08.00)	**173** As Tuesday arr Guild 07.05 (09.00)	**173** As Tuesday arr Guild 07.05 (09.00)	**173** As Tuesday arr Guild 07.05 (09.00)	**CS14** See Sunday box	**CS14(Sat)** 00.25le Guildford loco- Yard Failed in Guildford Yard- replaced by D6522 SUN:Guildford Repairs

	MONDAY 5/6	TUESDAY 6/6	WEDNESDAY 7/6	THURSDAY 8/6	FRIDAY 9/6	SATURDAY 10/6	SUNDAY 11/6
80011 (F)	FSpl c11.30le Bo'mouth-Poole 12.10tweedkiller Poole- Swanage-Wareham- Hamworthy Goods-Poole- Blandford Forum-Poole- Ringwood-Poole(a17.07) c.18.30le to Bournemouth	FSpl c08.30le Bo'mouth-Poole 09.10tweedkiller Poole- Weymouth-Poole c.18.30le to Bournemouth	Bournemouth- No Diagram	394(1)/396(2) 06.45 Poole-Bo'mouth 08.08 Christ'ch-Brockhst 16.03 Brockhst-Christ'ch 17.00e Christ'ch-Bo'mouth e.c.s Bo'mouth area to 20.20	394(1)/396(2) 06.45 Poole-Bo'mouth 08.08 Christ'ch-Brockhst F & C.S. 09.00-09.50/ 16.03 Brockhst-Christ'ch 17.00e Christ'ch- Bournemouth e.c.s Bo'mouth area to 20.20	**400** 06.48 Bo'mouth-Brockhst 07.56 Brock'hst-Bo'mouth 09.38e Bomo-Branksome 0953le to Bournemouth 14.0ebro Poole-Bailey Gate 15.20milk Bailey Gate-Poole	400 SAT (cont) 17.01bank Poole- Branksome (16.00 Wey Quay-Wloo) 17.27bank Poole- Branksome (16.15 Wey Quay-Wloo) ECS between Branksome and Bomo West 17.50-22.45
80016 (D)	308 01.57 Eleigh-Port & S'sea 06.30 Fareham-Fratton 17.20 Eastleigh-Fratton 23.32 Port & S-Eleigh Also freight & vans in Portsmouth & Eastleigh areas	308 As Monday	Eastleigh- No Diagram	314 As 80133 Tuesday	314 As 80133 Tuesday	Eastleigh- No Diagram	Eastleigh- No Diagram
80133 (D)	314(MO) P.A.D Pilot 08.00 - 16.00 18.57v Sot W. Dks-Soton C 20.45v West Docks- Bevois Park C. S. 21.05 - 21.45 22.00v Bevois Park- Northam 22.10le to Eastleigh	314(Tu-Fri) 00.25v Eleigh-Soton Cent 01.34 Soton Cent-Eleigh 04.10f Eleigh-Sot W. Dks 06.00le to Eastleigh Then as Monday	**308** As 80016 Monday but including: 07.30le Eleigh-Brockhst 09.00e Brockhst-Eleigh 15.06e Eleigh-Brockhst 16.15e Brockhst-Eleigh (D/H 280 loco)	Eastleigh- No Diagram	DS15/DSpl 10.00le Eastleigh- Redbridge Engrs Yd 11.00dep Red-Romsey 11.30dep Romsey- Redbridge Engrs Yd/ xx.xxle to Winchester 14.00bst Winch-Eleigh (turn ballast cleaner) 15.35bst Eleigh-M'dever 16.59le to Eastleigh	314 00.25v Eleigh-Soton Cent 01.34 Soton Cent-Eleigh Local frieghts and C. S. until 13.15f Soton West Docks- Eastleigh 14.15le to Basingstoke *	Basingstoke-No Diagram
80139 (D)	Eastleigh- Wash Out?	Eastleigh- Wash Out?	314 As 80133 Tuesday	**308** 01.57 Eleigh-Port & S'sea 06.30 Fareham-Eleigh 17.20 Eleigh-Fareham 23.32 Port & S'sea-Eleigh Also freight & vans in Portsmouth & Eastleigh areas	308 As Thursday	308(or 80016) 01.57 Eleigh-Port & S'sea 04.05v Ports&S-Havant 04.55o Havant-Fratton 22.53o Fratton-Ports&S 23.32 Ports & S-Eastleigh 01.57 Eleigh-Port & S'sea	308(Sat)cont/308 03.10e Ports & S-Fratton/ 22.50e Fratton-Ports & S. 23.25 Ports & S-Eastleigh 00.25le to Eleigh loco

	Monday	Tuesday	Wednesday	Thursday	Friday	Saturday	Sunday
80145 (A)	**108** 01.30le Nine Elms-Clapham Jcn ECS between Clapham Junction and Waterloo and Carriage Shunting 02.30 - 18.07 18.35le Wloo-Nine Elms	**108** As Monday	**108** As Monday	**108** As Monday	*108* As Monday	**112** 07.18 Wloo-Salisbury C. S. 14.05 - 14.35	113 C.S. at Salisbury 16.50 - 23.00 23.45le Salisbury-Eastleigh 01.50 Eastleigh-Salisbury
80146 (F)	**401** *As Tuesday*	**401** 07.37 Bo'mouth-Eastleigh 14.02 Eastleigh-Bo'mouth 17.02 Bomo-Dorch Sth 18.22e Dorch Sth-Poole 19.30le to Bournemouth	400 06.48 Bo'mouth-Brockhst 07.56 Brockhst-Bo'mouth ECS to 12.20 Bailey Gate Milk(if reqd) 17.01bank Poole-Branksome 17.35f Poole-Bo'mouth Central Goodss	**401** 07.37 Bo'mouth-Eastleigh 14.02 Eastleigh-Bo'mouth 17.02 Bomo-Dorch Sth 18.22e Dorch Sth-Poole 19.30le to Bournemouth	*401* As Thursday	**401** 05.55f Cent Goods-Poole 07.23e Branksome-Bomo 07.37 Bo'mouth-Eastleigh 14.10 Eastleigh-Bo'mouth	**FS12** 06.15e Brockenhurst-Bournemouth 11.38se Branksome-Bomo West 13.00le to Wareham On rear 14.00sp to Swanage 14.45sp Swanage-Wareham 15.30le to Bournemouth
80152 (D)	313 06.20f Basing-Andover 09.00f Andover-Ludgershall 10.30f Ludgershall-Andover F.S. at Ludgers& Andover 15.05f Andover-Basing C. S. 19.30 - 01.05	313 As Monday	313 As Monday	313 As Monday	*313* As Monday	**313** 09.50le Basingstoke-Eastleigh	*DS19 08.30bst Eastleigh Ballast Sdgs. - Bevois Pk. 09.30le to Eleigh. Bst. Sdgs 10.35bst to Bevois Park 11.22le to Eastleigh loco*

Rosters, 12 – 18 June

	MONDAY 12/6	TUESDAY 13/6	WEDNESDAY 14/6	THURSDAY 15/6	FRIDAY 16/6	SATURDAY 17/6	SUNDAY 18/6
34001 (A)	Bournemouth-Repairs	Bournemouth-Repairs	Bournemouth-Repairs	Bournemouth-Repairs	Bournemouth-Repairs	*11.55le Bournemouth-Eastleigh*	Eastleigh-Repairs
34004 (F)	**137(1)** 05.30f Weymouth-Poole 09.08f Poole-Wareham-Wool-Wareham-Furzebrook-Poole 15.16f(bank) Poole-Branksome	Bournemouth- *Repairs or wash out*	**394(1)/396(2)** 06.45 Poole-Bo'mouth 08.08 Christ'ch-Brockst F & C.S. 09.00-09.50/ 16.03 Brockhst-Christ'ch 17.00e Christchurch-Poole? xx.xxle to Bournemouth	394(1)/396(2) 06.45 Poole-Bo'mouth 08.08 Christ'ch-Brockst F & C.S. 09.00-09.50/ 16.03 Brockhst-Christ'ch 16.59le Christ'ch-Brockst c&w shunting 18.45-19.45	394(1)/396(2) *As Thursday*	Bournemouth- *No Diagram*	397 *21.20v Bournemouth-Weymouth*
34013 (E)	**147(2)** 18.54 Wloo-Salisbury	**148** 06.49 Salisbury-Wloo 11.38v Wloo-Basingstoke 19.06 Basing-Soton Cent 21.18e Soton C.-Brockst 22.00le Brockhst-Weymth	**137** 05.30f Weymouth-Poole 09.08f Poole-Wareham-Wool-Wareham-Furzebrook-Poole 17.42 Bo'mouth-Eastleigh 20.50f Eastleigh-Soton East Docks	**138(1)/146** 00.54 Eleigh-Weymouth (22.35 Ex Wloo)/ 14.45sf Weymouth-Westbury (banked by 80011 to Bincombe 17.30le to Weymouth	**138(mid)/254(2)** 06.43 Weymth-Bo'mouth 08.46 Bournemouth-Waterloo/ 17.23 Wloo-Bournemouth 20.15e Bomo-Branksome 20.30e to Bournemouth	**FS24** 07.50e Branksome-Bomo 08.46 Bournemouth-Wloo 14.24sp Wloo-Weymouth 19.00le to Bournemouth	394 19.36 Bournemouth-Waterloo
34018 (A)	**254(1)** 11.27 Soton West Docks-Waterloo (B-33 "S. A. Vaal")	Nine Elms-Wash Out	**DS3(2)** 17.23 Wloo-Sot East Dks (B40 – "Statendam") *xx.xxle Eastleigh-Nine Elms* (Also conveyed ordinary passengers for Basing, Winchester and Eastleigh	**AS2** 10.00 Waterloo-Southampton East Dks (B43-"Queen Elizabeth") 14.28se Soton East Dks-Clapham Jcn	**AS1/Spl** 07.40e Clap Jcn-Andover 09.20p Andover-Salisbury 11.15le to Nine Elms/ 17.00 Waterloo-Salisbury	**ES22** 06.10(bst) Salis East Yd-Woking Up Yard. 08.28le to Basing West Yd 10.36sf Basingstoke-Salisbury East Yard	*Salisbury-No Diagram*
34021 (A)	**145** 08.35 Wloo-Weymouth 17.41 Weymth-Bo'mouth 21.00 Bo'mouth-Weymth	**147** 07.49 Weymth-Bo'mouth 12.34 Bournemouth-Wloo 18.54 Wloo-Salisbury	**148** 06.49 Salisbury-Wloo 11.38v Wloo-Basingstoke 19.06 Basing-Soton Cent 21.18e Soton C.-Brockst 22.00le Brockhst-Weymth	**137** 05.30f Weymouth-Poole 09.08f Poole-Broadstone-Poole-Wareham-Furzebrook-Poole 17.42 Bo'mouth-Eastleigh 20.50f Eastleigh-Soton East Docks	*138(1)/147(1)/138(2)* 00.54 Eastleigh-Weymth/ 07.49 Weymth-Bo'mouth 12.34 Bournemouth-Waterloo/ 18.22 Wloo-Bournemouth 20.49e Bo'mouth-Weymth	139 Carriage Shunting and Banking as required at Weymouth 10.00 - 18.30	139(1) Carriage Shunting at Weymouth 09.30 - 14.00

Loco							
34023 (A)	**395** 02.45 Waterloo-Bournemouth 07.08 Bo'mouth-Weymth	**396(1)/394(2)** 08.27 Weymouth-Bournemouth 15.01 Bo'mouth-Weymth 18.15 Weymouth-Wloo	Nine Elms-Exams	**D91** 02.15v Wloo-Bournemouth-Wloo 06.22 Bournemouth-Wloo 12.30 Wloo-Bournemouth 16.37 Bournemouth-Wloo (Down and Up "Belles")	**140** 10.30sf Nine Elms Goods-Soton East Docks 16.20sf Soton West Docks-Nine Elms "H" Shed	– *Nine Elms-No Diagram*	**AS1(railtour)** 09.10sp Wloo-Fareham (D/H 73029) 11.30le to Weymouth 16.20sp Weymouth-Salisbury (D/H 34108) 20.00le to Nine Elms
34024 (F)	**DS13/136(2)** 09.10weedkiller Eleigh-Salisbury-Gosport Eastleigh (arr 15.30)/ 19.50 Eastleigh-Bo'mouth 22.05e Bo'mouth-Poole 22.40le to Weymouth	**137** 05.30f Weymouth-Poole 09.08f Poole-Broadstone-Poole-Wareham-Furzebrook-Poole 17.42 Bo'mouth-Eastleigh 20.50f Eastleigh-Soton East Dks	**138(1)/146** *00.54 Eleigh-Weymouth/* 14.45sf Weymth-Westbury 17.30le to Weymouth	**138(2)** 06.43 Weymth-Bo'mouth 08.46 Bournemouth-Wloo	**Spl 4(ptD91)** 12.30 Wloo-Bournemouth-Wloo 16.37 Bournemouth-Wloo (Down and Up "Belles")	**113** 04.40 Wloo-Woking 06.30 Woking-Salisbury	*148* *Salisbury- Spare*
34025 (F)	Nine Elms - *No Diagram*	**254** 09.20 Wloo-Soton E Dks (B34-"Southern Cross") (Service and turn at Eleigh) 17.41 Soton E Dks.-Wloo (B38-"Qeen Elizabeth") 20.59se Waterloo-Clapham Jcn.	**136(1)/165(2)** 02.30 Wloo-Ports. Harb/ 10.15v Fratton-Basing 16.51 Basing-Salisbury 19.20v Salisbury-Northam 21.22f Soton W Dks-Eleigh 23.10v Northam-Ports Harb	*Spl 5?* *05.10le Eleigh-Redbridge-* *06.10engrs Redbridge-Wimbledon* *c11.00le to Nine Elms*	**DS9**/part 280 07.22e Clapham Jcn.-Waterloo 09.20 Wloo-Soton West-Docks (B46-"Edinburgh Castle")/ 19.04f Northam-Eastleigh	*137* *Eastleigh-Spare* *xx.xxle to Basing(pm)?*	*Basingstoke-No Diagram*
34034 (A)	Nine Elms-Repairs	Nine Elms-Repairs	Nine Elms-Repairs	Nine Elms-Repairs	Nine Elms-Repairs	Nine Elms-Repairs	Nine Elms- *Light Engine Test Run?*
34036 (A)	Weymouth-Repairs	**146** 14.45sf Weymth-Westbury 17.30le to Weymouth	**138(2)** 06.43 Weymth-Bo'mouth 08.46 Bournemouth-Wloo	– Nine Elms-Exams	**145** 08.35 Wloo-Weymouth 17.41 Weymth-Bo'mouth 21.00 Bo'mouth-Weymth (18.30 Ex Wloo)	*147* *Weymouth- Spare*	*Spl* *10.20sf Weymth-Westbury (to Crewe)* *xx.xxle to Weymouth* *or 147* *Weymouth- Spare*
34037 (D)	Eastleigh-Repairs	**DS10** 17.40le Eastleigh-Soton East Dks 18.40 Soton East Docks-Waterloo (B39-"Queen Elizabeth")	**395** 02.45 Wloo-Bournemouth 07.08 Bo'mouth-Weymth	**396(1)/394(2)** 08.27 Weymth-Bo'mouth/ 15.01 Bournemouth-Weymouth 18.15 Weymouth-Wloo	**395**/Dsl or Spl? 02.45 Waterloo-Bournemouth 07.08 Bo'mouth-Weymth/ xx.xxse Weymth-Bo'mouth/ 16.28 Bo'mouth-Eastleigh or xx.xxse Weymth-Eastleigh	*Eastleigh-No Diagram*	**AS4** 09.50le Eastleigh-Southampton Central 10.32sp Soton Cent-Wloo (via Petersfield)

	MONDAY 12/6	TUESDAY 13/6	WEDNESDAY 14/6	THURSDAY 15/6	FRIDAY 16/6	SATURDAY 17/6	SUNDAY 18/6
34052 (E)	**462** 21.00f Salis-Basingstoke 00.35f Basing-Salisbury	**462** As Monday	**ES8/462** 09.40le Salisbury-Grateley 10.50bst Grateley-Basing Up Yard 13.00le to Salisbury / Then as Monday	**462** As Monday	Salisbury-Wash Out	_Salisbury-Repairs_	_Salisbury-Repairs_
34060 (D)	**148** 06.49 Salisbury-Wloo xx.xxle 9 Elms-Basing* 19.06 Basing-Soton Cent 21.18e Soton C.-Brockhst 22.00le Brockhst-Weymth * Photographed running light loco near Winchfield in down direction.	**149** 17.30 Weymouth-Wloo	_Nine Elms-Repairs_	Nine Elms-Repairs	**136/Spl 122?** 02.30 Waterloo-Ports Harbour 07.30 Ports & Southsea-Eastleigh/ 19.07 Soton East Docks-Wloo (B51 - "Carmania")	**AS1** 01.40le Nine Elms-Mitre Bridge 03.08 M B-Ports Harbour (22.33 Ex Castleton) 06.15e Ports Harbour-Fratton 07.20e Fratton-Weymouth 11.00le Weymth-Eastleigh	**AS3** 10.48 Soton East Docks-Waterloo (B102 - "Aurelia")
34087 (D)	Eastleigh-Repairs	Eastleigh-Repairs	**DSpl/412(2)** 12.37sf Soton East Dks-Basingstoke 14.50le to Eastleigh/ 18.30 Soton Central-Bournemouth 20.15e Bomo-Branksome	280 05.15v Bo'mouth-Weymth 10.13 Weymth-Bo'mouth 15.00le to Brockenhurst 16.15e Brockhst-Eastleigh 19.04f Northam-Eastleigh 20.40v Eastleigh-Clapham Jcn	**135** 08.10 Wloo-Weymth Jcn 16.23 Weymth Jcn-Wloo (16.00 Ex Quay)	**136** 02.30 Waterloo-Ports Harbour 06.00e Ports Harb-Fratton 18.10v Fratton-Basing 22.30v Basingstoke-Wloo	Nine Elms-No Diagram
34089 (E)	**ES12** _09.46bst Salis-Grateley_ _10.45le to Salisbury_ 14.30le Salisbury-Southampton East Dks 16.50sf Soton East Dks-Westbury 19.20le to Salisbury	**463** 08.31v Salis-Basingstoke 10.45v Basingstoke-Ports & S'sea C. S. 13.20 - 15.00 16.00v Port & S-Fratton 19.06v Port & S-Salisbury	**463** As Tuesday	**463** As Tuesday	**463** As Tuesday	_Salisbury-_ _No Diagram_	**ES14(railtour)** 09.00le Salisbury-Fareham 11.12p Fareham-Swanage (D/H 34108 Soton-Wareham 14.10p Swanage-Wareham (o/r) 14.45p Wareham-Weymouth 16.30le to Salisbury

34090 (D)	**136(1)** 02.30 Waterloo—Ports Harbour 07.30 Port & S'sea-Eleigh	**DS4/DS6** 12.37sf Soton East Dks-Basingstoke 15.15le to Eastleigh 18.00(weedkiller) Eastleigh loco depot-Southampton Terminus-Fratton Yard-Northam-Eastleigh	*DS?* Recorded at Poole between 08.45 and 09.20. Working unknown	**254(1)/Spl.10** 10.07 Soton E Dooks-Waterloo (B49 – "Rotterdam")/ 16.40 Waterloo-Soton E Docks (B48 – "France")	*138* *Eastleigh - Spare*	*Eastleigh - Spare*	*Eastleigh - Spare*
34093 (D)	**FS10** 08.55ebv Bomo-Wareham 10.08sf Wareham-Basingstoke	**FS8** 06.05sf Basing-Wareham 10.45ebv Wareham-Bournemouth	*Bournemouth-Repairs*	*FS10* 20.00le Bomo-Wareham 21.05sf Wareham-Basing 05.00sf Bas-Weymouth	*146* 14.45sf Weymth-Westbury 17.30le to Weymouth	*396* *Weymouth - Spare*	*395(2)* 22.13 Weymth-Bo'mouth (D/H D65xx)
34095 (D)	Weymouth-Repairs	Weymouth-Repairs	Weymouth-Repairs	Weymouth-Repairs		*Weymouth–No Diagram*	*149* *Weymouth - Spare*
34102 (D)	**411** 07.51 Bo'mouth-Weymth 11.18 Weymth-Bo'mouth	**411/280(2)** 07.51 Bo'mouth-Weymouth/ 11.18 Weymth-Bo'mouth 15.00le to Brockenhurst 16.15e Brockhst-Eastleigh 19.04f Northam-Eastleigh 20.40v Eastleigh-Clapham Jcn	**281(1)/113(2)** 07.18 Wloo-Salisbury/ 18.38 Salisbury-Wloo	**147(2)** 18.54 Wloo-Salisbury	**148** 06.49 Salisbury-Wloo 11.38v Wloo-Basingstoke 19.06 Basing-Soton Cent 21.18e Soton C.-Brockhst 22.00le Brockhst-Weymth	*149* *Weymouth - Spare*	**139(2)** 15.00sf Weymth-Westbury (D6544 pilot - to Dorchester West?) 17.35le to Weymouth
34108 (E)	**463** 08.31v Salis-Basingstoke 10.45v Basingstoke-Port & S'sea C.S. 13.20 - 15.00 16.00v Ports & S-Fratton 19.06v Ports&S-Salisbury	Salisbury-Wash Out	**ES11**/Spl 05.55(dep) Salis East Yard -Micheldever 09.15(dep) Micheldever-Salisbury Carriage Sdgs./ 20.42sf Salis-Northam Yard 22.10le to Salisbury	**462** 21.00f Salis-Basingstoke 00.35f Basing-Salisbury	Salisbury-Boiler Inspection	*- Salisbury-No Diagram*	**ES15(railtour)** 10.30le Salis-Soton Cent. 11.53sp Soton-Wareham (D/H 34089) 13.25le to Weymouth 16.20sp Weymth-Salisbury (D/H 34023)
35003 (A)	**280(1)** 07.15le Bo'mouth-Christ'ch 08.08 Christ'ch-Brockhst F. & CE/S 09.00-09.50 09.55le to Eastleigh	**136(2)** 19.50 Eastleigh-Bo'mouth 22.05e Bo'mouth-Poole 22.40le to Weymouth	**149** 17.30 Weymouth-Wloo	Nine Elms-Wash Out	Nine Elms-Boiler Inspection	Nine Elms-Boiler Inspection	Nine Elms-No Diagram

	MONDAY 12/6	TUESDAY 13/6	WEDNESDAY 14/6	THURSDAY 15/6	FRIDAY 16/6	SATURDAY 17/6	SUNDAY 18/6
35007 (A)	FS13(Sun)/149 00.54 Eleigh-Weymouth/ 17.30 Weymouth-Wloo	136(1)/166 02.30 Waterloo-Ports Harbour 07.30 Ports & Southsea-Eastleigh/ 10.43 Soton C.-Bo'mouth 13.08 Bo'mouth-Weymth 16.46 Weymth-Bo'mouth 18.51 Bo'mouth-Woking	165(1)/136(2) 02.28le Guildford-Woking 03.18v Woking-Fratton/ 07.30 Port & S'sea-Eastleigh/ 19.50 Eastleigh-Bo'mouth 22.05e Bo'mouth-Poole 22.40le to Weymouth	149 17.30 Weymouth-Wloo	Nine Elms-Exams	AS2 08.30 Wloo-Weymouth 16.18 Weymth Jcn.-Wloo (15.55 Ex Quay) Banked to Bincombe by D65xx?	Nine Elms-No Diagram
35008 (A)	Nine Elms-Exams	281 07.18 Wloo-Salisbury C.S. 13.30 - 14.15 15. 55 Salis-Basingstoke	282 Basingstoke - Spare	162 09.02sf Basing-Feltham 12.45sf Feltham-Eastleigh 17.43sf Eastleigh-Basing or xx.xxle to Basing	162 09.02sf Basing-Feltham 12.45f Feltham-Eastleigh xx.xxle or a/o to Basingstoke	162 11.20sf Basing-Feltham 13.25le to Nine Elms 15.00le Nine Elms-Wloo 15.44v Wloo-Basingstoke	Basingstoke- No Diagram
35013 (A)	147(1) 07.49 Weymth-Bo'mouth- 12.34 Bournemouth- Waterloo	- Nine Elms-Exams	145 08.35 Wloo-Weymouth 17.41 Weymth-Bo'mouth 21.00 Bo'mouth-Weymth (18.30 Ex Wloo)	147(1) 07.49 Weymth-Bo'mouth 12.34 Bournemouth- Waterloo	Nine Elms- Boiler Inspection Then: 147(2) 18.54 Wloo-Salisbury	148 Salisbury- Spare	AS5(railtour) 18.55sp Salisbury-Wloo
35023 (A)	394 10.13 Weymth-Bo'mouth 15.01 Bo'mouth-Weymth 18.15 Weymouth-Wloo	395 02.45 Wloo-Bournemouth 07.08 Bo'mouth-Weymth	396(1)/394(2) 08.27 Weymth-Bo'mouth 10.32f Bomo-Cent Goods 10.57f Cent Goods-Bomo/ 15.01 Bo'mouth-Weymth 18.15 Weymouth-Wloo	395/145(2) 02.45 Wloo-Bournemouth 07.08 Bo'mouth-Weymth/ 17.41 Weymth-Bo'mouth 21.00 Bo'mouth-Weymth (18.30 Ex Wloo)	396(1)/394(2) 08.27 Weymth-Bo'mouth 10.32f Bomo-Cent Goods 10.57f Cent Goods- Bournemouth 15.01 Bo'mouth-Weymth 18.15 Weymouth-Wloo	395 02.45 Waterloo- Bournemouth 07.08 Bournemouth- Weymouth 10.13 Bo'mouth-Weymth 21.00 Bo'mouth-Weymth (18.30 Ex Wloo)	396 Weymouth - Spare
35028 (A)	135 08.10 Wloo-Weymth Jcn 16.23 Weymth Jcn-Wloo (16.00 Ex Quay)	145 08.35 Wloo-Weymouth 17.41 Weymth-Bo'mouth 21.00 Bo'mouth-Weymth (18.30 Ex Wloo)	147 07.49 Weymth-Bo'mouth 12.34 Bournemouth-Wloo 18.54 Wloo-Salisbury	148(1)/AS4/136(2) 06.49 Salisbury-Wloo/ 11.20 Wloo-Soton W Dks (B45 - "Achille Lauro") 19.50 Eastleigh-Bo'mouth 22.05e Bo'mouth-Poole 22.40le to Weymouth	*Weymouth-Wash Out?*	Weymouth - Exams	*Weymouth-No Diagram*
35030 (A)	Nine Elms-No Diagram	135 08.10 Wloo-Weymth Jcn 16.23 Weymth Jcn-Wloo (16.00 Ex Quay)	135 As Tuesday	145(1) 08.35 Wloo-Weymouth	149 17.30 Weymouth-Wloo 21.25se Waterloo- Clapham Jcn	Nine Elms-Repairs (BIG END)	Nine Elms-Repairs

73018 (C)	Guildford - No Diagram	**171** 07.00le Guildford-Woking 07.23bst Woking-Shalford 09.28bst Shalford-Woking 11.10k&12.40f Woking-Farnham 21.40le Guildford-Shalford 22.20bst Shalford-Wimbledon	**171(tues)cont/171(2)** (W A O to) 05.30bst Wimbledon-Shalford 08.00le to Guildfd(08.40)/ 21.40le Guildford-Shalford	**171(weds)cont/173** 22.20bst Shalford-Wimbledon (W A O to) 05.30bst Wimbledon-Shalford 08.00le to Guildfd(08.45)/ 173(Thurs) - D/H 76031 '(see below)	**Dsl.15/CS6** xx(vans) Guildford-Redhill 16.34 Redhill-Reading c.20.00le to Guildford (arr 20.50)l 22.00le Guildford-Woking Up Yd 23.08crane Woking-Richmond	**CS6(Fri) cont** (WAO Richmond-Kew Gardens and return) 05.30crane Richmond-Woking Up Yard xx.xxle to Guildfd(09.25) SAT: Guildfd - No diagram	Guildford - Wash Out?
73020 (C)	Guildford - No Diagram	**161/165(2)** 04.32v Woking-Basing 06.50f Basing-Eastleigh 10.32v Bevois Park-Basingstoke 16.51 Basing-Salisbury 19.20v Salisbury-Northam 21.22f Soton West Dks-Eastleigh	**166** 10.15e Eleigh-Soton Cent 10.43 Soton C.-Bo'mouth 13.08 Bo'mouth-Weymth 16.46 Weymth-Bo'mouth 18.51 Bo'mouth-Woking 22.45le to Guildford	**165** 02.28le Guildford-Woking 03.18v Woking-Fratton 10.15v Fratton-Basing 16.51 Basing-Salisbury 19.20v Salisbury-Northam 21.22f Soton West Dks-Eastleigh	**DS11(1)** 10.59 Soton East Docks-Waterloo (B50-"Capetown Castle")/	Nine Elms-No Diagram	Nine Elms- Repairs or Wash Out
73029 (A)	**138** 00.54 Eleigh-Weymouth 06.43 Weymth-Bo'mouth 08.46 Bournemouth-Wloo 13.44e Waterloo-Clapham Jcn	- Nine Elms- Wash Out	**113** 04.40 Wloo-Woking 06.30 Woking-Salisbury 18.38 Salisbury-Wloo 21.15e Waterloo-Clapham Jcn.	**113** As Thursday	113	-	**AS2(railtour)** 08.40le Nine Elms-Wloo 09.10sp Wloo-Fareham (D/H 34023) 11.30e to Eastleigh/
						Nine Elms-No Diagram	
73037 (A)	**282/138(2)** 07.58bst Basing W Yd-Eastleigh Ballast Sdgs/ 10.14 Eastleigh-Wloo 13.44e Wloo-Clapham Jcn (replaced 76031)	**AS1** 12.30le Nine Elms-Wloo 13.15se Waterloo-Clapham Jcn 15.57se Clapham Jcn-Waterloo 17.26le to Nine Elms	**AS1** xx.xxse Clap Jcn-Wloo 10.43 Wloo-Soton E Docks (B44-"Queen Elizabeth") xx.xxle or a/o to Nine Elms	**281(1)/Spl?/DS11(2)** 07.18 Waterloo-Basingstoke/ 14.36 Salisbury-Waterloo/ 18.55le 9 Elms-Clapham J 19.55se Clapham Jcn-Eastleigh	113	**DS17** 23.15le Eleigh-Fareham 00.15bst Fareham (WAO to Cosham) 06.25bst Cosham-Fareham 07.20le to Eastleigh	Eastleigh-No Diagram
73043 (A)	**140** 10.30sf Nine Elms Goods-Soton East Docks 16.20sf Soton West Docks-Nine Elms "H" Shed	**AS2** 10.00 Waterloo-Southampton East Dks (B35- "Southern Cross") 13.31se Soton East Docks-Clapham Jcn. 15.30le to Nine Elms	**140** As Monday	**136(1)/166** 02.30 Waterloo-Portsmouth Harb 07.30 Ports & Southsea-Eastleigh 10.43 Soton C.-Bo'mouth 13.08 Bo'mouth-Weymth 16.46 Weymth-Bo'mouth 18.51 Bo'mouth-Woking	**165** 02.28le Guildford-Woking 03.18v Woking-Fratton 10.15v Fratton-Basing 16.51 Basing-Salisbury 19.20v Salisbury-Northam 21.22f Soton West Dks-Eastleigh	**165(fri)cont** 23.10v Northam-Fratton 02.10le to Eastleigh/ SAT: Eastleigh-No Diagram	**140** 21.00le Eleigh-Basingstoke 22.02v Basingstoke-Waterloo

	MONDAY 12/6	TUESDAY 13/6	WEDNESDAY 14/6	THURSDAY 15/6	FRIDAY 16/6	SATURDAY 17/6	SUNDAY 18/6
73065 (A)	As Wednesday	As Wednesday	Salisbury-Repairs (STEAM BRAKE)	As Wednesday	As Wednesday	As Wednesday	As Wednesday
73085 (A)	281 07.18 Wloo-Salisbury C. S. 13.30 - 14.15 15.55 Salis-Basingstoke	162 09.02sf Basing-Feltham 12.45sf Feltham- Eastleigh 17.43sf Soton East Docks- Basingstoke	162 As Wednesday	282 Basingstoke - Spare	282 Basingstoke - Spare	282 Basingstoke - Spare	Basingstoke - No Diagram
73092 (C)	162/166(2) 09.02sf Basing-Feltham 12.45sf Feltham-Eastleigh 17.43sf Soton E Docks- Basingstoke/ 21.13 Basing-Woking (replaced 76064) 22.45le to Guildford	Guildford - No Diagram	Spl. dep Guildford 05.30 (Breakdown Vans - poss. Guildford area) arr Guildford 15.15	Guildford - No Diagram	CS5 07.30le Guild-Woking 09.28 Woking-Eleigh- Woking (weedkiller) 17.40le to Guildford C. S. at Guildford 23.30 - 01.15	CS4/CS7 04.00le Guildford-Woking 04.45v Woking-Guildford (C. S. 05.50-0705) 07.15f Guild-Wokingham (F. S. 09.35-c10.45) c10.45le to Guildford/	CS7 (Sat) 19.55le Guildford- Woking c20.35bst Woking- Wimbledon (WAO to 17.00 Sun) 17.00bst Wim'don- Clap Jcn 17.38bst Clapham Jcn- Woking Up Yd 18.50le to Guildford
73093 (C)	FSpl xx.xxle to Wool 11.10sf Wool-Poole Yd (layover at Bournemouth) 19.47sf Poole Yd-Eleigh xx.xxle to Bournemouth	394(1)/396(2) 06.45 Poole-Bo'mouth 08.08 C'hrist'ch-Brockhst F & C.S. 09.00-09.50/ 16.03 Brockhst-Christ'ch 16.59le Christ'ch-Brockhst c&rw shunt 18.45-19.45	F57 05.50le to Brockhst 07.08bst Brockhst-Wool (WAO to Dorch. South) 10.10le to Weymth(Turn) 11.44bst Dorch South (WAO to Wool) 12.46bst Wool-Brockhst. 14.50le to Bournemouth	Bournemouth-Repairs	412 09.20 Bournemouth- Weymouth (05.30 Ex Wloo) 12.12 Weymth-Bo'mouth 13.52 Bomo-Southampton 18.30 Soton C.-Bo'mouth 20.15e Bomo-Branksome	412 05.00le Bo'mouth-Poole 06.45 Poole-Bo'mouth 07.51 Bo'mouth-Weymth 12.12 Weymth-Bo'mouth	Bournemouth - No Diagram
73118 (C)	171(1)/172 07.00le Guildford- Woking Up Yard 07.23bst Woking- Shalford 09.28bst Shalford- Woking 11.10f Woking-Farnham 13.30le to Guildfd(16.00)/ Then as Tuesday	172 22.00le Guildford- Woking Up Yard 23.08bst Wok-Wimbledon (WAO to Clapham Jcn) 06.15bst Clap Yard- Woking 07.28le to Guildfd(08.35)	Guildford - No Diagram	Guildford - Wash Out?	171alt? (D/H 76031) 21.40le Guild-Shalford 22.20bst Shalfd- Wimb'don (WAO) 05.30bst Wimb'don- Shalfd 08.00le to Guild(11.45)	165(2) 20.45crane Guildfd- Fratton 23.35crane Fratton (WAO to Ports & S'sea) 06.40crane Ports & S'sea- Guildford	Guildford - No Diagram

73155 (C)	**CS2** 10.25le Guildford-Soton E Dks 14.00sf Soton East Dks-Feltham 17.00le to Guild(18.50) 20.50bst Woking-Basing-Hook (WAO to Winchfield) 06.00bst Winch-Wok UpYd	**CS2(Mon)cont/CS3** 07.00le to Guildfd(08.40)/ 23.00le Guild-Wok.Up Yd 23.48bst Woking-Aldershot (W A O to Alton) 0520bst Alton-Woking xx.xxle to Guild(06.30)	**172** 22.00le Guildford-Woking Up Yd 23.08bst Wok-Wimbledon (WAO to Clapham Jcn) 06.15bst Clapham Yd-Woking 07.28le to Guildfd (08.45)	**Spl./Dsl.622/172** dep dep Guildford 09.20 (Shalford shunting?) arr Guildford 11.00 12.40le Guildford-North Camp 13.20tanks North Camp-Guildford (arr 16.40)/ Then as Weds(arr. 08.15)	**Spl.** dep Guildford 08.35 (Shalford shunting?) arr Guildford 11.30 dep Guildford 11.45 (Shalford shunting?) arr Guildford 15.00	**165(1)** 03.18v Woking-Fratton 10.30le Fratton-Chichester 11.44bst Chichester Yd-Redbridge 13.56le to Eastleigh 14.25le to Guildford	**CS8/CS9** 03.55le Guildford-Woking 04.38V Woking-Aldershot 05.30ev Aldershot-Woking 06.05le to Guildford/ 3 x Woking-Farnham trips 10.30 - 17.25
75068 (D)	404 *As Thursday*	404 *As Thursday*	404 *As Thursday*	404	404 *As Thursday*	**FS21** 06.30le Bomo-Christ'ch 08.00le to Bournemouth 16.10le Bo'mouth-Poole 17.00bank Poole-Branksome 17.30le to Hamworthy Jcn	**FS21(Sat) cont** 18.34e Hamworthy Jcn -Bomo West sdgs 20.00le to Bo'mouth loco *SUN: Bomo - No Diagram*
75074 (D)	**412** 09.20 Bo'mouth-Weymth (05.30 Ex Wloo) 12.12 Weymth-Bo'mouth 13.52 Bomo-Southampton 18.30 Soton C.-Bo'mouth 20.15e Bomo-Branksome	**412** As Monday	**412(1)/Spl 9?** 09.20 Bo'mouth-Weymth (05.30 Ex Wloo) 12.12 Weymth-Bo'mouth 13.52 Bournemouth-Southampton xx.xxle Elgh loco-Ballast S. 00.05engrs Ball Sdgs-*Botley*	**Spl (Weds)cont/Spl Thurs** (WAO to Fareham 06.15) 06.50le to Eastleigh/ 23.10le Eastleigh-Fareham 00.05engrs (WAO to and from Botley to 06.54) 07.20le Fareham-Eastleigh	**166** 10.15e Eleigh-Soton Cent 10.43 Soton C.-Bo'mouth 13.08 Bo'mouth-Weymth 16.46 Weymth-Bo'mouth 18.51 Bo'mouth-Woking 22.05e Woking-Clapham Jcn.	**167** 02.15v Clapham Jcn-Wloo 03.40v Wloo-Guildford 05.10v Guildford-Ports & S'sea 08.45le to Guildford North Sdgs 1035sf GNS-Godalming 12.18sf Godalming-GNS	**CS7** 03.05le Guildford-Woking Up Yd 04.00bst Woking-Hook (Work as Ordered) 11.00bst Hook-Basingstoke 11.40bst Basingstoke-Woking Up Yd 13.00le to Guildford
75075 (D)	**DS9/280(2)** 11.25le Eleigh-Soton E Dks 12.37sf Soton East Docks-Basingstoke/ 14.50le to Eastleigh/ 19.04f Northam-Eastleigh 20.4?o Eleigh-Clapham Jcn	Nine Elms-Wash Out	Nine Elms-Wash Out	**140** 10.30sf Nine Elms Goods-Soton East Docks 16.20sf Soton West Docks-Nine Elms "H" Shed	**AS14/DS13?** 08.25le to Battersea Yard 09.45/materials/ Battersea Yard- xx.xxle to Eastleigh/ 23.10le Eleigh-Fareham 00.15bst Fareham-*Netley*	**DS13(Fri)cont** (WAO to and from Woolston 00.40-04.45) 05.50bst Netley-Eleigh *Sat: Eastleigh - No Diagram*	*Eastleigh- No Diagram*

	MONDAY 12/6	TUESDAY 13/6	WEDNESDAY 14/6	THURSDAY 15/6	FRIDAY 16/6	SATURDAY 17/6	SUNDAY 18/6

75076 (D)	161(2)/282
	10.32v Eastleigh-Basing/
	
	Basingstoke - Spare
		282
		
		Basingstoke - Spare
			283
			11.29v Basing West Yard-Soton West Docks
			16.20 Soton C.-Bo'mouth
			E. C. S. Bo'mouth Area
			17.30 – 23.00
				412
				09.20 Bo'mouth-Weymth (05.30 Ex Wloo)
				12.12 Weymth-Bo'mouth
				13.52 Bomo-Southampton
				18.30 Soton C.-Bo'mouth
				20.15e Bomo-Branksome
					407
					06.48 Bo'mouth-Brockenhurst
					07.56 Brockhst-Bournemouth
					08.35e Bomo-Branksome
					09.17le to Weymouth
					17.00v Weymth-Bo'mouth
						Bournemouth -
						    No Diagram
							FS12
							07.55le Bo'mouth-
							    Brockenhurst
							09.00bst (WAO to Totton)
							13.20bst to Bevois Park
							  (CCE/S 13.35-14.05)
							14.05le to Eastleigh(turn)
							15.35le to Bournemouth

75077 (D)	**290** Local freights & vans Eleigh and Soton area 08.00 – 14.00 16.22 Eleigh-Soton Cent 17.16 Soton Central-Bo'mouth & ECS 20.45le to Eastleigh Local freights 23.25 – 02.00	**290(Mon)cont/290** 04.40f Eastleigh-Winchester 05.30le to Eastleigh / As Monday	**290** As Monday	**290** As Monday	**290** As Monday	**DS16** 08.10le Eastleigh-Redbridge 09.15bst Red-Winchester (D/H 75077) 10.30le to Eastleigh 21.00crane Basing Up Yard-Houndsmills Bridge (WAO)	DS16 (sat) cont 08.00crane to Basing Up Yd 11.34crane to Eastleigh/ SUN: Eleigh - No Diagram

76005 (F)	396(2)
	14.32le Bomo-Brockhst
	16.03 Brock-Christ'ch
	16.59le to Brockenhurst
	C&W shunt 18.45-19.45
		Bournemouth-No Diagram	**411**
			07.51 Bo'mouth-Weymth
			11.18 Weymth-Bo'mouth
				411
				07.51 Bo'mouth-Weymth
				11.18 Weymth-Bo'mouth
					411
					07.51 Bo'mouth-Weymth
					11.18 Weymth-Bo'mouth
						Bournemouth -
						    No Diagram
							Bournemouth -
							    No Diagram

76006 (F)	*Weymouth - Repairs*	*Weymouth - Repairs*	Weymouth - Repairs	Weymouth - Repairs	Weymouth - Repairs	Weymouth - Repairs	Weymouth - Repairs
76007 (F)	**165** 02.28le Guildford-Woking 03.18v Woking-Fratton 10.15v Fratton-Basing 16.51 Basing-Salisbury 19.20v Salisbury-Northam 21.22f Soton West Dks-Eastleigh	DS5 / DS7 *14.00sf Soton East Docks-Feltham Yard.* *17.00le to Eastleigh/* *23.00(weedkiller)* *Eastleigh-Woking(via Alton)*	**DS7(tues)cont** CCE/S Woking Up Yard. (01.20 - 02.20) 02.25le to Guildfd (08.35) WEDS: *Guildford - No Diagram*	**Spl/148(2)** 17.15le Guildford-Basing/ 19.06 Basing-Soton Cent 21.18e Soton C.-Brockhst 22.00le Brockhst-Weymth	**137** 05.30f Weymouth-Poole 09.08f Poole-Wareham-Wool-Wareham-Furzebrook-Poole 17.42 Bo'mouth-Eastleigh 20.50f Eastleigh-Soton East Dks	**DS23** 08.10le Eleigh-Redbridge 09.15bst Red-Winchester (D/H 76007) 10.39le to Micheldever Engrs. Shunt 11.00-15.00 15.03le to Eastleigh	*Eastleigh-Repairs*
76009 (F)	283 11.29v Basing West Yard-Soton West Docks 16.20 Soton C.-Bo'mouth E. C. S. Bo'mouth Area 17.30 – 23.00	280(1) 05.15v Bo'mouth-Weymouth 10.13 Weymth-Bournemouth			*400(all or part)* *13.23e Branksome-* *Bournemouth*		

Loco							
76011 (F)	**163** 14.05v Basing-Surbiton 14.59le to Guildford	**165(1)/163** 02.28le Guildford-Woking 03.18v Woking-Fratton 10.15v Fratton-Basing/ 14.05v Basing-Surbiton 14.59le to Guildford	**161/163** 03.30le Guildford-Woking 04.32v Woking-Basing 06.50f Basing-Eastleigh 10.32v Bevoir Pk-Basing/ 14.05v Basing-Surbiton 14.59le to Guildford	**161/163** As Wednesday	**161/163** As Wednesday	**161** 03.30le Guildford-Woking 04.32v Woking-Basing	*Basingstoke -* *No Diagram*
76026 (F)	**113** 04.40 Wloo-Woking 06.30 Woking-Salisbury 18.38 Salisbury-Wloo 21.15e Waterloo-Clapham Jcn	*Nine Elms - Repairs*	*Nine Elms - Repairs*	Nine Elms - Repairs	Nine Elms - Repairs	Nine Elms - Repairs	Nine Elms - Repairs
76031 (C)	**138(1)/282(2)/171(2)** 06.43 Weymth-Bo'mouth 08.46 Bomo-Eastleigh/ 12.37f Soton Dks-Basing xx.xxle to Guildford/ 20.00le Guildfd-Shalford 20.33bst Shalford-Surbiton 22.42bst Surbiton-Walton-on Thames	**171(Mon)cont** (WAO to West Byfleet) 06.15bst to Woking Up Yd 07.18le to Guildford *TUES: Guildford -* *No Diagram*	**171** 21.40le Guildford-Woking Yd 22.08bst Woking-Clapham Jcn (WAO to Wimbledon) 05.45bst Wimbledon-Woking Down Yd 07.10le to Guildfd(09.00) (D/H 73018)	**172 (D/H 73118)** 21.40le Guild-Shalford 22.20bst Shalfd-Wimb'don (WAO) 05.30bst Wimb'don-Shalfd 08.00le to Guild (11.45)	*Guildford - Wash Out*	*- Guildford - No Diagram*	**CS17** 05.00le Guildford-Woking 05.30bst Wok Up Yd-Wimbledon (WAO to Clap Jcn) 18.08bst Clap Jcn-Woking Dn Yd 19.20le to Guildford (arr 20.45)
76064 (D)	**161(1)/166(1)** 06.50f Basing-Eastleigh/ 10.15e Eleigh-Soton Cent 10.43 Soton C.-Bo'mouth 13.08 Bo'mouth-Weymth 16.46 Weymth-Bo'mouth 18.51 Bo'mouth-Basing	*283* 11.29v Basing West Yard-Soton West Docks 16.20 Soton C.-Bo'mouth E. C. S. 17.30 - 23.00	**280** 05.15v Bo'mouth-Weymth 10.13 Weymth-Bo'mouth 15.00le to Brockenhurst 16.15e Brockhst-Eastleigh 19.04f Northam-Eastleigh 20.40v Eastleigh-Clapham Jcn	**281** 07.18 Wloo-Salisbury C. S. 13.30 - 14.15 15.55 Salis-Basingstoke	**283** 11.29v Basing West Yard-Soton West Docks 16.20 Soton C.-Bo'mouth C&WE Shunt at Brock 18.45 - 19.45 19.45le to Bournemouth	**280** 05.55f Cent. Gds-Poole 07.23e Branksome-Bomo 07.37 Bo'mouth-Eastleigh 10.29 Eastleigh-Bo'mouth 12.20e to Branksome (ECS Bomo area to 18.45)	*280?* *Bournemouth - Spare*
76066 (D)	*113* 04.40 Wloo-Woking 06.30 Woking-Salisbury 18.38 Salisbury-Wloo 21.15e Waterloo-Clapham Jcn	*Nine Elms-No Diagram*	**113(1)/467(2)** 04.40 Wloo-Woking 06.30 Woking-Salisbury/ 15.15le to Soton East Docks 16.50sf East Dks-Westbury 19.20le to Salisbury	**467** 10.00le Salis-Warminster F. S. 11.00 - 12.00 12.00le to Salisbury	**467** As Thursday	*Salisbury - No Diagram*	*Salisbury - No Diagram*

	MONDAY 12/6	TUESDAY 13/6	WEDNESDAY 14/6	THURSDAY 15/6	FRIDAY 16/6	SATURDAY 17/6	SUNDAY 18/6
76067 (F)	**343** (Diesel diag) Carriage shunting at Fratton Yd 06.30-23.00	Fratton - Repairs	Fratton - Repairs	Fratton - Repairs xx.xxle to Eastleigh (or Friday a.m.)	DS16 06.45le Eastleigh-Basing 08.25sf Basing-Chichester 11.40le to Eastleigh/	DS18 23.35le Eastleigh loco -Marshalling Yd 00.15bst Marsh Yd-Station (WAO to St Denys) 08.00bst to Northam Yard 08.40le to Eastleigh	
76069 (C)	*Weymouth - Repairs*	*Weymouth - Repairs*	Weymouth - Repairs	Weymouth - Repairs	Weymouth - Repairs	Weymouth - Repairs	*WITHDRAWN*
77014 (C)	*Guildford - Repairs*	*Guildford - Repairs*	**171(1)** 07.00le Guildford-Woking 07.23bst Woking-Shalford 09.28bst Shalford-Woking 11.10f Woking-Farnham 12.40f Woking-Farnham 13.30le to Guildfd (17.50)	*Guildford - No Diagram*	*- Guildford - No Diagram*	**CS10** 20.35le Guild-Wok Up Yd 21.18bst Wok-Wimbledon 22.45bst Wimbledon-New Malden (WAO to Surbiton) 08.30bst Surbiton-Wok Up Yard 09.20le to Guildford	*Guildford - No Diagram*
80011 (F)		*Bank CIBT Poole-Branksome*		407 06.48 Bo'mouth-Brockhst 07.56 Brockhst-Bo'mouth 08.35e Bomo-Branksome 09.17le to Weymouth (banked 34013 to Binc) 17.00v Weymth-Bo'mouth			
80016 (D)	*Eastleigh- No Diagram*	**343** (Diesel diag) xx.xxle Eleigh-Fratton Carriage Shunting at Fratton Yd 06.30-23.00	**343** As Tuesday	**343** As Tuesday	**343** As Tuesday then: xx.xxle to Eastleigh	DS19 00.40le(Sun) Eastleigh -Winchester City 01.28bst Winchester-St Cross (WAO to Shawford) 08.00bst Shawford -Redbridge Engrs Yd	DS19(Sat) cont xx.xxle to Eastleigh SUN: Eastleigh -No Diagram
80133 (D)	313 As Wednesday	313 As Wednesday	**313** 06.20f Basing-Andover 09.00f Andover-Ludgershall 10.30f Ludgershall-Andover F. S. at Ludgers & Andover 15.05f Andover-Basing C. S. 19.30 - 01.05	**313** As Wednesday	**313** As Wednesday	314(2) 19.00le Basing-Woking C. S. 21.20 - 23.25 23.39sp Woking-Basing	*Basingstoke - No Diagram*

80139 (D)	As Thursday	308 As Thursday	**308 As Thursday** Also Weds only 07.00le Eastleigh- Brockhst 09.00e Brockhst-Eastleigh 15.06e Eastleigh-Brockhst 16.15e Brockhst-Eastleigh	**308** 01.57 Eastleigh- Ports & Southsea 06.30 Fareham-Eastleigh 17.20 Eastleigh-Fratton 23.32 Port & S'sea-Eleigh Also freights & Vans in Portsmouth & Eleigh areas	308 As Thursday	*308 alt* *01.57 Eleigh-Port & S'sea* *04.05v Ports&S-Havant* *04.55v Havant-Fratton* *22.53v Fratton-* *Ports&S'sea* *23.32 Ports & S-Eastleigh* *01.57 Eastleigh-Fareham*	*308 (Sat)cont/308 alt* *02.45le Fareham-* *Eastleigh/* *06.15le Eastleigh-* *Fareham* *07.00se Fareham-Fratton* *07.35sev Frat-Ports & S* *22.50e Fratton-Ports&S* *23.25 Ports & S-Eastleigh*
80145 (A)	467 As Wednesday	467 As Wednesday	**467**/281(2) 10.00le Salis-Warminster F. S. 11.00 - 12.00 12.00le to Salisbury / 15.55 Salis-Basingstoke	**283** 11.29v Basing West Yard- Soton West Docks 16.20 Soton C.-Bo'mouth E. C. S. Bo'mouth Area 17.30 - 23.00	**280** 05.15v Bournemouth- Weymouth 10.13 Weymth-Bo'mouth 15.00le to Brockenhurst 16.15e Brockhst-Eastleigh (19.04f worked by 34025) 20.40v Eastleigh- Clapham Jcn	102 or 106 London E. C. S.	105 or 106 London E. C. S.
80146 (F)	407 As Tuesday	**407** 06.48 Bo'mouth-Brockhst 07.56 Brockhst-Bo'mouth 08.35e Bomo-Branksome 09.17le to Weymouth 17.00v Weymouth- Bournemouth	407 As Tuesday	**407** *Bournemouth-Wash Out?*	– *Bournemouth-No diagram*	– *Bournemouth-No diagram*	**FS13** 12.30le Bomo-Wareham 13.32(O/R)Ware'm- Swanage 14.10sp Swanage- Wareham 14.35le Wareham- Branksome 15.20e Branksome- Bomo West 16.00le to Bournemouth
80152 (D)	**314(MO)** P.A.D Pilot 08.00 - 16.00 Soton West Dks- Central 18.57v Soton West Docks- Bevois Park 20.45v West Docks- C. S. 21.05 - 21.45 22.00v Bevois Pk- Northam 22.10le to Eastleigh	**314**(Tu-Fri) 00.25v Eastleigh- Soton Cent 01.34 Soton C.-Eastleigh 04.10f Eastleigh- Soton West Dks 06.00le to Eastleigh Then as Monday	314 As Tuesday	314 As Tuesday	314 As Tuesday	314 As Tuesday	**314(1)** 00.25v Eleigh-Soton Cent 01.34 Soton C.-Eastleigh Local freights & C. S. until; 13.15f Soton West Docks- Eastleigh Main Yard

Rosters, 19 – 25 June

	MONDAY 19/6	TUESDAY 20/6	WEDNESDAY 21/6	THURSDAY 22/6	FRIDAY 23/6	SATURDAY 24/6	SUNDAY 25/6
34001 (A)	Eastleigh-Repairs	Eastleigh-Repairs	Eastleigh-Repairs	**DS4** 05.10le Eleigh-Redbridge 06.10engrs Redbridge-Wimbledon 10.45le to Nine Elms	Nine Elms-Boiler Inspection	**AS1** 07.45 Waterloo-Southampton East Dks (B70 - "Ellinis") 10.57 Soton West Dks-Waterloo (B73 - "Chusan")	*Nine Elms-No Diagram*
34004 (F)	**394(1)** 10.13 Weymth-Bournemouth	*Bournemouth-No Diagram*	**394(1)/396(2)** 06.45 Poole-Bo'mouth 08.08 Christ ch-Brockhst F & CS 09.00-09.50 09.50le to Bo'mouth/ 14.32le to Brockenhurst 16.03 Brockhst-Christ'ch 16.59le to Brockenhurst Shunting 18.45-19.45 19.45le to Bournemouth	*Bournemouth-No Diagram*	**ES10** 07.30le Bomo-Branksome 08.07e Branks-Bo'mouth 08.20sp Bournemouth-Waterloo 17.23 Waterloo-Bournemouth 20.15e Bomo-Branksome 20.30le to Bournemouth	*Bournemouth -* *No Diagram*	*Bournemouth -* *No Diagram*
34013 (E)	**395** 02.45 Waterloo-Bournemouth 07.08 Bo'mouth-Weymth	**137** 05.30f Weymouth-Poole 09.08f Poole-Broadstone-Poole-Wareham-Furzebrook-Poole 17.42 Bo'mouth-Eastleigh 20.50f Elgh-Soton E Docks	**138** 00.54 Eastleigh-Weymth 06.43 Weymth-Bo'mouth 08.46 Bo'mouth-Woking *(Replaced by 35003)* *xx.xxle to Nine Elms*	Nine Elms-Repairs	Nine Elms-Repairs	**AS10** 01.40le Nine Elms-Mitre Bdge 03.19sp Mitre Bridge-Portsmouth Harbour (23.15 Ex Bolton Trinity St) 06.15e Ports Harb-Fratton 07.10le to Eastleigh	137 *Eastleigh - Spare*
34018 (A)	**ES13** 14.30le Salisbury-Soton East Docks 16.50sf Soton East Docks-Westbury 19.20le to Salisbury	**148** 06.49 Salisbury-Wloo 11.38v Wloo-Basingstoke 19.06 Basing-Soton Cent 21.18e Soton C.-Brockhst 22.00le Brockhst-Weymth	**149** FS 08.00-13.00 17.30 Weymouth-Wloo	**AS9** 08.20 Waterloo-Southampton East Dks (B64 - Queen Mary) *17.30le Eleigh-Wareham* *21.05sf Wareham-Basingstoke* *01.30le to Eastleigh*	**FS11** 14.00sf Soton East Docks-Feltham 19.00le Feltham-Woking 20.58f Woking-Millbrook (F. S. 22.45-23.30) 23.35le to Bournemouth	395(2) 21.00 Bo'mouth-Weymth	139 *Weymouth - Spare*

Loco							
34021 (A)	- Nine Elms-Repairs	**138(2)** 06.43 Weymth-Bo'mouth 08.46 Bournemouth- Waterloo 13.44e Wloo-Clapham Jcn.	**254/147(2)** 08.54 Wloo-Southampton West Docks (B60 - "United States") 11.45le to Nine Elms (or as ordered)/ 18.54 Wloo-Salisbury	**148** 06.49 Salisbury-Wloo 11.38v Wloo-Basingstoke 19.06 Basing-Soton Cent 21.18e Soton C.-Brockhst 22.00le Brockhst-Weymth	**149** 17.30 Weymouth-Wloo	**39(1)** 02.45 Wloo-Bournemouth- 07.08 Bo'mouth- Weymouth 10.13 Weymth-Bo'mouth	280 Bournemouth - Spare
34023 (A)	**135** 08.10 Wloo-Weymth Jcn 16.23 Weymth Jcn-Wloo (16.00 Ex Quay)	**136(1)/AS4** 02.30 Wloo- Ports Harbour 07.30 Ports & S'sea- Eastleigh/ 14.00sf Soton East Dks- Feltham 16.50le to Nine Elms	**AS2** 10.06sp Willesden Jcn-Soton West Docks (09.23 Ex Hemel Hemps) 17.41sp Soton East Docks- Willeden Junction (to Hemel Hempstead) 20.25le to Nine Elms (Coupled to 34024)	**AS2** 10.43 Waterloo- Southampton East Dks (B65 - "Capetown Castle") 14.00sf Soton East Docks- Feltham 16.50le to Nine Elms	**113** 04.40 Wloo-Woking 06.30 Woking-Salisbury 18.38 Salisbury-Wloo	**136** 02.30 Waterloo- Ports Harbour 18.10v Fratton-Basing 22.07v Basingstoke-Wloo	*OUT OF SERVICE* (Withdrawn w/e 9th July)
34024 (F)	**148** 06.49 Salisbury-Wloo 11.38v Wloo-Basingstoke 19.06 Basing-Soton Cent 21.18e Soton C.-Brockhst 22.00le Brockhst- Weymouth	**149** FS 08.00-13.00 17.30 Weymouth-Wloo WEDS: Empty stock berthed at Bracknell	**AS1** 09.58le Nine Elms- Mitre Bridge 11.09p Mitre Bridge- Ascot 13.20le Bracknell- Guildford 15.45le Guildford- Bracknell 18.42sp Ascot- Mitre Bridge 20.25le Willesden Jcn- Nine Elms	**281** 07.18 Wloo-Salisbury C. S. 13.30 - 14.15 15. 55 Salis-Basingstoke	**282/148(2)** Basingstoke - Spare / 19.06 Basing-Soton Cent. 21.18e Soton C.-Brockhst 22.00le Brockhst- Weymouth	*Dsl.* 06.23 *Weymth Jcn-Wloo*	*Dsl.* 22.35 *Wloo-Eastleigh*
34025 (F)	**162** 09.02sf Basing-Feltham 12.45le to Basingstoke	**283** 11.29v Basingstoke- Soton West Dks 16.20 Soton Central- Bournemouth E. C. S. Bo'mouth Area 17.30 - 23.00	Bournemouth-Wash Out	Bournemouth-Repairs	Bournemouth-Repairs	*Bournemouth-Repairs*	*Bournemouth-Repairs*
34034 (A)	**113** 04.40 Wloo-Woking 06.30 Woking-Salisbury 18.38 Salisbury-Wloo	Nine Elms-Repairs *(PONY TRUCK BEARING)*	Nine Elms-Repairs	Nine Elms-Repairs	Nine Elms-Repairs	*OUT OF SERVICE*	

	MONDAY 19/6	TUESDAY 20/6	WEDNESDAY 21/6	THURSDAY 22/6	FRIDAY 23/6	SATURDAY 24/6	SUNDAY 25/6
34036 (A)	Weymouth-Repairs	**138(2)** 06.43 Weymth-Bo'mouth / 08.46 Bournemouth-Waterloo	**136** 02.30 Waterloo-Ports Harbour / 07.30 Ports & Southsea-Eastleigh / 19.50 Eastleigh / 22.05e Bo'mouth-Poole	**137** 05.30f Weymouth-Poole / 09.08f Poole-Broadstone-Poole-Wareham-Furzebrook-Poole / 17.42 Bo'mouth-Eleigh / 20.50f Elgh-Soton E Dks	**138(1)** 00.54 Eleigh-Weymouth / 06.43 Weymth-Bo'mouth / 08.46 Bournemouth-Wloo	*Nine Elms-No Diagram*	*Nine Elms-No Diagram*
34037 (D)	D92(part) 02.15 Waterloo-Bournemouth / 06.22 Bournemouth-Waterloo	**AS2** 07.00 Waterloo-Soton West Dks (B54-"Aurelia") / 17.38 Soton West Docks-Waterloo (B58 "United States")	Nine Elms-Wash Out	Nine Elms-Repairs	Nine Elms-Repairs	Nine Elms-Repairs	Nine Elms-Repairs
34052 (E)	Salisbury-Repairs	Salisbury-Repairs	Salisbury-Repairs	Salisbury-Repairs	Salisbury-Repairs	*Salisbury-No Diagram*	*Salisbury-No Diagram*
34060 (D)	**AS4** 16.05se Clapham Jcn-Soton West Docks / 18.30le to Eastleigh	*DS8* 03.30le Eleigh-Basing / 06.05sf Basing-Wareham / 10.45le to Bournemouth / 12.30le to Eastleigh *(Seen at Poole c.17.30-suspect train ran late and loco left at Bo'mouth)*	396(mid)/394(2) 10.32f Bomo-Central Gds / 10.57f Central Gds-Bomo/ 15.01 Bomo-Weymth / 18.15 Weymouth-Wloo	**395/146** 02.45 Wloo-Bo'mouth / 07.08 Bomo-Weymth/ 14.45sf Wey-Westbury / 17.30le to Weymouth	**396(1)/394(2)** 08.27 Weymth-Bo'mouth / *10.32f Bomo-Cent Goods / 10.57f Cent Goods-Bomo/* 15.01 Bo'mouth-Weymth / 18.15 Weymouth-Wloo	*Nine Elms-No Diagram*	*Nine Elms-No Diagram*
34087 (D)	**281(1)** 07.18 Wloo-Salisbury / C. S. 13.30 - 14.15 / 15. 55 Salis-Basingstoke	**162** 09.02sf Basing-Feltham / 12.45sf Feltham-Eastleigh / 17.43sf Soton E Dks-Basing/	283 11.29v Basingstoke-Soton West Docks / 16.20 Soton C.-Bo'mouth / E. C. S. Bo'mouth Area / 17.30 - 23.00	280 05.15v Bo'mouth-Weymouth / 10.13 Weymth-Bo'mouth / 15.00le to Brockenhurst / 16.15e Brockhst-Eastleigh / 19.04f Northam-Eastleigh / 20.40v Eastleigh-Clapham Jcn	**254(1)** 09.20 Waterloo-Southampton West Dks (B67 - "S. A. Vaal")	*Eastleigh-No Diagram*	*395(1)* 00.54 Eleigh-Weymouth
34089 (E)	Spl. 1? 08.26 Salisbury-Wloo / *13.00 Wloo-Salisbury (or l.e. to Salisbury)*	**463** 08.31v Salis-Basingstoke / 10.45v Basing-Port & S'sea / C. S. 13.20 - 15.00 / 16.00v Port & S-Fratton / 19.06v Port & S-Salisbury	**463** As Tuesday	**463** As Tuesday	**463** As Tuesday	*Salisbury-No Diagram* / *Poss. Warminster shunt*	*Salisbury-No Diagram*

34090 (D)	**254** 11.27 Soton West Docks-Wloo (B52-"Pendennis Castle")	**AS3** 08.54 Wloo-Sot E Docks-Wloo (B55 - "Caronia") 16.52 Soton W Docks-Waterloo (B57 - "United States") xx.xx London-Eastleigh (ecs or departmental)	**SpL6/162(2)** 09.38 Soton E Dks-Wloo (B62 - "Queen Mary")/ xx.xxle 9E then Feltham 12.45sf Felt-Bas or Eleigh 17.43sf Soton E Dks- Basing or le Eastleigh-Basing	**282/283** Basingstoke - Spare/ 11.29v Basing- Soton West Docks 16.20 Soton C.-Bo'mouth E. C. S. Bo'mouth Area 17.30 - 23.00	**280** 05.15v Bo'mouth- Weymth 10.13 Weymth-Bo'mouth 15.00le to Brockenhurst 16.15e Brockhst-Eastleigh 19.04f Northam-Eastleigh 20.40v Eastleigh- Clapham Jcn	*281* *Nine Elms - Spare*	*Nine Elms-No Diagram*
34093 (D)	**394(2)** 15.01 Bo'mouth-Weymth 18.15 Weymouth-Wloo	**395** 02.45 Wloo-Bournemouth 07.08 Bo'mouth-Weymth	– Weymouth-Repairs	**138(2)** 06.43 Weymth-Bo'mouth 08.46 Bournemouth- Wloo	**136/254(2)** 02.30 Waterloo- Ports Harbour 07.30 Ports & S'sea- Eastleigh 16.55 Soton East Docks- Waterloo (B68 - "Ellinis")	*Nine Elms-No Diagram*	*Nine Elms-No Diagram*
34095 (D)	**137** 05.30f Weymouth-Poole 09.08f Poole-Wareham- Wool-Wareham- Furzebrook-Poole 17.42 Bo'mouth- Eastleigh 20.50f Eastleigh- Soton E Docks	**138(1)146** 00.54 Eleigh-Weymouth 14.45sf Wey-Westbury 17.30le to Weymouth	**396(1)/FS11** 08.27 Weymth-Bomo/ 11.30sp Bomo West-Wey 13.10sp Yeovil Pen Mill 14.20sp Pen Mill-Yeo J. 14.38sp Yeo Jcn-Salis 16.10sp Salisbury-Wloo	**136(1)** 02.30 Waterloo- 07.30 Port & S'sea-Eleigh	**138(2)** Eastleigh-Wash Out	*DSpl* xx.xxle Eastlgh-Redbridge 13.20lxr Redbdge Engrs Yd- Woking Up Yard xx.xxle to Eastleigh	*140* 21.00le Eastleigh-Basing 22.02v Basingstoke-Wloo
34102 (D)	**396(1)** 08.27 Weymth-Bo'mouth 10.32f Bomo-Cent Goods 10.57f Cent Goods-Bomo	**411/394(2)** 07.51 Bo'mouth-Weymth 11.18 Weymth- Bo'mouth/ 15.01 Bo'mouth-Weymth 18.15 Weymouth-Wloo	**395** 02.45 Waterloo- Bournemouth 07.08 Bo'mouth-Weymth	**396(1)/394(2)** 08.27 Weymth-Bo'mouth 15.01 Bo'mouth-Weymth 18.15 Weymouth-Wloo	**395** 02.45 Waterloo- Bournemouth 07.08 Bo'mouth-Weymth	*396* Weymouth - Spare	***396/395(2)*** 10.20sf Weymth- Westbury (to Crewe) xx.xxle to Weymouth/ 22.13 Weymth-Bo'mouth (D/H D65xx)
34108 (E)	**467/462** 10.00le Salis-Warminster F. S. 11.00 - 12.00 12.00le to Salisbury 21.00f Salis-Basingstoke 00.35f Basing-Salisbury	**462** 21.00f Salis-Basingstoke 00.35f Basing-Salisbury	**Dsl./462** 08.35 Salisbury-Wloo 13.00 Wloo-Salisbury Then as Tuesday	**462** As Tuesday	**462** As Tuesday	*ES14* 05.30le Sal loco-East Yard 05.55bst East Yd-Bevois Pk (Eastleigh loco to turn) 10.03bst Bevois Park -Salisbury East Yd xx.xxle to loco	*Salisbury-No Diagram* *(OFFICIAL* *WITHDRAWAL DATE)*

	MONDAY 19/6	TUESDAY 20/6	WEDNESDAY 21/6	THURSDAY 22/6	FRIDAY 23/6	SATURDAY 24/6	SUNDAY 25/6
35003 (A)	Nine Elms-Repairs	**281(1)** 07.18 Wloo-Salisbury C. S. 13.30 - 14.15 15. 55 Salis-Basingstoke	**162(1)/138(2)** 09.02sf Basing-Feltham 11.04le to Woking/ 11.32 Woking-Waterloo (Replaced 34013) xx.xxse Wloo-Clap Jcn or xx.xxle Wloo-Nine Elms	**145** 08.35 Wloo-Weymouth 17.41 Weymth- 21.00 Bo'mouth- Weymth (18.30 Ex Wloo)	**147(1)/138(2)** 07.49 Weymth-Bo'mouth 12.34 Bournemouth- Waterloo/ 18.22 Waterloo- Bournemouth 20.49e Bo'mouth-Weymth	149 *Weymouth - Spare*	**Spl2** /147 xx.xxle to Bournemouth xx.xxsf Bo'mouth- Weymth (towing condemned locos 76008,41230 & 41295)/ 15.00sf Weymth-Westbury xx.xxle to Weymouth
35007 (A)	**145** 08.35 Wloo-Weymouth 17.41 Weymth-Bo'mouth 21.00 Bo'mouth-Weymth (18.30 Ex Wloo cancelled -start from Bo'mouth?)	**147** 07.49 Weymth-Bo'mouth 12.34 Bournemouth- Waterloo 18.54 Wloo-Salisbury	**148** 06.49 Salisbury-Wloo 11.38v Wloo-Basingstoke 19.06 Basing-Soton Cent 21.18e Soton C.-Brockhst 22.00le Brockhst-Weymth	**149** 17.30 Weymouth-Wloo	Nine Elms-Repairs	*Nine Elms-Repairs*	*Nine Elms-Repairs*
35008 (A)	**283** 11.29v Basingstoke- Southampton West Dks 16.20 Soton C.-Bo'mouth E. C. S. Bo'mouth Area 17.30 - 23.00	**280** 05.15v Bo'mouth-Weymth 10.13 Weymth-Bo'mouth 15.00le to Brockenhurst 16.15e Brockhst-Eastleigh 19.04f Northam-Eastleigh 20.40v Eastleigh- Clapham Jcn	–	**135** 08.10 Wloo-Weymth Jcn 16.23 Weymth Jcn-Wloo (16.00 Ex Quay)	**135** As Thursday (banked by 41320 on Parkstone bank)	*Nine Elms-No Diagram*	*Nine Elms-No Diagram*
35013 (A)	Nine Elms-No Diagram	**135** 08.10 Wloo-Weymth Jcn 16.23 Weymth Jcn-Wloo (16.00 Ex Quay)	**135** As Tuesday	– Nine Elms-Exams	**145** 08.35 Wloo-Weymouth 17.41 Weymth- Bo'mouth 21.00 Bo'mouth-Weymth (18.30 Ex Wloo)	146 *Weymouth - Spare*	146 *Weymouth - Spare*
35023 (A)	**147(1)** 07.49 Weymth-Bo'mouth 12.34 Bournemouth- Waterloo	**145** 08.35 Wloo-Weymouth 17.41 Weymth-Bo'mouth 21.00 Bo'mouth-Weymth (18.30 Ex Wloo)	**147(1)** 07.49 Weymth-Bo'mouth 12.34 Bournemouth- Waterloo	– *Nine Elms- Repairs or wash out*	**147(2)** 18.54 Wloo-Salisbury	148 *Salisbury - Spare*	148 *Salisbury - Spare*
35028 (A)	**149** FS 08.00-13.00 17.30 Weymth-Wloo	–	**145** 08.35 Wloo-Weymouth 17.41 Weymth-Bo'mouth 21.00 Bo'mouth-Weymth (18.30 Ex Wloo)	**147** 07.49 Weymth-Bo'mouth 12.34 Bournemouth- Waterloo 18.54 Wloo-Salisbury	**148(1)** 06.49 Salisbury-Wloo 11.38v Wloo-Basingstoke	283 Basingstoke - Spare	*Basingstoke - No Diagram*

35030 (A)	Nine Elms-Repairs	**113** 04.40 Wloo-Woking 06.30 Woking-Salisbury 18.38 Salisbury-Wloo	**281(1)** 07.18 Wloo-Salisbury C.S. 13.30 - 14.15 15.55 Salis-Basingstoke	**162** 09.02sf Basing-Feltham 12.45le to Basingstoke	**283** 11.29v Basing-Soton West Docks 16.20 Soton C.-Bo'mouth C&WE Shunt at Brock 18.45 - 19.45 19.45le to Bournemouth	**280** 05.55 Bomo Cent Gds-Poole Yard 06.35le Poole-Branksome 07.23e Branks-Bo'mouth 07.37 Bo'mouth-Eastleigh 10.29 Eastleigh-Bo'mouth	**280(Sabcont)/394** 12.20e Bomo-Branksome E.C.S. Bomo Area to 16.30 18.53e Hamworthy Jcn-Bournemouth West/ 19.36 Bournemouth-Wloo
73018 (C)	**CS7** 08.30le Guildford-Woking Up Yard 09.20 Woking-Portsmouth Harbour (Weedkiller) 11.35le to Fratton 12.30le to Soton E Dks 14.00sf Soton East Dks-Feltham 16.50le to Nine Elms	*Spl.* *xx.xxsf (am) Nine Elms-Southampton Docks*	**166** 10.15e Eleigh-Soton Cent 10.43 Soton C.-Bo'mouth-Weymth 13.08 Bo'mouth-Weymth 16.46 Weymth-Bo'mouth 18.51 Bo'mouth-Woking 22.45le to Guildford	**161**/282 04.32v Woking-Basing 06.50f Basingstoke-Eleigh 10.32v Eastleigh-Basing/ *Basingstoke - Spare*	**162** 09.02sf Basing-Feltham 12.45le to Basingstoke	162 *Basingstoke - Spare*	Basingstoke - *No Diagram*
73020 (C)	*Nine Elms-* *Repairs or Wash Out*	**AS5** 17.23 Waterloo-Soton East Docks (B56 - "Rotterdam")	**Spl.4** 09.00 Soton East Docks - Waterloo (B61 - "Queen Mary") 11.59se Waterloo-Clapham Jcn	**Spl.5** 07.45 Waterloo-Southampton East Dks (B63 - "Queen Mary")	**166** 10.15e Eleigh-Soton Cent 10.43 Soton Central-Bo'mouth 13.08 Bo'mouth-Weymth 16.46 Weymth-Bo'mouth 18.51 Bo'mouth-Woking 22.45le to Nine Elms	**167(1)** 02.15v Clapham Jcn-Waterloo 03.40v Wloo-Guildford 05.10v Guildford-Ports & S'sea 08.45le to Guildfd(10.40)* (*D/H 73085)	*Guildford - No Diagram*
73029 (A)	**CS2** 09.45 Eastleigh-Portsmouth Harb 11.29 Ports Harbour-Woking (weedkiller) CCE shunt 13.17-14.15 14.15le to Guild(18.00)	**172** 22.05le Guildford-Woking Up Yd 222.42bst Woking-Wimbledon West Yd 23.45bst Wimbledon-New Malden (WAO to Subriton) 06.15bst Surbiton-Wok Up Yard 07.08le to Guildfd(08.50)	**171(2)** 20.45le Guild-Farnham 21.50bst Farnham-Surbiton (WAO to New Malden) 05.46bst to Wim'don West Yard 06.10bst to Woking Down Yard 07.26le to Guildfd(09.45)	**CSpl(no number?)** 21.55le Guildford-Woking Up Yd 22.43bst Woking-Wimbledon (WAO to Raynes Pk) 05.43bst Raynes Park-Wok Up Yard 07.05le to Guildfd(09.40)	**171** 21.10le Guildford-Shalford 21.50bst Shalford-Surbiton (WAO to New Malden) 05.46bst to Wim'don 06.10bst to Woking 07.26le to Guildfd(08.15)	**CS5** 21.40le Guildford-Wok Up Yard 22.47bst Woking-Alton (WAO to Bentley) 07.00bst Bentley-Woking Up Yd 08.23le to Guildfd(10.40)	*Guildford - No Diagram*

	MONDAY 19/6	TUESDAY 20/6	WEDNESDAY 21/6	THURSDAY 22/6	FRIDAY 23/6	SATURDAY 24/6	SUNDAY 25/6
73037 (A)	138(1)/146/404(2) 00.54 Eleigh – Weymouth/ Weymouth - Spare/ 22.13 Weymth-Bo'mouth (D/H D65xx)	**412** 09.20 Bournemouth- Weymouth (05.30 Ex Wloo) 12.12 Weymth-Bo'mouth 13.52 Bo'mouth-Soton C. 18.30 Soton C.-Bo'mouth 20.15e Bomo-Branksome	**412** As Tuesday	**412** As Tuesday	**412** 09.20 Bournemouth- Weymouth (05.30 Ex Wloo) 12.12 Weymth-Bo'mouth 13.52 Bo'mouth-Soton C. 19.45 Eastleigh-Bo'mouth 22.05e Bo'mouth-Poole	*Bournemouth -* *No Diagram*	*Bournemouth -* *No Diagram*
73043 (A)	**136** 02.30 Waterloo- Ports Harbour 07.30 Port & S'sea- Eleigh/ 19.50 Eastleigh-Bo'mouth 22.05e Bo'mouth-Poole 22.40le to Weymouth	396(1) 08.27 Weymth-Bo'mouth	280/ **pt137**/ 280 05.15v Bo'mouth-Weymth 10.13 Weymth- Bo'mouth/ 17.42 Bo'mouth- Eastleigh/ 20.40v Eastleigh- Clapham Jcn.	*Nine Elms - No Diagram*	281 07.18 Wloo-Salisbury C. S. 13.30 - 14.15 15. 55 Salis-Basingstoke	282	*Basingstoke -* *No Diagram*
73065 (A)	*Salisbury-Repairs* (STEAM BRAKE)	*As Monday*	*As Monday*	*As Monday*	*As Monday*	*As Monday*	*As Monday*
73085 (A)	282/281(2) *Basingstoke - Spare/* 22.55le Basingstoke- Woking Up Yd 00.30bst Woking- Brookwood (WAO to Farnborough) 0600bst to Basing West Yard	282/ /281(2) *Basingstoke - Spare/* 23.25le Bas-Farnborough 00.25bst Farn-Winchfield (WAO to Basing a 06.00)	282/281(2) *Basingstoke - Spare /* 23.35bst Basingstoke- Hook (WAO to Winchfield) 05.30bst Winch- Wok Up Yd) 06.33bst Woking-Basing	163/171 14.05v Basing-Surbiton 14.59le to Guildford / 21.50bst Farnboro- Surbiton (WAO to New Malden) 05.46bst to Wim'don West Yard 06.10bst to Woking Down Yard	171(Thurs)cont 07.26le to Guildfd(09.20) *FRI: Guildford -* *No Diagram*	165(1)/CS9 02.28le Guildford- Woking 03.18v Woking-Fratton 08.45le to Guildford arr 10.40 (*D/H 73020)/ 00.30(Sun)le to Farnham 01.40bst Farnham- Surbiton	CS9(Sat) cont (WAO to New Malden) 08.00bst New Malden- Wimbledon West Yd 09.07bst Wimbledon- Wok Dn Yard 10.20bst Woking- Farnham 11.10le to Guildford *SUN: Guild -* *No Diagram*
73092 (C)	**172** 22.05le Guildford- Woking Up Yd 22.42bst Woking- Wimbledon West Yd 23.45bst Wimbledon- New Malden (WAO to Surbiton) 06.15bst Surbiton- Wok Up Yard 07.08le to Guildford (arr 08.55)	**173** 21.50le Guildford- Shalford 22.22bst Shalford- Surbiton (WAO to New Malden) 05.55bst New Malden- Wimbledon West Yd '06.24bst Wimbledon- Shalford 07.58le to Guildfd(09.45)	**173** As Tuesday(arr.11.00)	**173** As Tuesday(arr. 10.50)	**173** As Tuesday(arr. 11.45)	165(2) 20.20le Guildford- Woking Up Yd 21.45bst Woking- Guildford 22.15bst Guildford- Wokingham (WAO) 07.40bst Wokingham- Guildford 09.00bst Guildford- Woking Up Yd	165(Sat)cont 09.50le to Guildfd(11.30) SUN: *Guildford -* *No Diagram*

Loco							
73093 (C)	**411/396(2)** 07.51 Bournemouth-Weymouth Bo'mouth/ 11.18 Weymth-Bo'mouth/ 14.32le to Brockenhurst 16.03 Brockenhurst-Christchurch 16.59le to Brockhst (C.S.) 19.45le to Bournemouth	**394(1)/396(2)** 06.45 Poole-Bo'mouth 08.08 Christ'ch-Brockhst F & C.S. 09.00-09.50/ 16.03 Brockhst-Christ'ch 17.00e Christ'ch-Bo'mouth e.c.s Bo'mouth area to 20.20	*FS8* 05.44 Bournemouth-Eastleigh 08.29 Eastleigh-Bournemouth 10.15e Bournemouth-Branksome 10.31le to Bo'mouth	**394(1)/396(2)** *As Wednesday*	**394(1)/396(2)** 06.45 Poole-Bo'mouth 08.08 Christ'ch-Brockhst F & C.S. 09.00-09.50/ 16.03 Brockhst-Christ'ch 17.0e Christ'ch-Bo'mouth e.c.s Bo'mouth area to 20.20	**412** 05.00le Bo'mouth-Poole 06.45 Poole-Bo'mouth 07.51 Bournemouth-Weymouth 12.12 Weymth-Bo'mouth Work MP Crane at Bomo Central 21.45-07.00	*Bournemouth-* *No Diagram*
73118 (C)	*Guildford - No Diagram*	**171(2)** 20.45le Guildford-Farnham 21.50bst Farnham-Surbiton (WAO to New Malden) 05.46bst to Wimbledon West Yard 06.10bst to Woking Down Yd 07.26le to Guildfd(09.15)	**172** 22.05le Guildford-Woking Up Yd 22.42bst Woking-Wimbledon West Yd 23.45bst Wimbledon-New Malden (WAO to Surbiton) 06.15bst Surbiton-Woking Up Yd 07.08le to Guildfd(09.50)	**Spl** dep Guildford 11.30 *Shalford Shunt?* arr Guildford 15.30	**CS7** 22.10le Guildfd-Wok Up Yd 23.13bst Woking-Richmond (WAO) 05.30bst Rich-Wok Up Yard xx.xxle to Guildfd(09.00) (Coupled to 77014)	**167(2)** 21.43le Guildford-Woking Up Yd 22.38bst Woking-Waterloo (WAO to Loco Jcn) 07.35bst Loco Junction-Woking Up Yard 08.58le to Guildford	*Guildford - No Diagram*
73155 (C)	**171** 20.45le Guildford-Farnham Surbiton (WAO to New Malden) 05.46bst to Wimbledon West Yd 06.10bst to Woking Down Yd 07.26le to Guildford (arr 08.55)	*Guildford - No Diagram*	**172** 22.05le Guildford-Woking Up Yd 22.42bst Woking-Wimdn W Yd 23.45bst Wimbledon-New Malden (WAO to Surbiton) 06.15bst Surbiton-Woking Up Yd 07.08le to Guildfd(09.40)	- *Guildford -* *Wash Out?*	**172** As Thursday(arr. 08.30)	*Guildford - No Diagram*	
75068 (D)	**404** 07.52le Bo'mouth-Poole 08.30f Poole-Ringwood 12.10f Ringwood-Poole 15.35f Poole-Weymouth 22.13 Weymth-Bo'mouth Bo'mouth- (D/H D65xx)	*Weymouth-* *No Diagram*	**146** 14.45f Wey-Westbury 17.30le to Weymouth	*Weymouth-* *No Diagram*	**146** *As Wednesday*	**139** (C. S. and banking at Weymouth 10.00-14.00) 22.00ebv Weymouth-Dorchester South 23.30bst Dorch-Wareham (WAO to Hamworthy Jcn) 08.20le to Bournemouth	**139Sat) cont** 09.30le Bournemouth-Hamworthy Jcn 10.15bst Hamworthy J-Dorchester South 11.30ebv Dorchester Sth-Weymouth SUN: Weymouth- *No Diagram*

	MONDAY 19/6	TUESDAY 20/6	WEDNESDAY 21/6	THURSDAY 22/6	FRIDAY 23/6	SATURDAY 24/6	SUNDAY 25/6
75074 (D)	**165** 02.28le Guild-Wok 03.18v Woking-Fratton 10.15v Fratton-Basing 16.51 Basing-Salisbury 19.20v Salis-Northam 21.22f Sot W. Dks-Eleigh	166(1) 10.15e Eleigh-Soton Cent 10.43 Soton Central-Bournemouth	*Bournemouth - Repairs*	*Bournemouth - Repairs*	*Bournemouth - Repairs*	Bournemouth - *No Diagram*	397 21.20v Bomo-Wey
75075 (D)	DS11 12.37sf Soton E Dks-Basingstoke 14.50le to Eastleigh 17.43sf Soton E Dks-Basingstoke 20.15le to Eastleigh	136(2) 19.50 Eastleigh-Bo'mouth 22.05e Bo'mouth-Poole 22.40le to Weymouth	137/pt280/137 05.30f Weymouth-Poole 09.08f Poole-Wareham-Wool-Wareham-Furzebrook-Poole 16.15e Brockhst-Eastleigh 19.04f Northam-Eastleigh/Soton E Docks 20.50f Eastleigh	136(2) 19.50 Eastleigh-Bo'mouth 22.05e Bo'mouth-Poole 22.40le to Weymouth	137 05.30f Weymouth-Poole 09.08f Poole-Wareham-Wool-Wareham-Furzebrook-Poole 17.42 Bo'mouth-Eastleigh 20.50f Eastleigh-Soton E Docks	*Spl/DS12* *xx.xxle Eleigh-Redbridge* *c09.30sf R'bridge-Eastleigh/* *20.10crane Eastleigh loco-Bournemouth loco* *00.05crane Loco-Station* *(WAO Bomo to 07.00)*	*DS12(Sat)cont* *07.20crane Bournemouth-Eastleigh loco* *SUN: Eastleigh-* *No Diagram*
75076 (D)	**412** 09.20 Bo'mouth-Weymth (05.30 Ex Wloo) 12.12 Weymth-Bo'mouth 13.52 Bo'mouth-Soton C. 18.30 Soton C.-Bo'mouth 20.15e Bomo-Branksome	**166(2)** 13.08 Bournemouth-Weymouth 16.46 Weymth-Bo'mouth 18.51 Bo'mouth-Woking 22.45le to Guildford	**165** 02.28le Guildford-Woking 03.18v Woking-Fratton 10.15v Fratton-Basing 16.51 Basing-Salisbury 19.20v Salisbury-Northam 21.22f Sot W. Dks-Eleigh	165(2) c11.15v Eleigh-Basing 16.51 Basing-Salisbury 19.20v Salis-Northam 21.22f Sot W Dks-Eleigh			*DSpl* *c.11.00le Eastleigh-Basing* *13.35bst Basing West Yard-Redbridge Engrs Yd* *c15.30le to Eastleigh*
75077 (D)	DS12 23.00le Eastleigh-Fareham (WAO at Fareham 00.01-04.55) 05.45le to Eastleigh	DS11/DS12 17.20sf Soton East Dks-Basingstoke 19.30le to Eastleigh/ 23.00le to Fareham (WAO at Fareham 00.01-04.55 05.45le to Eastleigh	DS7 10.22dep Eastleigh Ballast Sidings-Micheldever 12.05le to Eastleigh Then as Tuesday	DS7 11.26le Eastleigh-Soton E Dks 12.37sf Soton E Dks-Basing 15.10bst Baing Up Yard-Micheldever 16.00le to Eastleigh	**343** xx.xxle Eleigh-Fratton Carriage Shunting at Fratton Yd 06.30-23.00	*Fratton-Spare*	*Fratton-Spare*
76005 (F)			**411** 07.51 Bo'mouth-Weymth 11.18 Weymth-Bo'mouth	**411** As Wednesday	**411** As Wednesday	*Weymouth - Repairs*	*Weymouth - Repairs*
76006 (F)	*Weymouth - Repairs*	*Weymouth - Repairs*	*Weymouth - Repairs*	*Weymouth - Repairs*	*Weymouth - Repairs*	*Weymouth - Repairs*	*Weymouth - Repairs*

76007 (F)	308 / 01.57 Eleigh-Port & S'sea / 06.30 Fareham-Eastleigh / 17.20 Eastleigh-Fratton / 23.32 Port & S'sea-Eleigh / Also freights & Vans in / Portsmouth & Eleigh areas	308 / *As Monday*	**343** / xx.xxle Elgh-Fratton / Carriage shunting at / Fratton Yd 06.30-23.00	**343** / Carriage shunting at / Fratton Yd 06.30-23.00 / xx.xxle to Eastleigh	*Eastleigh- / No Diagram*	DS11 / 11.00le Eleigh- Ballast Sdgs / 11.30bst Eleigh Ballast Sdgs / -Basingstoke Up Yd / xx.xxle to Basing loco / 00.05le Basing loco- Up Yd / 00.35bst Up Yard-Station	DS11(Sat)cont / (WAO in stn to 07.30) / 07.30bst Stn-West Yard / 09.47bst Basingstoke- Eleigh Bst sdgs / xx.xxle to Eastleigh loco / SUN: *Eastleigh- / No Diagram*
76009 (F)		404 / 07.52le Bo'mouth-Poole / 08.30f Poole-Ringwood / 12.10f Ringwood-Poole / 15.35f Poole-Weymouth / 22.13 Weymth-Bo'mouth / (D/H D65xx)	404 / *As Tuesday*	404 / *As Tuesday*	404 / *As Tuesday*	*Bournemouth - / No Diagram*	*Bournemouth - / No Diagram*
76011 (F)	**161/163** / 06.50f Basingstoke- Eastleigh / 10.32v Eastleigh Basing/ / 14.05v Basing-Surbiton / 14.59le to Guildford	**161/163** / 03.30le Guildford- Woking / 04.32v Woking-Basing / 06.50f Basingstoke- Eastleigh / 10.32v Eastleigh-Basing / 14.05v Basing-Surbiton / 14.59le to Guildford	**161/163** / *As Tuesday*	- / Guildford - Repairs	**161/163** / *As Tuesday*	**161** / 03.30le Guildford- Woking / 04.32v Woking-Basing	*Basingstoke - No Diagram*
76026 (F)	Nine Elms - Repairs	Nine Elms - Repairs	Nine Elms - / *Repairs or Spare*	**113** / 04.40 Wloo-Woking / 06.30 Woking-Salisbury / 18.38 Salisbury-Wloo	**105(1)/106(2)** / 03.00e Clapham Jcn-Wloo / C. S. at Waterloo / 04.45 - 08.00/ / C. S. at Waterloo / 17.45 - 23.59	**113** / 04.40 Wloo-Woking / 06.30 Woking-Salisbury / 11.00le or A/O to / Nine Elms	
76031 (C)	**173** / 21.50le Guildford- Shalford / 22.22bst Shalford- Surbiton / (WAO to New Malden) / 05.55bst New Malden- Wim'don W Yd / '06.24bst Wimbledon- Shalford / 07.58le to Guildtd(11.30)	*Guildford - No Diagram*	**171(1)** / 06.40le Guild-Wok Up Yd / 07.28bst Wok-Shalford / 09.28bst Shalfd-Woking / 11.10bst Wok-Farnham / 12.40bst Wok-Farnham / c15.00le to Guildford	**165(1)/308(2)** / 02.28le Guildford- Woking / 03.18v Woking-Fratton / 10.15v Fratton-Eleigh / 17.20 Eleigh-Fratton / Vans in area / 23.32 Ports & S-Eleighh	*308* / 01.57 Eleigh-Ports & S / 06.30 Fareham-Eleigh / 17.20 Eleigh-Fratton / 23.32 Ports & S-Eleigh / Also freight and vans in / Ports and Eleigh areas	166	*Eastleigh-Spare*

	MONDAY 19/6	TUESDAY 20/6	WEDNESDAY 21/6	THURSDAY 22/6	FRIDAY 23/6	SATURDAY 24/6	SUNDAY 25/6
76064 (D)	**280** 07.15le Bomo-Christ'ch 08.08 Christ'ch-Brock F. & CE/S 09.00-09.50 09.55le to Eastleigh 19.04f Northam- Eastleigh 20.40v Eastleigh- Clapham Jcn	**AS1/AS9** 06.06se Clap Jcn-Wloo 07.03le to Clapham Jcn 08.10se Clap Jcn-Wloo 09.00le to Nine Elms/ FS at Nine Elms Goods Yd (14.30-21.30)	**113** 04.40 Wloo-Woking 06.30 Woking-Salisbury 18.38 Salisbury-Wloo	*Nine Elms - No Diagram*	*Nine Elms - No Diagram*	*Nine Elms - No Diagram*	*Nine Elms - Wash out?*
76066 (D)	**463** 08.31v Salisbury-Basing 10.45v Basingstoke- Portsmouth & Southsea C. S. 13.20 - 15.00 16.00v Port & S-Fratton 19.06v Port & S-Salisbury	**467/ES12** 10.00le Salis-Warminster F. S. 11.00 - 12.00 12.00le to Salisbury/ 20.42sf Salisbury- Northam Yard 22.10le to Salisbury	**467** *As Tuesday*	**467/ES13** *As Tuesday /* 20.42sf Salis-Northam Yard 22.10le to Eastleigh 23.15le to Salisbury	**467/ES12** *As Tuesday /* 14.30le Salis-Soton E. Dks 16.50sf Sot. E. Docks- Westbury 19.20le to Salisbury		
76067 (F)	**166** 10.15e Eleigh-Soton Cent 10.43 Soton C.-Bo'mouth 13.08 Bo'mouth-Weymth 16.46 Weymth-Bo'mouth 18.51 Bo'mouth-Woking 22.45le to Guildford	**165** 02.28le Guildford- Woking 03.18v Woking-Fratton 10.15v Fratton-Basing 16.51 Basing-Salisbury 19.20v Salisbury- Northam 21.22f Sot W. Dks-Eleigh	-	**166** 10.15e Eleigh-Soton Cent 10.43 Soton C.-Bo'mouth 13.08 Bo'mouth-Weymth 16.46 Weymth-Bo'mouth 18.51 Bo'mouth-Woking 22.45le to Guildford	**165** 02.28le Guildford- Woking 03.18v Woking-Fratton 10.15v Fratton-Basing 16.51 Basing-Salisbury 19.20v Salisbury- Northam 21.22f Sot W. Dks-Eleigh	**DS13** 23.30le Eastleigh-Fareham 00.30bst Fareham (WAO to Cosham 06.30) 07.13bst Cosham- Eleigh Ballast sdgs xx.xxle to loco	*Eastleigh - No Diagram*
77014 (C)	**Spl** dep Guild 09.45 1 Woking- Farnham Freight? arr Guild 13.00	- *Guildford - No Diagram*	- *Guildford - No Diagram*	- *Guildford -Wash Out?*	**CS8** 22.25le Guild-Wok Up Yd 23.10bst Woking-Staines 00.20bst Staines- Windsor&Eton (WAO) 05.15bst Winds&E-Staines 06.02bst Staines- Woking Up Yd	**CS8(Fri) cont** 07.28le to Guildfd(09.00) Coupled to 73118 SAT: *Guildford -* *No Diagram*	*Guildford - No Diagram*
80011 (F)		**400** 07.13e Bomo. West-Cent. 08.15f Cent Gds- Branksome Branks & Bomo West ecs 09.15 - 13.20 13.23e Branks=Bomo Cent.	**400** First part only or all as Tuesday	**400** First part only or all as Tuesday			*Bournemouth -* *No Diagram*

Loco	Monday	Tuesday	Wednesday	Thursday	Friday	Saturday	Sunday
80016 (D)	**343** xx.xxle Eleigh-Fratton Carriage Shunting at Fratton Yd 06.30-23.00	**343** Carriage shunting at Fratton Yd 06.30-23.00 xx.xxle to Eastleigh	**314** 00.25v Eleigh-Soton Cent 01.34 Soton Cent-Eleigh 04.10f Eleigh-Sot W Dks 06.00le to Eleigh P.A.D pilot 08.00-16.00 18.57v Sot W Dks-Cent 20.45 W Dks-Bevois Pk 22.00v Bev Pk-Northam 22.10le to Eastleigh	**314** As Wednesday	**314** As Wednesday	**308** 01.57 Eleigh-Port & S'sea 04.05v Ports&S-Havant 04.5v Havant-Fratton 22.53v Fratton-Ports&S 23.32 Ports & S-Eastleigh 01.57 Eleigh-Port & S'sea 03.30e Ports&S-Fratton	**308** 22.50le Fratton-Ports & S 23.32 Ports&S-Eleigh
80133 (D)	**313** 06.20f Basing-Andover 09.00f Andover-Ludgershall 10.30f Lud-Andover F. S. at Lud & Andover 15.05f Andover-Basing C. S. 19.30 - 01.05	**313** As Monday	**313** As Monday	**313** As Monday	**313** As Monday	**313** 09.50le Basing-Eastleigh	
80139 (D)	**314(MO)** P.A.D Pilot 08.00 - 16.00 18.57v Sot W Dks-Soton C 20.45v West Dks-Bevoir Pk C. S. 21.05 - 21.45 22.00v Bevois Pk-Northam 22.10le to Eastleigh	**314(Tu-Fri)** 00.25v Eleigh-Soton Cent 01.34 Soton C.-Eleigh 04.10f Eleigh-Sot W Dks 06.00le to Eastleigh *Then as Monday*	**308** 01.57 Eleigh-Ports & S 06.30 Fratton-Eleigh 07.30le to Brockenhurst 09.00e Brock-Eleigh 15.06e Eleigh-Brock 16.15e Brock-Eleigh 17.20 Eleigh-Fratton 23.32 Ports & S-Eleigh	**308(1)** 01.57 Eleigh-Ports & S 06.30 Fratton-Eleigh 12.05f Elgh-Bevois Pk 13.40f Bevois Pk-Elgh	**314** Eastleigh - *Repair or Wash Out*	**314** 00.25v Eleigh-Soton Cent 01.34 Soton C.-Eleigh Local freights & C. S. *until;* 13.15f Soton West Dks- Eastleigh Main Yard 14.25le to Basingstoke	**314(Sat) cont** 22.00le Basing-Woking (C. S. 23.00-23.25) 23.30 Woking-Basing SUN: *Basingstoke-* *No Diagram*
80146 (F)	**407** 06.48 Bo'mouth-Brockhst 07.56 Brockhst-Bo'mouth 08.35e Bomo-Branksome 09.17le to Weymouth 17.00v Weymth-Bo'mouth	**409** Bournemouth West pilot and ecs trips to and from Branksome 05.40 - 22.00	**407** 06.48 Bo'mouth-Brockhst 07.56 Brockhst-Bo'mouth 08.35e Bomo-Branksome 09.17le to Weymouth 17.00v Weymth-Bo'mouth	**407** As Monday	**407** As Monday	**407** As Monday	
80152 (D)	**290** As Tuesday	**290** Local friegths and vans Eastleigh and Soton area 08.00-14.00 16.22 Eleigh-Soton Cent 17.16 Soton-Bomo & ecs 20.45le to Eastleigh Local freights 23.25 - 02.00	**Tues(290)cont/290** 04.40f Eleigh-Winchester 05.30le to Eastleigh/ As Tuesday	**290** As Tuesday	**290** As Tuesday	**290** *Eastleigh - No Diagram*	

Rosters, 26 June – 2 July

	MONDAY 26/6	TUESDAY 27/6	WEDNESDAY 28/6	THURSDAY 29/6	FRIDAY 30/6	SATURDAY 1/7	SUNDAY 2/7
34001 (A)	**281** 07.18 Wloo-Salisbury C. S. 13.30 - 14.15 15.55 Salis-Basingstoke	**283** 11.29v Basing-Soton West Docks 16.20 Soton C.-Bo'mouth E. C. S. Bo'mouth Area 17.30 - 23.00	**394(1)/Spl** 05.00le Bo'mouth - Poole 06.45 Poole-Bo'mouth 08.08 Christ'ch-Brockhst F&C.S.to09.50 le to Bomo/ 19.30le Bomo- Dn Direction (work not known)	**394(2)** 15.01 Bo'mouth- Weymouth 18.15 Weymouth-Wloo	**395/149** 02.45 Waterloo- Bournemouth 07.08 Bo'mouth- Weymouth/ 16.15bank Wey Quay- Waterloo (To Bincombe) 17.30 Weymouth-Wloo	Nine Elms - Repairs	*Nine Elms - Repairs*
34004 (F)	*Bournemouth - No Diagram*	**411** 07.51 Bo'mouth- Weymth 11.18 Weymth- Bo'mouth	**411** *As Tuesday*	**411** *As Tuesday*	**411** *As Tuesday*	*Bournemouth - No Diagram*	*Bournemouth - No Diagram*
34013 (E)	**138(1)/254**/*Spl.* 00.54 Eastleigh-Weymth 06.43 Weymth-Bo'mouth 08.46 Bo'mouth-Eleigh (or Southampton?)/ 11.27 Sot. W. Dks-Wloo (B76 "Reina del Mar")/ *xx.xxse Wloo-Soton Dks*	**DS10** 10.00 Soton East Docks- Waterloo (B79 - "Queen Elizabeth")	**DS9** 08.54 Waterloo- Southampton East Dks (B83-"Nieuw Amsterdam")	Eastleigh- Wash Out	**DS10/DS14(2)** 05.10le Eleigh-Redbridge 06.10sf Redbridge- Wimbledon 10.45le to Nine Elms/ 16.40 Waterloo- Soton E Docks (B93 - "France")	138 *Eastleigh - Spare*	140 21.00le Eastleigh-Basing 22.02v Basingstoke- Waterloo
34018 (A)	Weymouth - Repairs Then **145(2)**: 17.41 Weymth-Bo'mouth *21.00 Bo'mouth-Weymth (18.30 Ex Wloo)*	**138(2)** 06.43 Weymth-Bo'mouth 08.46 Bournemouth- Waterloo 13.15se Waterloo- Clapham Jcn	**136** 02.30 Waterloo- Ports Harbour 07.30 Port & S'sea-Eleigh 19.50 Eastleigh-Bo'mouth 22.05e Bo'mouth-Poole 22.40le to Weymouth	**137** 05.30f Weymouth-Poole 09.08f Poole- Broadstone-Poole- Wareham-Furzebrook -Poole 17.42 Bo'mouth-Eastleigh 20.50f Eleigh-Sot E. Docks	**138(1)** 00.54 Eleigh-Weymouth (22.35 Ex Wloo)	**AS4(2)** 16.18 Weymth Jcn.-Wloo (15.55 Ex Quay) (Off at Woking - Hot Box-Replaced by E6026) c21.40le to Guildford	Guildford - Repairs
34021 (A)	Bournemouth-Repairs	Bournemouth-Repairs	*Bournemouth - No Diagram*	**394(1)** 05.00le Bo'mouth - Poole 06.45 Poole-Bo'mouth 07.18le to Christchurch 08.08 C'hrist'ch-Brockhst F & C.S. 09.00-09.50 09.50le to Bournemouth	**394** As Thurs. Then: 15.01 Bo'mouth- Weymouth 18.15 Weymouth-Wloo	**395** 02.45 Wloo-Bo'mouth 07.08 Bo'mouth- Weymth/ 10.13 Weymth-Bo'mouth 12.33e Bo'mouth Central -Bo'mouth West Sdgs 21.00 Bo'mouth-Weymth	**396** Carriage shunting at Weymouth 09.30-14.00 15.06sf Weymth- Westbury (Banked by 34093 to Bincombe) 17.35le to Weymouth

Loco	Col 1	Col 2	Col 3	Col 4	Col 5	Col 6	Col 7
34024 (F)	**138(2)** 10.14 Eastleigh(or Soton)-Waterloo (replaced 34013) 13.44e Waterloo-Clapham Jcn	**101(part?)** xx.xxle Nine Elms-Wloo 12.18se Waterloo-Clapham Jcn 12.50le to Nine Elms/ Repairs	Nine Elms - Repairs	**145** 08.35 Wloo-Weymouth 17.41 Weymth-Bo'mouth 21.00 Bo'mouth-Weymth	**147(1)** 07.49 Weymth-Bo'mouth 12.34 Bournemouth-Waterloo	**AS7**(after repairs) 22.00le 9 Elms-Surbiton 23.45bst Surbiton-New Malden (WAO to Raynes Park) 07.30bst to Wimbledon West Yard 08.05bst to Surbiton xx.xxle to Nine Elms	Nine Elms - No Diagram
34025 (F)	Bournemouth - No Diagram	**280(1)/396(2)/145(2)** 05.15v Bournemouth-Weymouth 10.13 Weymth-Bo'mouth/ 16.03 Brockhst-Christ'ch 16.59le to Brock(Shunt) 19.45le to Bournemouth/ 21.00 Bo'mouth-Weymth	**147(1)/135(2)** 07.49 Weymth-Bo'mouth/ 10.36 Bo'mouth-Wey Jcn (Replaced 35030) 16.23 Weymouth Jcn-Waterloo (16.00 Ex Quay)	**395** 02.45 Waterloo-Bournemouth 07.08 Bo'mouth-Weymth	**137** 05.30f Weymouth-Poole 09.08f Poole-Wareham-Wool-Wareham-Furzebrook-Poole 15.36le to Bournemouth 17.42 Bo'mouth-Eastleigh 20.50f Eastleigh-Soton East Docks xx.xxle to Bournemouth	**E.M.U. Cover** 09.24 Bournemouth-Waterloo	**ASpl.** 09.33 Waterloo-Bournemouth 19.59 Bournemouth-Waterloo
34036 (A)	Nine Elms-Wash Out xx.xxsf Nine Elms Goods-Feltham xx.xxle to Nine Elms	**136(1)/DS13** 02.30 Waterloo-Ports Harbour 07.30 Ports & S-Eleigh/ 13.05le Eleigh-Soton E Dks 14.00sf Soton East Docks-Feltham 17.00le to Nine Elms	**DS13/412(2)** 13.20 Waterloo-Soton East Docks (B84-"Montserrat") 17.40le Eastleigh-Soton C. 18.30 Soton C.-Bo'mouth 20.15e Bomo-Branksome	**412(1)** 09.20 Bo'mouth-Weymth 12.12 Weymth-Bo'mouth 13.52 Bo'mouth-Soton C. 15.00le to Eastleigh	**DS11** 10.00 Sot. East Dks-Wloo (B94 - "Statendam") 12.21le Wloo-Nine Elms 13.30le to Stewarts Lane 14.40se Stewarts Lane-Eastleigh Carriage Works	Eastleigh - No Diagram	Eastleigh - No Diagram
34037 (D)	Nine Elms - Repairs		**281** 07.18 Wloo-Salisbury C. S. 13.30 - 14.15 15.55 Salis-Basingstoke	**162** 09.02sf Basing-Feltham 12.45sf Feltham-Eastleigh 17.43sf Eastleigh-Basing	**283** 11.29v Basing West Yard-Soton West Docks 16.20 Soton C.-Bo'mouth C&WE Shunt at Brockhst 18.45 - 19.45 19.45le to Bournemouth	**280** 05.55f Cent. Gds-Poole 07.23e Branksome-Bournemouth 07.37 Bo'mouth-Eastleigh 10.29 Eastleigh-Bo'mouth E.C.S. Bournemouth Area to 18.45	**394** 18.18le Bournemouth-Hamworthy Jcn. 18.55e Ham Jcn-Bo'mouth 19.36 Bournemouth-Wloo

	MONDAY 26/6	TUESDAY 27/6	WEDNESDAY 28/6	THURSDAY 29/6	FRIDAY 30/6	SATURDAY 1/7	SUNDAY 2/7
34052 (E)	467 10.00le Salis-Warminster F. S. 10.50 - 12.00 12.00le Warm-Salisbury 15.15le to Soton East Docks 16.50sf E Docks-Westbury 19.20le to Salisbury	ES14 20.42sf Salisbury-Northam Yard 22.10le to Salisbury	462 21.00f Salis-Basingstoke 00.35f Basing-Salisbury	462 As Wednesday	462 As Wednesday	462 addl 22.20le Salisbury-Andover 23.30bst Andover-Whitchurch (WAO to Oakley) 02.30bst Oakley-Basing 03.00bst Basing-Oakley (WAO to Whitchurch)	462(Sat)cont 08.00bst Whitchurch-Salisbury East Yard SUN: Salisbury - No Diagram
34060 (D)	135 08.10 Wloo-Weymth Jcn 16.23 Weymth Jcn-Wloo (16.00 Ex Quay)	135 As Monday	395/146/404(2) 02.45 Wloo-Bo'mouth 07.08 Bo'mouth-Wey / 14.45f Wey-Wesbury 17.30le to Weymouth / 22.13 Wey-Bo'mouth (D/H Cl. 33)	147(Mid) 12.34 Bournemouth-Waterloo	254(1)/147(2) 09.20 Wloo-Southampton West Docks (B91-"Pendennis Castle) 13.27se Soton West Dks - Clapham Jcn 18.54 Wloo-Salisbury	148	148
34087 (D)	149 F. S. 08.00 - 13.00 17.30 Weymouth-Wloo	145(1)/149(2) 08.35 Wloo-Weymouth/ 17.30 Weymouth-Wloo	Nine Elms - Repairs	135 08.10 Wloo-Weymth Jcn 16.23 Weymth Jcn-Wloo (16.00 Ex Quay)	136/AS2/254(2) 02.30 Wloo-Ports Harbour 07.30 Ports & S'sea-Eastleigh/ 11.27 Soton West Dks-Waterloo (B97 "Himalaya") 17.23 Wloo-Bournemouth 20.15e Bomo-Branksome	Fri(254)cont 21.35le Bo'mouth-Eastleigh SAT: 137	137 Eastleigh - Spare
34089 (E)	463 08.31v Salis-Basingstoke 10.45v Basingstoke-Ports & S'sea C. S. 13.20 - 15.00 16.00v Port & S-Fratton 19.06v Ports & S'sea-Salisbury	463 As Monday	463 As Monday	463 As Monday	148 06.49 Salisbury-Wloo 11.38v Wloo-Basingstoke 19.06 Basing-Soton Cent 21.18e Soton C.-Brockhst 22.00le Brockhst-Weymth	149/spl? Wey – Spare/ 19.15v Weymth Jcn-Westbury (18.45 Ex Quay) xx.xxle to Weymouth	149 Wey – Spare
34090 (D)	145(1) 08.35 Wloo-Weymouth Short of steam-Off at Eastleigh (replaced by 75076)	DS12 10.55 Soton West Docks-Waterloo (B82 - "Andes")	AS10 10.40p Wloo-Salisbury 17.35p Salisbury-Wloo (Salisbury Races)	AS7(1)/DS11 10.40p Wloo-Salisbury (Salisbury Races)/ 20.42sf Salisbury-Northam 22.10le to Salisbury	467 10.00le Salis-Warminster F. S. 10.50 - 12.00 12.00le Warm-Salisbury	OUT OF USE (INJECTORS)	

34093 (D)	*Nine Elms - Repairs*	**AS2** 08.54 Waterloo - Soton East Docks (B77 - "Reina del Mar")	**DS11/147(2)** 11.28 Soton East Docks- Waterloo (B88 - "Montserrat")/ 18.54 Wloo-Salisbury	**148** 06.49 Salisbury-Wloo 11.38v Wloo-Basingstoke 19.06 Basing-Soton Cent 21.18e Soton Cent- Brockhst 22.00le Brockhst-Weymth	**138(2)** 06.43 Weymth-Bo'mouth 08.46 Bournemouth- Wloo 13.15e Waterloo- Clapham Jcn 18.22 Waterloo- Bournemouth 20.49e Bo'mouth- Weymth	**139** 22.40e Weymth- Dorchester South 23.30bst Dorchester South.- Worgret Jcn (WAO to Hamworthy Jcn.)	**139 Sat(cont)** 10.48bst Hamworthy Jcn- Dorchester South 12.05le to Weymouth Bank 15.06sf Wey- Westbury (to Bincombe)
34095 (D)	**136** 02.30 Waterloo- Ports Harbour 07.30 Ports & S'sea- Eastleigh 19.50 Eastleigh- Bo'mouth 22.05e Bo'mouth-Poole 22.40le to Weymouth	**137** 05.30f Weymouth-Poole 09.08f Poole-Broadstone- Poole-Wareham- Furzebrook-Poole 17.42 Bo'mouth- Eastleigh 20.50 Elgh-Sot. East Dks	**138** 00.54 Eastleigh-Weymth 06.43 Weymth-Bo'mouth 08.46 Bournemouth- Waterloo	**136(1)/DS8** 02.30 Waterloo- Ports Harbour 07.30 Ports & S'sea- Eastleigh 10.42sp Soton Cent- East Docks (passrs. for "Bremen") 12.45sf Eleigh-Poole Yard xx.xxle to Eastleigh	**DS13/171(2)** 10.24 Soton West Dks- Waterloo (B95 - "Himalaya") xx.xxle to Guildford/ c14.15le to Guildford/ 23.55le to Woking? (c/o 73018)	**Fri (17)cont** xx.xxbst Woking- Wimbledon (WAO Surbiton- New Malden 06.10bst Wimbledon- Woking 07.26le to Guildfd(08.15)/ SAT-Spl(Dsl.672) Ballast- dep Guildford 19.30	**Spl(Sat)cont** (worked in London area- loco turned at Nine Elms arr Guildford 13.15 SUN: *Guildford -* *No Diagram*
34102 (D)	**280** 07.15le Bomo-Christ'ch 08.08 Christ'ch-Brockhst F. & CE/S 09.00-09.50 09.55le to Bournemouth	**394(1)** 05.00le Bo'mouth - Poole 06.45 Poole-Bo'mouth 07.18le to Christchurch 08.08 Christ'ch-Brockst F & C.S. 09.00-09.50 09.50le to Bournemouth	*Bournemouth - Repairs*	**FS13** 20.00le Bournemouth- Wareham 21.05sf Wareham- Basingstoke 01.20le to Eastleigh	**DS14(1)/DS15** 10.59 Soton East Docks- Waterloo (B96 - "Iberia")/ 16.00 Waterloo- Soton East Docks (B92 - "France")	*Eastleigh - No Diagram* *Used for trip working* *Eastleigh Works-Main* *yard?*	*Eastleigh - No Diagram*
34108 (E)	**462** 21.00f Salis-Basingstoke 00.35f Basing-Salisbury	**462** As Monday	*OUT OF USE*				
35003 (A)	**396(1)/394(2)** 08.27 Weymth-Bo'mouth 10.32f Bomo loco- Cent Gds 10.57f Cent Gds- Bomo loco/ 15.01 Bo'mouth-Weymth 18.15 Weymouth-Wloo	**395/146** 02.45 Wloo- Bournemouth 07.08 Bo'mouth-Weymth/ 14.45sf Weymth- Westbury 17.30le to Weymouth	**396(1)/394(2)** 08.27 Weymth-Bo'mouth 10.32f Bomo loco- Central Goods 10.57f Cent Gds- Bomo loco/ 15.01 Bo'mouth-Weymth 18.15 Weymouth-Wloo	**135** 08.10 Wloo-Weymth Jcn 16.23 Weymth Jcn-Wloo (16.00 Ex Quay) 20.45e Waterloo- Clapham Jcn	*Nine Elms - Repairs*	**AS4(1)** 08.30 Wloo-Weymouth	*Weymouth - Repairs*

	MONDAY 26/6	TUESDAY 27/6	WEDNESDAY 28/6	THURSDAY 29/6	FRIDAY 30/6	SATURDAY 1/7	SUNDAY 2/7
35007 (A)	Nine Elms - Repairs	**113** 04.40 Wloo-Woking 06.30 Woking-Salisbury 18.38 Salisbury-Wloo 21.15e Waterloo-Clapham Jcn.	**145** 08.35 Wloo-Weymouth 17.41 Weymth-Bo'mouth 21.00 Bo'mouth-Weymth (18.30 Ex Wloo)	*147(1)/146* 07.49 Weymth-Bo'mouth xx.xxle to Wey/ 14.45sf Weymth- Westbury 17.30le to Weymouth	**146** 14.45sf Weymth- Westbury 17.30le to Weymouth or Weymouth - Spare (May not have run)	*147* *Weymouth - Spare*	*147* 15.00sp Weymth- Bo'mouth (Pilot to 35008) 17.30le to Weymouth
35008 (A)	Nine Elms - No Diagram	Nine Elms - Repairs	Nine Elms - No Diagram HELD FOR SUNDAY	Nine Elms - No Diagram SPECIAL	Nine Elms - No Diagram	Nine Elms - No Diagram	**AS1(1)** 09.55sp Wloo-Weymouth 15.00sp Weymouth-Wloo
35013 (A)	**147** 07.49 Weymth-Bo'mouth 12.34 Bournemouth-Wloo 18.54 Wloo-Salisbury	**148** 06.49 Salisbury-Wloo 11.38v Wloo-Basingstoke 19.06 Basing-Soton Cent 21.18e Soton C.-Brock'hst 22.00le Brockhst-Weymth	**149** F. S. 08.00 - 13.00 17.30 Weymouth-Wloo	*OUT OF USE* *(BOILER TUBES)*			
35023 (A)	**148** 06.49 Salisbury-Wloo 11.38v Wloo-Basingstoke 19.06 Basing-Soton Cent 21.18e Soton C.-Brockhst 22.00le Brockhst-Weymth	**147** 07.49 Weymth-Bomo 12.34 Bo'mouth-Wloo 18.54 Wloo-Salisbury	**148** 06.49 Salisbury-Wloo 11.38v Wloo-Basingstoke 19.06 Basing-Soton Cent 21.18e Soton C.-Brockhst 22.00le Brockhst-Weymth	**149** F. S. 08.00 - 13.00 17.30 Weymouth-Wloo	**145** 08.35 Wloo-Weymouth 17.41 Weymth-Bo'mouth 21.00 Bo'mouth-Weymth (18.30 Ex Wloo)	*146* *Weymouth - Spare*	*146/395(1)* *Weymouth - Spare* 10.20sf Weymth-Westbury (to Crewe) 12.40le to Weymouth
35028 (A)	**283** 11.29v Basingstoke- Soton West Docks 16.20 Soton C-Bo'mouth E. C. S. Bournemouth area 17.30 - 23.00	**394(2)** 15.01 Bo'mouth-Weymth 18.15 Weymouth-Wloo	Nine Elms - No Diagram HELD FOR SUNDAY	Nine Elms - No Diagram SPECIAL	Nine Elms - No Diagram	Nine Elms - No Diagram	**AS2/106(part)** 12.20sp Wloo-Bo'mouth 16.30sp Bo'mouth-Wloo/ 19.13se Waterloo- Clapham Jcn xx.xxle to Nine Elms
35030 (A)	**395** 02.45 Wloo-Burne'mouth 07.08 Bo'mouth-Weymth	**396(1)/280(2)** 08.27 Weymth-Bo'mouth/ 15.00le to Brockenhurst 16.15e Brockhst-Eastleigh 19.04f Northam-Eastleigh 20.40v Eastleigh- Clapham Jcn.	**135(1)/147(Mid)** 08.10 Wloo-Weymouth (Replaced by 34025 at Bomo)/ 12.34 Bournemouth- Waterloo	Nine Elms - Repairs	Nine Elms - Repairs	**AS5** 09.15sp Wloo-Bo'mouth 18.30sp Bo'mouth-Wloo	*Nine Elms - No Diagram*

73018 (C)	**161(1)** 06.50f Basingstoke- Eastleigh	*162(2)* *17.43sf Soton East Dks-* *Basingstoke*	**163** 14.05v Basing-Surbiton 14.59le to Guildford	*Guildford - No Diagram*	**171(1)** 06.40le Guildford- Woking Up Yd 07.28bst Woking- Shalford 09.28bst Shalford- Wok Up Yd xx.xxle to Guildford (a. 13.10) 22.50le Guildford- Woking (Failed)	**171(Sat)cont/161** c.01.00le to Guildford/ 03.30le Guildford- Woking 04.32v Woking-Basing	*Basingstoke - No Diagram*
73020 (C)	*Guildford - No Diagram*	**171(1)/Spl/171(2)** As 73029 Monday xx.xxle to Woking/ c12.45sf Woking - Feltham xx.xxle Feltham- Guildfd(16.45)/ 20.45le Guildford- Farnham 21.50bst Farnham - Surbiton	**Tues171(2)cont/171(2)** (WAO to New Malden) 05.46bst N Malden- Wim'don 06.10bst Wim'don- Woking 07.26le to Guildford (arr 08.45)/ Weds -As Tues from 20.45	**AS2/13(6)2)** xx.xxle to Nine Elms 13.20 Wloo-Soton E. Dks (B90-"Queen Elizabeth")/ 19.50 Eastleigh-Bo'mouth 22.05e Bo'mouth-Poole 22.40le to Weymouth	**171(1)** 396 08.27 Weymth-Bo'mouth 10.32f Bomo loco- Central Goods 10.57f Cent Gds- Bournemouth loco/ 16.03 Brockhst-Christ'ch 17.00e Christchurch- Bo'mouth ECS Bo'mouth area to 20.20	**Spl2/FS13(2)** xx.xxam(Crane) Bournemouth-Poole (Work As Ordered) xx.xxcrane Poole-Bo'mouth/ 23.45Crane in Bournemouth Loco Work As Ordered Loco and Station Area to 07.00	397 20.50v Bournemouth- Weymouth
73029 (A)	**171(1)** 06.40le Guildford- Woking Up Yd 07.28bst Woking- Shalford 09.28bst Shalford- Woking Up Yard xx.xxbst Woking-Farnham? xx.xxle to Guildfd (a. 13.10)	**CS16** 008.30le Guildford- Woking Up Yd 09.38 (Weedkiller) Woking- Staines- Aldershot-Ascot- Wokingham- Twickenham-Feltham Yd (arr 15.05) 15.20le to Guildfd (17.40)	*Guildford - No Diagram*	**161** 03.30le Guildford- Woking 04.32v Woking-Basing 06.50f Basing-Eastleigh 10.32v Bevois Park- Basingstoke	**162** 09.02sf Basing-Feltham- 12.45sf Feltham- Eastleigh 16.45le to Basingstoke/	*Basingstoke - Spare* 162	*Basingstoke-* *No Diagram*
73037 (A)	**411** 07.51 Bo'mouth-Weymth 11.18 Weymth-Bo'mouth	**404** 07.52le Bo'mouth-Poole 08.30f Poole-Ringwood 12.10f Ringwood-Poole 15.35f Poole-Weymouth 22.13 Weymth-Bo'mouth (D/H D65xx)	**404(1)** 07.52e Bo'mouth-Poole 08.30f Poole-Ringwood 12.10f Ringwood-Poole 15.35f Poole-Weymouth	**396/290(2)** 08.27 Weymth-Bo'mouth 14.32le to Brockenhurst 16.03 Brockhst-Christ'ch/ xx.xxle Brockhst-Eastleigh *Local freights 23.25 - 02.00* *04.40f Eleigh-Winchester*	**290** Local freights & vans Eastleigh and Soton area 08.00 - 14.00 16.22 Eleigh-Soton Cent 17.16 Soton-Bomo & ecs 20.45le to Eastleigh Local freights 23.25 - 02.00	**290(Fri)/Spl/DS19** 04.40f Eastleigh- Winchester City xx.xxle to Eastleigh/ xx.xxle Eleigh-Redbridge c.10.30sf R'bridge- Eastleigh/ 22.25le Elgh- Micheldever (W. A. O. 23.30 - 07.15)	*DS19(Sat)cont* *07.45le to Eastleigh* *(or v. v. 75075)* SUN: *Eastleigh - No Diagram*

	MONDAY 26/6	TUESDAY 27/6	WEDNESDAY 28/6	THURSDAY 29/6	FRIDAY 30/6	SATURDAY 1/7	SUNDAY 2/7
73043 (A)	**162** 09.02sf Basing-Feltham 12.45le to Basingstoke	282 Basingstoke - Spare	162 09.02sf Basing-Feltham 12.45sf Feltham-Basing	282 Basingstoke - Spare	282 Basingstoke - Spare	283 Basingstoke - Spare	DS5 10.20bst Basingstoke-Bramley (W. A. O.) 11.10bst Bramley-Basingstoke
73065 (A)	*Salisbury - Repairs or spare*	467 10.00le Salis-Warminster F. S. 10.50 - 12.00 12.00le Warm-Salisbury	467/**DS15** 07.00dep Salis E.Yd-Grately 08.00le to Salisbury Then as Tues/ 15.15le Salis-Sot East Dks 16.50le Soton East Dks-Westbury 19.20le to Salisbury	467/**113(2)** 04.00bst Salis-Tunnel Jcn (WAO to Dean and back) 07.00bst to Salis. East Yard Then as Tues/ 18.38 Salisbury-Wloo 21.15e Wloo-Clapham Jcn	**113** 04.40 Wloo-Woking 06.30 Woking-Salisbury 18.38 Salisbury-Wloo 21.15e Waterloo-Clapham Jcn	**136** 02.30 Waterloo-Portsmouth Harb 18.10v Fratton-Basing 22.07v Basingstoke-Wloo	Nine Elms - Wash Out
73085 (A)	**165(1)**/282 02.28le Guildford-Woking 03.18v Woking-Fratton 10.15v Fratton-Basing/ Basing - Spare	162(1) 09.02sf Basing-Feltham 12.45sf Feltham-Eastleigh	DS14 14.00sf Soton East Docks-Feltham 16.50le to Eastleigh	DS10 14.00sf Soton East Docks-Feltham 16.50le to Eastleigh	DS12? 09.10le Eastleigh-Micheldever CCE shunt 10.00-11.00 11.19dep Micheldever-Feltham 13.55le to Eastleigh	*OUT OF USE?*	
73092 (C)	*Guildford - No Diagram*	**173** 21.50le Guildford-Shalford 22.22bst Shalford-Surbiton (WAO to New Malden) 05.55bst New Malden-Wim West Yd 06.24bst Wimbledon-Shalford 07.58le to Guildfd(09.00)	173 As Tuesday	**172** 22.05le Guildford-Woking Up Yd 22.42bst Woking-Wimbledon 23.45bst Wimbledon-New Malden (WAO to Surbiton) 06.15bst Surbiton-Woking Up Yd 07.08le to Guildfd(09.00)	**172** As Thursday (Arrive Guildford 09.15)	**CS10** 21.30le Guildford-Woking Up Yard 22.08bst Up Yd.-Surbiton 23.25bst Surbiton-Hampton Court Jcn (W. A. O. to Weybridge) 07.00bst Weybridge-Woking Down Yd 07.35le to Guildfd(09.45)	*Guildford - No Diagram*
73093 (C)	404 07.52le Bo'mouth-Poole 08.30f Poole-Ringwood 12.10f Ringwood-Poole 15.35f Poole-Weymouth 22.13 Weymth-Bo'mouth (D/H D65xx)	**DS11** 10.27 Soton East Docks-Waterloo (B81 - "France")	**AS2** 14.00 Waterloo-Soton East Docks (B85 - Andes") 16.32se Soton East Docks-Weymouth	*Weymouth-No diagram*	**AS3** 16.38 Weymth Jcn-Wloo (16.15 Ex Quay)	**D90** 12.35 Wloo-Weymouth 17.57v Weymouth-Wloo	D91 02.15v Wloo-Bournemouth 08.50 Bournemouth-Wloo (may not have worked)

73118 (C)	**173** 21.50le Guildford- Shalford- 22.22bst Shalford- Surbiton (WAO to New Malden) 05.55bst New Malden- Wimbledon West Yd 06.24bst Wimbledon- Shalford 07.58le to Guildfd(08.45)	**172** 22.05le Guildford- Woking Up Yd 22.42bst Wok-Wimbledon- New Malden (WAO to Surbiton) 06.15bst Surbiton- Woking Up Yd 07.08le to Guildford(09.00)	**172** *As Tuesday* *(Arrive Guildford 09.30)*	*Guildford - No Diagram*	**CS8** 23.05le to Farnham 00.20bst Farnham- Aldershot (WAO to Farnham) 05.30le to Guildfd(07.00)	**CS11(2)** 22.35le Guildford- Woking Up Yard- Aldershot 23.25bst Up Yard- 00.10bst Aldershot-Ash (WAO to Guildford) 07.35bst Guildford- Woking Up Yd 08.20 le to Guildfd(09.45)	*Guildford - No Diagram*
73155 (C)	**172** 22.05le Guildford- Woking Up Yd 22.42bst Woking- Wimbledon 23.45bst Wimbledon- New Malden (WAO to Surbiton) 06.15bst Surbiton- Woking Up Yd 07.08le to Guildfd(08.30)	*Guildford - No Diagram*	**171(1)/CS6** *As 73029 Monday/* 21.55le Guildford- Woking Up Yd 22.43bst Woking Up Yd- Wimbledon West Yd (WAO to Raynes Park) 05.43bst Raynes Park- Woking Up Yd 07.05le to Guildford	**173(2)** 21.50le Guildford- *Shalford-* 22.22bst *Shalford-* *Surbiton* (WAO to New Malden) 05.55bst New Malden- Wimbledon West Yard 06.24bst Wimbledon- *Shalford* 07.58le to Guildfd(09.00)	**173** *As Thursday* *(Arrive Guildford 11.15)*	**CS9(2)** 18.45le Guildford- Farnham 19.50le Farnham- Woking-Basingstoke (WAO to Winchfield) 08.00bst Winch-Woking 09.13bst Woking- Farnham 10.30le to Guildfd(12.20)	*Guildford - No Diagram*
75068 (D)	**137** 05.30f Weymouth-Poole 09.08f Poole-Wareham- Wool-Wareham- Furzebrook-Poole 17.42 Bo'mouth-Eastleigh 20.50f Eleigh-Sot. E. Dks	**138(1)** 00.54 Eastleigh-Weymth	*OUT OF USE?*			*WITHDRAWN*	
75074 (D)	**394(1)/280(2)** 10.13 Weymth-Bo'mouth *xx.xxle to Brockenhurst* *16.15se Brock-Eastleigh* *19.04f Northam-Eastleigh* *20.40v Eleigh-Clapham Jcn*	**101(1)/106(part)/101(2)** 04.45e 9 Elms-Clapham J 05.47ecs Clapham Jcn- Waterloo ECS Wloo & CJ to 10.55/ 12.44se Waterloo- Clapham Jcn/ 17.23le 9E to Clapham Jcn ECS Clapham Jcn and Waterloo to 03.00	**AS1** 08.10se Clapham Jcn- Wloo 10.03se Clapham Jcn- Wloo 12.38se Clapham Jcn- Wloo 13.44se Wloo- Clapham Jcn 15.03se Clapham Jcn- Twickenham 17.32se Wloo- Clapham Jcn	**113(1)** 04.40 Wloo-Woking 06.30 Woking- Salisbury	**ES18** 09.30se Salisbury-Grateley 10.30deptl. Grateley- Feltham Yard. 13.05le to Nine Elms.	**AS1 / AS8** 01.10le 9 Elms-Mitre Bdge 02.15sp Mitre Bridge- Ports Harb 05.15se Ports Harb- Fratton 11.00le to Ports Harbour 11.28 Ports H-Willsdn Jcn 13.50le to Nine Elms/ 23.30le to Wimbledon 00.15bst (W. A. O. to Clapham Jcn.) 06.10bst to Wimbledon Yd *xx.xxle to Nine Elms*	*Nine Elms - No Diagram*

	MONDAY 26/6	TUESDAY 27/6	WEDNESDAY 28/6	THURSDAY 29/6	FRIDAY 30/6	SATURDAY 1/7	SUNDAY 2/7
75075 (D)	DS55/DS57 13.53sv Sot W Dks-Wloo 18.48se Clapham Jcn.- Soton West Docks/ 23.31le Eleigh-M'dexer 00.30bst M'dexer-Winch'r (WAO to Shaw'ford) 03.40bst Shaw-Bevois Pk 04.10le to Eastleigh	DS9/136(2) 08.45le to Havant 09.50bst to Farlington Jcn. (WAO to Cosham) le to Fratton(turn). le to Havant (WAO Farlington-Cosham) 15.40le to Eastleigh/ 19.50 Eleigh-Bomo 22.05e Bo'mouth-Poole 22.40le to Weymouth	137 05.30f Weymouth-Poole 09.08f Poole-Wareham- Wool-Wareham- Furzebrook-Poole 17.42 Bo'mouth-Eastleigh 20.50f Eastleigh- Soton East Docks	**138/147(2)** 00.54 Eleigh-Weymouth 06.43 Weymth-Bo'mouth 08.46 Bournemouth- Waterloo/ 18.54 Wloo-Salisbury	463(1) 08.31v Salis-Basingstoke 10.45v Basingstoke- Portsmouth & S'sea C. S. 13.20 - 15.00 16.00v Port & Southsea- Fratton (repairs?)	DS12 xx.xxle Fratton-Eastleigh 21.35(M.P.Crane) Eastleigh-Fratton (W. A. O.) 08.05(M.P.Crane) Fratton-Eastleigh	Eastleigh - No Diagram
75076 (D)	**145(part)** c11.00 Eastleigh-Weymth (08.35 Ex Wloo) Replaced 34090	149(1) Carriage shunting 08.00-13.00	OUT OF USE?				
75077 (D)	343 Carriage shunting at Fratton Yd 06.30-23.00	343 As Monday	343 As Monday	343 As Monday	343/463(2) As Monday to c.18.45 then: 19.06v Ports & S'sea- Salisbury	ES22/DS20 06.30le Salisbury- Andover 07.25bst Andover- Salisbury 08.10bst Salisbury- Eleigh Ballast Sdgs Ballast Sidings./ 23.30le Eastleigh- Brocklst	DS20 (sat)cont (Ballast - W. A. O. to Totton and return) 04.30le to Eastleigh (or v.v. 73037)
76005 (F)			396(2) 14.32le Bo'mouth-Brocklst 16.03 Brock-Christ'ch 16.59le to Brockenhurst C&W Shunt 18.45 - 19.45 19.45le to Bournemouth (or 80011)	404 As Friday	**404** 07.52le Bo'mouth-Poole 08.30f Poole-Ringwood 12.10f Ringwood-Poole 15.35f Poole-Weymouth 22.13 Weymth-Bo'mouth (D/H D65xx)	**412** 06.45 Poole-Bo'mouth 07.51 Bo'mouth-Weymth 12.12 Weymth- Bo'mouth	280
76006 (F)	Weymouth - Repairs or spare	Weymouth - Repairs or spare	Weymouth - Repairs or spare	Weymouth - Repairs or spare	Weymouth - Repairs or spare	Weymouth-No Diagram	Weymouth-No Diagram
76007 (F)	166 10.15e Eleigh- Southampton 10.43 Soton C.-Bo'mouth 13.08 Bo'mouth-Weymth 16.46 Weymth-Bo'mouth 18.51 Bo'mouth-Woking 22.45le to Guildford	**165(1)** 02.28le Guildford-Woking 03.18v Woking-Fratton 10.15v Fratton- Basingstoke	282 Basingstoke - Spare	**283** 11.29v Basing-Soton West Docks 16.20 Soton C.-Bo'mouth E. C. S. Bo'mouth Area 17.30 - 23.00	280 05.15v Bomo-Weymouth 10.13 Weymth-Bo'mouth 15.00le to Brockenhurst 16.15e Brockhst-Eastleigh 19.04f Northam-Eastleigh 20.40v Eastleigh- Clapham Jcn.	**ES16** 04.40 Wloo-Woking 06.30 Woking-Salisbury (C. S. 08.40 - 10.10)	Salisbury - No Diagram

Loco							
76009 (F)	**412** 09.20 Bo'mouth-Weymth (05.30 Ex Wloo) 12.12 Weymth-Bo'mouth 13.52 Bomo-Southampton 18.30 Soton C.-Bo'mouth 20.15e Bomo-Branksome	**412** *As Monday*	**412(1)** 09.20 Bo'mouth-Weymth 12.12 Weymth-Bo'mouth 13.52 Bomo-Southampton 18.30 Soton C.-Bo'mouth 20.15e Bomo-Branksome	**412(2)** 17.40le Eleigh-Southampton 18.30 Soton C.-Bo'mouth 20.15e Bomo-Branksome 20.30le to Bournemouth	**400 (all or part 2)** E. C. S. 06.00 - 13.45 inc 08.15f Central Goods - Branksome.	*Bournemouth -* *No Diagram*	
76011 (F)	**282/165(2)** Basingstoke - Spare / 16.51 Basing-Salisbury 19.20v Salisbury-Northam 21.22f Sot W. Dks-Eleigh 23.10v Northam-Ports & S'sea	**166** 10.15e Eleigh-Soton Cent 10.43 Soton C.-Bo'mouth 13.08 Bo'mouth-Weymth 16.46 Weymth-Bo'mouth 18.51 Bo'mouth-Woking 22.45le to Guildford	**165** 02.28le Guildford-Woking 03.18v Woking-Fratton 10.15v Fratton-Basing 16.51 Basing-Salisbury 19.20v Salisbury-Northam 21.22f Sot W. Dks-Eleigh	**166** 10.15e Eleigh-Soton Cent 10.43 Soton C.-Bo'mouth 13.08 Bo'mouth-Weymth 16.46 Weymth-Bo'mouth 18.51 Bo'mouth-Woking 22.45le to Guildford	**165** 02.28le Guildford-Woking 03.18v Woking-Fratton 10.15v Fratton-Basing 16.51 Basing-Salisbury 19.20v Salisbury-Northam 21.22f Sot W. Dks-Eleigh	**166** Eastleigh - Spare	**DS4** *05.00le Eastleigh-Fareham* *06.00bst (WAO Fareham-* *Cosham)* *08.20bst. Cosham-Fareham* *09.00le to Eastleigh*
76026 (F)	**113** 04.40 Wloo-Woking 06.30 Woking-Salisbury 18.38 Salisbury-Wloo 21.15e Waterloo- Clapham Jcn.	**281** 07.18 Wloo-Salisbury C. S. 13.30 - 14.15 15. 55 Salis-Basingstoke	**283** 11.29v Basingstoke- Southampton West Dks 16.20 Soton C.-Bo'mouth E. C. S. Bo'mouth Area 17.30 - 23.00	**280** 05.15v Bomo-Weymouth 10.13 Weymth-Bo'mouth 15.00le to Brockenhurst 16.15e Brockhst-Eastleigh 19.04f Northam- Eastleigh- Clapham Jcn	**281(1)/FS16** 07.18 Wloo-Basingstoke/ *(Replaced by 76031)* *le to Eastleigh(repairs?)* c12.00le to Redbridge 12.40materials Redbridge Engrs Yd- Bournemouth Goods Yd	*Bournemouth -* *No Diagram*	
76031 (C)	*Eastleigh - No Diagram*	**DS6/145(mid)** 03.30le Eastleigh-Basing 06.05sf Basing-Wareham 10.45le to Weymouth/ 17.41 Weymth-Bo'mouth	**280** 05.15v Bomo-Weymouth 10.13 Weymth-Bo'mouth 15.00le to Brockenhurst 16.15e Brockhst-Eastleigh 19.04f Northam- Eastleigh xx.xxle to Nine Elms*	**281** 07.18 Wloo-Salisbury C. S. 13.30 - 14.15 15. 55 Salis-Basingstoke *Weds-20.40v cancelled?* *Observed at Basingstoke* *light engine in up* *direction*	**281(2)** 08.52 Basing-Salisbury C. S. 13.30 - 14.15 15. 55 Salis-Basingstoke	**282** Basingstoke - Spare	*Basingstoke -* *No Diagram*
76064 (D)	*Nine Elms - No Diagram*	**113** 04.40 Wloo-Woking 06.30 Woking-Salisbury 18.38 Salisbury-Wloo 21.15e Waterloo- Clapham Jcn.	**AS1** 10.03se Clapham Jcn- Wloo 12.38se Clapham Jcn- Wloo 14.02se Clapham Jcn- Strawberry Hill 15.06le to Nine Elms	**AS19** 08.15le N. Elms-Feltham 09.45(Weedkiller) Feltham-Windsor - Staines-Surbiton- Woking-Wimbledon- Chessington- Wimbledon West Yard 14.35le to Nine Elms	**AS3** 06.55e Clapham Jcn- Wloo 08.54 Waterloo- Soton East Docks (B1 - "Iberia") 11.20le to Nine Elms	*OUT OF USE*	

	MONDAY 26/6	TUESDAY 27/6	WEDNESDAY 28/6	THURSDAY 29/6	FRIDAY 30/6	SATURDAY 1/7	SUNDAY 2/7
76066 (D)	xx.xxle Salisbury-Basingstoke (or Tuesday a. m.)	**163** 14.05v Basing-Surbiton 14.59le to Guildfd(17.35)	**161** 03.30le Guildford-Woking 04.32v Woking-Basing 06.50f Basing-Eastleigh 10.32e Bevoir Park-Basingstoke	**163** 14.05v Basing-Surbiton 14.59le to Guildfd(16.55)	**161/163** 03.30le Guildford-Woking 04.32v Woking-Basing 06.50f Basing-Eastleigh 10.32v Bevoir Pk-Basing/ 14.05v Basing-Surbiton 14.59le to Guildford	**165** 03.18v Woking-Fratton 07.50se Fratton-Ports.Harb 09.20le to Guildford 21.55le Guildfd-Woking 22.38bst Woking-Wloo (WAO)	**Sat (165)cont** 08.02bst Wloo-Woking 09.20le to Guildford SUN: *Guildford-* *No Diagram*
76067 (F)	161(2)/**163** 10.32v Bevois Park-Basingstoke/ 14.05v Basing-Surbiton 14.59le to Guildford	**161/165(2)** 04.32v Woking-Basing 06.50f Basing-Eastleigh 10.32v Bevois Park-Basingstoke/ 16.51 Basing-Salisbury 19.20v Salisbury-Northam 21.22f Sot W. Dks-Eleigh	**166** 10.15 Eastleigh-Southampton Central 10.43 Soton C.-Bo'mouth 13.08 Bo'mouth-Weymth 16.46 Weymth-Bo'mouth 18.51 Bo'mouth-Woking 22.45le to Guildford	**165** 02.28le Guildford-Woking 03.18v Woking-Fratton-Basing 10.15v Fratton-Basing 16.51 Basing-Salisbury 19.20v Salisbury-Northam 21.22f Sot W. Dks-Eleigh	**166** 10.15e Eleigh-Soton Cent 10.43 Soton C.-Bo'mouth 13.08 Bo'mouth-Weymth 16.46 Weymth-Bo'mouth 18.51 Bo'mouth-Woking 22.45le to Guildford	**167** 02.15 Clapham Jcn-Waterloo 03.40v Wloo-Guildford 05.10v Guildford-Ports & S'sea 16.30se Fratton-Clapham Jcn xx.xxle to Nine Elms 20.30le to Guildford	*Guildford - No Diagram*
77014 (C)	*Guildford - No Diagram*	*Guildford - No Diagram*	*Guildford - No Diagram*	**173(1)/171** 06.50bst Woking-Godalming (WAO) 15.50bst Godalming-Wok Up Yard 16.35le to Guild(17.45)/ 20.45le Guildford-Farnham 21.50bst Farnham-Surbiton	**171(Thurs)cont/CS5** (WAO to New Malden) 05.46bst N Malden-Wimbledon 06.10bst Wim'don-Woking 07.26e to Guildfd(08.40)/ 20.10le Guildford-Woking Up Y'd 20.50bst Woking-Basing	**CS5(Fri)cont** 23.15bst Basingstoke-Hook (WAO to Winchfield) 06.00bst Winchfield-Woking Up Yd 07.00le to Guildfd(08.40) SAT: *Guildford-* *No Diagram*	*Guildford - No Diagram*
80011 (F)	**396(2)** 14.32le Bo'mouth-Brockhst 16.03 Brockhst-Christ'ch 16.59le to Brockenhurst C&W Shunt 18.45 - 19.45 19.45le to Bournemouth	**400** 07.13e Bomo West-Cent. 08.15f Central Goods-Branksome ECS Branksome & Bournemouth West 09.15 - 13.20 13.23e Branksome-Bournemouth Central	**400** As Tuesday	**FS12** 07.30le Bo'mouth-Brockhst 08.37 Brockenhurst-West Moors (Hauling WD loco 8212) 16.00le to Bournemouth	**412** 09.20 Bo'mouth-Weymth 12.12 Weymth-Bo'mouth 13.52 Bomo-Soton Cent. C. S. 16.45 - 17.15 19.45 Eastleigh-Bo'mouth 22.05e Bo'mouth-Poole	**FS13(1)** 16.10le Bo'mouth-Poole 17.00(Bank) Poole-Branksome (15.55 Weymouth Quay -Waterloo) 17.30le Branks-Ham Jcn 18.34e Ham J-Bomo West 20.00le to Bournemouth	Bournemouth - *No Diagram*

	Monday	Tuesday	Wednesday	Thursday	Friday	Saturday	Sunday
80016 (D)	**290** As Tuesday	**290** Local freights & vans Eastleigh and Soton area 08.00 - 14.00 16.22 Eleigh-Soton Cent. 17.16 Soton-Bomo & ecs 20.45le to Eastleigh Local freights 23.25 - 02.00	**Tues(290)cont/290** 04.40f Eleigh-Winchester 05.30le to Eastleigh/ As Tuesday	**290(1)** As Tuesday to: 17.16 Soton C.-Bo'mouth	*Repairs, then* *xx.xxle Bomo-Eleigh*	*Eastleigh - No Diagram*	*Eastleigh - No Diagram*
80133 (D)	308 As Friday	308 As Friday	308 As Friday Also Weds only 07.00le Eastleigh-Brockhst 09.00e Brockhst-Eastleigh 15.06e Eastleigh-Brockhst 16.15e Brockhst-Eastleigh	308 As Friday	**308** 01.57 Eleigh-Port & S'sea 06.30 Fareham-Eastleigh 17.20 Eastleigh-Fratton 23.32 Port & S'sea-Eleigh Also freights & Vans in Portsmouth & Eleigh areas	308 alt 01.57 Eleigh-Port & S'sea 04.05v Ports & S'sea-Havant 04.55v Havant-Fratton xx.xxle to Fratton loco.	308 22.50e Fratton-Portsmouth & S'sea 23.25 Portsmouth and Southsea-Eastleigh
80139 (D)	**313** 06.20f Basing-Andover 09.00f Andover-Ludgershall 10.30f Ludgershall-Andover F. S. at Ludgers& Andover 15.05f Andover-Basing C. S. 19.30 - 01.05	**313** As Monday	**313** As Monday	**313** As Monday	**313** As Monday	*313/Spl?* *09.50le Basing-Eastleigh (towing D6536)/* *xx.xxlur Redbridge - Eastleigh?* *(poss. part of 314)*	*Eastleigh - No Diagram*
80146 (F)	**407** 06.48 Bo'mouth-Brockhst 07.56 Brockhst-Bo'mouth 08.35e Bomo-Branksome 09.17le to Weymouth 17.00v Weymth-Bo'mouth	**407** As Monday	**407** As Monday	**407** As Monday	**407** As Monday	*Bournemouth -* *No Diagram*	*Bournemouth -* *No Diagram*
80152 (D)	314(MO) P.A.D Pilot 08.00 - 16.00 18.57v Soton W Dks-Soton Cent 20.45v West Dks-Bevois Park C. S. 21.05 - 21.45 22.00v Bevois Pk.-Northam 22.10le to Eastleigh	314(Tu-Fri) 00.25v Eastleigh-Soton C. 01.34 Soton C.-Eastleigh 04.10f Eastleigh-Soton West Docks 06.00le to Eastleigh Then as Monday	314 As Tuesday	314 As Tuesday	314 As Tuesday	314 00.25v Eastleigh-Soton C. 01.34 Soton C.-Eastleigh Local freights & C. S. until; 13.15f Soton West Docks-Eastleigh Main Yard 14.25le to Basingstoke	Basingstoke - No Diagram

Rosters, 3 – 9 July

	MONDAY 3/7	TUESDAY 4/7	WEDNESDAY 5/7	THURSDAY 6/7	FRIDAY 7/7	SATURDAY 8/7	SUNDAY 9/7
34001 (A)	**135** 08.10 Wloo-Weymth Jcn / 16.23 Weymth Jcn-Wloo (16.00 Ex Quay) / Banked by 41320 from Poole to Branksome	**395(1)/146** 02.45 Waterloo-Bournemouth/ c.10.15le to Weymouth (with D65xx & 80146) / 14.45sf Weymth-Westbury / 17.00le to Weymouth	**396(1)/394(2)** 08.27 Weymth-Bo'mouth / 10.32f Bomo loco-Cent Gds / 10.57f Cent Gds-Bomo Loco/ 15.01 Bo'mouth-Weymth / 18.15 Weymouth-Wloo	*OUT OF USE* (failed on shed prior to working 02.45 from Waterloo)			
34004 (F)	**Dsl / 280(1)** 05.00le Bo'mouth-Poole / 06.45 Poole-Bo'mouth/ *07.15le Bomo-Christ'ch* / 08.08 Christ'ch-Brocklst *F. & CE/S 09.00-09.50* / 09.55le to Bournemouth	**394(1)** 05.00le Bo'mouth-Poole / 06.45 Poole-Bo'mouth/ *07.15le Bomo-Christ'ch* / 08.08 Christ'ch-Brockhst *F. & CE/S 09.00-09.50* / 09.55le to Bournemouth	**396(2)** 14.32le Bo'mouth-Brockenhurst / 16.03 Brockhst-Christ'ch / 16.59le to Brockenhurst C. S. 18.45 - 19.45 / 19.45le to Bournemouth	**394** As Tuesday, then: / 15.01 Bo'mouth-Weymth / 18.15 Weymouth-Wloo (Assisted by Cl.33/1 Weymth to Dorchester South)	**136/Dsl** 02.30 Waterloo-Portsmouth Harbour / 07.30 Ports & S'sea-Eastleigh/ 18.30 Soton Central-Bournemouth	**412** *07.51 Bournemouth-Weymouth*	*OUT OF USE*
34013 (E)	**136** 02.30 Waterloo-Portsmouth Harb / 07.30 Port & S'sea-Eleigh / 19.50 Eastleigh-Bo'mouth / 22.05e Bo'mouth-Poole / 22.40le to Weymouth	**137** 05.30f Weymouth-Poole / 09.08f Poole-Broadstone-Poole-Wareham-Furzebrook-Poole / 17.42 Bo'mouth-Eastleigh / 20.50f Eastleigh-Soton E Docks	**138/147(2)** 00.54 Eleigh-Weymouth / 06.43 Weymth-Bo'mouth / 08.46 Bournemouth-Wloo/ 18.54 Wloo-Salisbury	**148** 06.49 Salisbury-Wloo / 11.38v Waterloo-Basingstoke / 19.06 Basing-Soton Cent / 21.18e Soton Central-Brockenhurst / 22.00le Brockenhurst-Weymouth	**149** 16.38(bank) Wey Jcn-Bincombe (16.15 Ex Quay) / xx.xxle to Weymouth / 17.30 Weymouth-Wloo	*OUT OF USE*	
34018 (A)	Guildford - Repairs (HOT BOX AT WOKING SAT 1st JULY)	Guildford - Repairs (AUTHORISED LIGHT DUTIES ONLY)	**177** 21.35le Guildford-Woking / 22.36bst Woking-Wimbledon / 23.45bst Wimbledon-New Malden (WAO to Surbiton) / 06.00bst Surbiton-Woking / 06.50le to Guildfd(08.00)	**177(weds)cont/177** As Wednesday	**171** 20.35le Guildford-Shalford / 21.28bst Shalford-Woking / 22.40bst Woking-Farnborough (work as ordered) / 05.30bst Farnborough-Woking / 06.00bst Woking-Shalford	**171(fri)cont** 06.40le to Guildfd(08.20) / SAT: Guildford - No Diagram	Spl/**CS3** Shunting at Guildford? 07.00-08.00/ 10.54(stores) Guildford-Woking / 11.35le to Salisbury

Engine							
34021 (A)	**396(1)/145(2)** 08.27 Weymth-Bo'mouth/ 11.33 Bo'mouth-Weymth (Replace 35030) 17.41 Weymth-Bo'mouth (D842 pilot Wey-Dorch S.) 21.00 Bo'mouth-Weymth	**147(1)** 07.49 Weymth-Bo'mouth/ 12.34 Bournemouth-Waterloo	Nine Elms - Boiler Inspection	**138** Eastleigh - Spare	**AS9/136(2)** 08.20 Waterloo-Southampton East Dks (B16 - "Queen Mary")/ 19.50 Eastleigh-Bo'mouth 22.05e Bo'mouth-Poole 22.40le to Weymouth	**137** 05.30f Weymouth-Poole 09.08f Poole-Wareham-Wool-Wareham-Furzebrook-Poole 17.42 Bo'mouth-Eastleigh 20.50f Eastleigh-Southampton East Dks	**DS9** 11.07 Soton East Docks-Waterloo (B27-"Ellinis") 13.17le to Nine Elms 14.30le Nine Elms-Salisbury
34024 (F)	**AS2** 09.25se Clapham Jcn-Willesden 10.00le to Nine Elms	**D93(1)** 05.30 Waterloo-Bournemouth 11.07 Bournemouth-Waterloo	**D91(1)/137(2)** 02.15v Waterloo-Bournemouth 06.22 Bournemouth-Waterloo 12.30 Waterloo-Bournemouth (Down "Belle")/ 17.42 Bo'mouth-Eastleigh 20.50f Eastleigh-Soton E Docks	**DS16** 14.10le Eastleigh-Salisbury (towing 34089)	**138** 00.54 Eleigh-Weymouth 06.43 Weymth-Bo'mouth 08.46 Bournemouth-Waterloo	*OUT OF USE*	
34025 (F)	**D91** 02.15v Waterloo-Bournemouth 06.22 Bournemouth-Waterloo 12.30 Waterloo-Bournemouth 16.37 Bournemouth-Waterloo (Down and Up "Belles") 22.35 Wloo-Eastleigh	**138(1)/149** 00.54 Eleigh-Weymouth (22.35 Ex Wloo cont.) 06.43 Weymth- Bo'mouth/ (possibly 34060) xx.xxle to Weymouth 17.30 Weymouth-Wloo	**DS4(1)** 07.22se Clapham Jcn-Waterloo 08.54 Waterloo-Southampton West Dks (B11 -"United States")	**Spl(82)** Eastleigh- Steam Test Then: 17.41 Soton E Dks-Wloo (B20 - "Carmania")	**254(1)/147(2)** 07.22se Clapham Jcn-Waterloo 08.54 Wloo-Soton E Dks (B22-"Castel Felice?") 12.25se Soton W Docks-Clapham Jcn/ 18.54 Waterloo-Salisbury	*OUT OF USE*	
34036 (A)	**DSpl2** c.12.00le Eastleigh-Southampton West Dks c13.00 Bullion to Wloo c.15.00le to Nine Elms (Turn) c.16.30le to Eastleigh	**165(part)/136(2)** xx.xxle Eastleigh-Fratton 10.15o Fratton-Eastleigh/ 19.50 Eastleigh-Bo'mouth 22.05e Bo'mouth-Poole 22.40le to Weymouth	**137(1)/D91(mid)** 05.30f Weymouth-Poole 09.08f Poole-Wareham-Wool-Wareham-Furzebrook-Poole/ 16.37 Bournemouth-Waterloo (Up "Belle")	**136(1)16(1)** 02.30 Waterloo-Ports Harbour 07.30 Ports & Southsea-Eastleigh/ 10.15e Eastleigh-Soton Central 10.43 Soton C.-Bo'mouth 13.08 Bo'mouth-Weymth	*OUT OF USE*		

	MONDAY 3/7	TUESDAY 4/7	WEDNESDAY 5/7	THURSDAY 6/7	FRIDAY 7/7	SATURDAY 8/7	SUNDAY 9/7
34037 (D)	**395** 02.45 Waterloo-Bournemouth 07.08 Bo'mouth-Weymth	**396** / D90(2) 08.27 Weymouth-Bo'mouth 16.03 Brockhst-Christ'ch 16.59le to Christchurch xx.xxle to Bournemouth/ 20.25v Bo'mouth- *xx.xxle to Bournemouth*	**394(1)/DS4(2)** 05.00le Bo'mouth-Poole 06.45 Poole-Bo'mouth 07.15le to Christchurch 08.08 Christchurch-Brockenhurst xx.xxle to Eastleigh/ 13.31 Soton East Dks-Waterloo (B14 - "Castel Felice?")	**AS3** 11.20 Waterloo-Southampton West Dks (B18 - "Fairsky") c14.00se Soton W Dks-Weymouth	**AS2** 16.38 Weymth Jcn-Wloo (16.15 Ex Quay) 20.45e Wloo-Clapham Jcn (on rear) C. S. 21.00 - xx.xx *xx.xxle to Nine Elms*	**136(1)/165(2)/AS33** 02.30 Waterloo-Portsmouth Harbour 06.00e Ports Harbour-Fratton/ 11.26sp Ports Harbour-Willesden Jcn. (to Colne)/ 18.20 Wloo-Soton E Dks (B25-"Rotterdam")	**AS33(Sat)cont** 21.35le to Salisbury *OUT OF USE*
34052 (E)	**467/462** 10.00le Salisbury-Warminster (FS) 12.00le to Salisbury loco 14.00le to Soton E. Docks 16.50sf East Dks-Westbury 19.20le to Salisbury/ 21.00f Salis-Basingstoke 00.35f Basing-Salisbury	**463** 08.31v Salis-Basingstoke 10.45v Basingstoke-Port & S'sea C. S. 13.20 - 15.00 16.00v Port & S-Fratton 19.06v Port & S-Salisbury	**463** As Tuesday	**463** As Tuesday	**148** 06.49 Salisbury-Wloo 11.38v Wloo-Basingstoke 19.06 Basing-Soton Cent 21.18e Soton C.-Brockhst 22.00le Brockhst-Weymth	**146** 22.40e&bv Weymouth-Dorch Sth 23.30bst Dorch South-Wareham (WAO to Hamworthy Jcn.) 08.35le to Bo'mouth(turn) 10.45bst Ham Jcn-Dorchester Sth 12.05e&bv to Weymouth/	**GS17** 14.20sf Weymth-Westbury (to Bescot) 16.40le to Weymouth
34060 (D)	**148** 06.49 Salisbury-Wloo 11.38v Wloo-Basingstoke 19.06 Basing-Soton Cent 21.18e Soton C.-Brockhst 22.00le Brockhst-Weymth (or Bournemouth?)	**138(2)** *06.43 Weymth- Bo'mouth* *(possibly 34025)* 08.46 Bomo-Wloo	**136(1)/166** 02.30 Waterloo-Portsmouth Harbour 07.30 Ports & S'sea-Eastleigh 10.43 Soton C.-Bo'mouth 13.08 Bo'mouth-Weymth 16.46 Weymth-Bo'mouth 18.51 Bo'mouth-Woking	**161/163** 03.30le Guildford-Woking 04.32v Woking-Basing 06.50f Basing-Eastleigh 10.32v Eastleigh-Basing/ 14.05v Basing-Surbiton 14.59le to Guildford	**161/163** As Thursday (arr Guild 18.50) then: C. S. 23.30 - 01.15	**161/283** 03.30le Guildford-Woking 04.32v Woking-Basing/ 12.55le Basing-Salisbury	*OUT OF USE*
34087 (D)	**254** / Spl? 11.27 Soton West Docks-Waterloo (B4 - "S. A. Oranje") *xx.xxes Waterloo-Southampton Docks*	**D92(2)/135** xx.xxle Eastleigh-Soton Central 01.20 Soton Cent-Wloo (Replace failed D1926)/ 08.10 Wloo-Weymth Jcn 16.23 Weymth Jcn-Wloo (16.00 Ex Quay)	**135(1)** 08.10 Wloo-Weymth Jcn	**396(1)/147(2)** 08.27 Weymth-Bo'mouth/ 12.34 Bournemouth-Wloo 18.54 Wloo-Salisbury	**462** *21.00f Salis-Basingstoke* *00.35f Basing-Salisbury*	*OUT OF USE?*	

				DS10	**AS8**	**DS17**	
34089 (E)	**Spl** xx.xx(am)le Weymouth-Eastleigh	Eastleigh - Repairs	Eastleigh - Repairs	**DS10** 10.59 Southampton Dks-Waterloo (B19 – "Caribia")	**AS8** 08.20 Waterloo-Southampton East Dks (B21 – "Caribia")	**DS17** 14.10le Eastleigh-Salisbury (with 34024)	OUT OF USE
34093 (D)	**137** 05.30f Weymouth-Poole 09.08f Poole-Wareham-Wool-Wareham-Furzebrook-Poole 17.42 Bo'mouth-Eastleigh 20.50f Eastleigh-Soton E Docks	**DS5/Spl** 10.07 Soton E. Dks-Wloo (B8 - "Rotterdam") 14.55se Stewarts Lane-Eastleigh/ xx.xxle to Salisbury 20.42sf Salis-Northam Yard	**DS5/412(2)** 08.15le Eastleigh-Redbridge 09.20sf R'bridge-Chichester 12.15le to Eastleigh/ 18.30 Soton C.-Bo'mouth 20.15e Bomo-Branksome 20.30le to Bournemouth	**280** 05.15v Bo'mouth-Weymth 10.13 Weymth-Bo'mouth 15.00le to Brockenhurst 16.15e Brockhst-Eastleigh 19.04f Northam-Eastleigh 20.40v Eastleigh-Clapham Jcn.	**254(2)** 17.23 Waterloo-Bournemouth 20.15e Bomo-Branksome 20.30le to Bournemouth	FS24? 16.10le Bournemouth-Weymouth	*May have been used for banking at Weymouth*
34095 (D)	**165** 02.28le Guildford-Woking 03.18v Woking-Fratton 10.15v Fratton-Basing 16.51 Basing-Salisbury 19.20v Salisbury-Northam 21.22f Soton West Dks-Eastleigh	**165(mon)cont/D9001** 23.10v Northam-Fratton 02.10le to Eastleigh/ 05.49 Eastleigh-Bo'mouth 09.40 Poole-Reading 16.03 Reading-Poole (see 76026)	Bournemouth - Repairs	Bournemouth - Repairs	**394(2)** 15.01 Bournemouth-Weymouth 18.15 Weymouth-Wloo	**395** 02.45 Wloo-Bournemouth 07.08 Bo'mouth-Weymth 10.13 Weymouth-Bomo 21.00 Bo'mouth-Weymth (18.30 Ex Wloo)	**396/139** Weymouth - Spare / Weymouth-Westbury 10.20sf Weymouth- (to Crewe) c.12.40le to Weymouth
34102 (D)	138 00.54 Eleigh-Weymouth (22.35 Ex Wloo) 06.43 Weymth-Bo'mouth 08.46 Bournemouth-Wloo 13.44se Waterloo-Clapham Jcn	Nine Elms - Repairs (BIG END) Then 147(2) 18.54 Wloo-Salisbury	148(1) 06.49 Salisbury-Wloo 11.38v Wloo-Basingstoke xx.xxle to Eastleigh	OUT OF USE	OUT OF USE		
35003 (A)	Weymouth - Repairs	Weymouth - Repairs	**146** 14.45sf Weymth-Westbury 17.30le to Weymouth	**135(2)** 16.23 Weymth Jcn-Wloo (16.00 Ex Quay)	**145** 08.35 Wloo-Weymouth 17.41 Weymth-Bo'mouth 21.00 Bo'mouth-Weymth (18.30 Ex Wloo)	OUT OF USE	
35007 (A)	**146/149(2)** 06.20se Weymouth-Christchurch 08.15le to Weymouth/ 17.30 Weymouth-Wloo	Nine Elms - Exams	**145** 08.35 Wloo-Weymouth 17.41 Weymth-Bo'mouth 21.00 Bo'mouth-Weymth (18.30 Ex Wloo)	*147(1)/149* *07.49 Weymth-Bo'mouth* *xx.xxle to Weymouth/* *17.30 Weymouth-Wloo* (BLEW L. H. VALVE COVER AND HOT BIG BROOKWOOD)	OUT OF USE		

	MONDAY 3/7	TUESDAY 4/7	WEDNESDAY 5/7	THURSDAY 6/7	FRIDAY 7/7	SATURDAY 8/7	SUNDAY 9/7
35008 (A)	Nine Elms - Repairs (BIG END)	Nine Elms - Repairs	**113** 04.40 Wloo-Woking 06.30 Woking-Salisbury 18.38 Salisbury-Wloo 21.15e Waterloo-Clapham Jcn.	**145** 08.35 Wloo-Weymouth 17.41 Weymth-Bo'mouth 21.00 Bo'mouth-Weymth (18.30 Ex Wloo)	**147(1)** 07.49 Weymth-Bo'mouth 12.34 Bournemouth-Waterloo	*OUT OF USE*	
35023 (A)	**147** 06.20se(bank) Weymth-Bincombe 06.50le to Weymouth 07.49 Weymth-Bo'mouth 12.34 Bournemouth-Waterloo 18.54 Wloo-Salisbury	**148** 06.49 Salisbury-Wloo 11.38v Wloo-Basingstoke 19.06 Basing-Soton Cent 21.18e Soton C.-Brockhst 22.00le Brockhst-Weymth	**149** F. S. 08.00-13.00 17.30 Weymouth-Wloo	Nine Elms -Exams	**135** 08.10 Wloo-Weymth Jcn 16.23 Weymth Jcn-Wloo (16.00 Ex Quay) Banked by 41320 from Poole to Branksome 20.45e Waterloo-Clapham Jcn	**AS1** 08.30 Wloo-Weymouth 16.18 Weymth Jcn-Wloo (15.55 Ex Quay)	*Nine Elms - Spare*
35028 (A)	Nine Elms - No Diagram	**145** 08.35 Wloo-Weymouth 17.41 Weymth-Bo'mouth 21.00 Bo'mouth-Weymth (18.30 Ex Wloo)	**147(1)** 07.49 Weymth-Bo'mouth 12.34 Bournemouth-Waterloo 15.42se Waterloo-Clapham Jcn	*OUT OF USE*			
35030 (A)	**145(1)/396(2)** 08.35 Wloo-Bo'mouth/ 14.32le Bo'mouth-Brockenhurst 16.03 Brockhst-Christ'ch 16.59le to Brockenhurst C. S. 18.45 - 19.45 19.45le to Bournemouth	**394(2)** 15.01 Bo'mouth-Weymth 18.15 Weymouth-Wloo	**395/135(2)** 02.45 Waterloo-Bournemouth 07.08 Bo'mouth-Weymth/ 16.23 Weymth Jcn-Wloo (16.00 Ex Quay)	**135(1)** 08.10 Waterloo-Weymouth Junction	Weymouth - Repairs (BROKEN BUSH)	**147** Weymouth - Spare	**147** 14.07 Weymouth-Wloo (Piloted by D65 (387) Weymouth-Dorchester South 18.18le to Nine Elms
73018 (C)	161/282 06.50f Basing-Eastleigh 10.32v Bevoir Pk-Basing/ Basingstoke - Spare	DS5/DS7 03.30le Eastleigh-Basing 06.05sf Basing-Wareham 10.45le to Bo'mouth(Turn)/ 12.30le to Soton 14.00sf Sot E. Dks-Feltham 17.00le to Basingstoke *East Docks*	282/148(1) Basingstoke - Spare 19.06 Basing-Soton Cent 21.18e Soton C.-Brockhst 22.00le Brockhst-Weymth	**146** 07.10e Wey-Dorch. South 07.40 Dorch. South-Wey 08.15 Wey-Dorch. South 09.20le to Weymouth 14.45sf Weymth-Westbury 17.30le to Weymouth	**396(1)** 08.27 Weymth-Bo'mouth 10.32f Bomo loco-Central Goods 10.57f Central Gds-Bomo loco	*Bournemouth -* *No Diagram*	**397** 08.50le Bomo-Bomo West 09.35e Bomo West-Branksome 09.45e Branks-Bo'mouth 10.02 Bo'mouth-Weymth

73020 (C)		**394** 10.13 Weymth- Bo'mouth C. S. 13.30 - 14.35 15.01 Bo'mouth-Weymth 18.15 Weymouth-Wloo	**136(1)/165(2)** 02.30 Wloo-Ports. Harb 07.30 Ports&S-Eastleigh/ c.11.15v Eastleigh- Basingstoke 16.51 Basing-Salisbury 19.20v Salisbury- Northam 21.22f Soton W Dks-Elgh	**40(2)** Weymouth- 17.00v Weymouth- Bournemouth	**394(1)/396(2)** 06.45 Poole-Bo'mouth 08.08 Christ'ch-Brockhst F&Engrs Shunt 09.00-09.50/ Bomo Loco 10.20-14.30 16.03 Brockhst-Christ'ch 17.00e Christchurch- Bo'mouth	**396 Fri(cont)** E.C.S. Bomo Area to 20.20 SAT - **FS26** 17.21e Bo'mouth-Weymth	*OUT OF USE*
73029 (A)	162 09.02sf Basing-Feltham 12.45sf Feltham-Eastleigh 17.43sf Soton East Docks- Basingstoke	283 11.29v Basingstoke- Southampton West Dks 16.20 Soton C.-Bo'mouth E. C. S. Bo'mouth Area 17.30 - 23.00	280 05.15v Bo'mouth- Weymth 10.13 Weymth- Bo'mouth 15.00le to Brockenhurst 16.15e Brockhst- Eastleigh 19.04f Northam-Eastleigh 20.40v Eastleigh- Clapham Jcn.	**395/166(2)** 02.45 Waterloo- Bournemouth 07.08 Bo'mouth- Weymth/ 16.46 Weymth- Bo'mouth 18.51 Bo'mouth-Woking 22.45le to Guildford C. S. 23.30 - 01.15	**165(1)/113(2)** 02.28le Guildford- Woking 03.18v Woking-Fratton 10.15v Fratton-Basing 16.51 Basing-Salisbury/ 18.38 Salisbury-Wloo	**167** 02.15v Clapham Jcn.- Waterloo 03.40v Wloo-Guildford 05.10v Guildford- Ports & S'sea 08.00le to Fratton	**CS2** 09.47se Fratton- Clapham Jcn 12.10le to Nine Elms 13.15le to Salisbury
73037 (A)	290 Local freights & vans Eleigh and Soton area 08.00 - 14.00 16.22 Eastleigh-Soton C. 17.16 Soton-Bomo & ecs 20.45le to Eastleigh Local freights 23.25 - 02.00	290 Mon(cont)/DS10 04.40f Eleigh-Winchester 05.30le to Eastleigh/ 17.38 Soton West Docks - Waterloo (B10 - "United States")	*OUT OF USE?*				
73043 (A)	282/163 *Basingstoke - Spare/* 14.05v Basing-Surbiton 14.59le to Guildfd(16.10)	161/163 As Wednesday	161/163 03.30le Guildford- Woking 04.32v Woking-Basing 06.50f Basing-Eastleigh 10.32v Bevoir Pk-Basing/ 14.05v Basing-Surbiton 14.59le to Guildfd(16.30)	165 03.18v Woking-Fratton 10.15v Fratton-Basing 16.51 Basing-Salisbury 19.20v Salisbury- Northam 21.22f Soton West Dks- Eastleigh 23.10v Northam-Fratton	165(cont) Fri-DS7/283(2) 02.10le to Eastleigh/ 06.10mts Redbridge-Wok 09.40le Woking-Eastleigh/ 16.20 Soton Central- Bo'mouth (C&WE Shunt at Brockhst 18.45 - 19.45)	280(1)/DS22 05.55f Cent. Gds-Poole 07.23e Branksome-Bomo 07.37 Bo'mouth-Eleigh/ 21.35MP crane Eleigh loco-Fratton Yard (Work as Ordered)	Sat(cont) 05.55le to Fratton loco 08.45 Loco-Yard 09.15MP crane Fratton Yard -Eastleigh loco 10.40 le to Salisbury

	MONDAY 3/7	TUESDAY 4/7	WEDNESDAY 5/7	THURSDAY 6/7	FRIDAY 7/7	SATURDAY 8/7	SUNDAY 9/7
73065 (A)	**AS1** 08.15le Nine Elms-Wimbledon 09.45(Weedkiller) Wimbledon-Windsor-Staines-Surbiton-Woking-Wimbledon-Chessington-Wim'don W. Yd 15.35le to Nine Elms	**281** 07.18 Wloo-Salisbury 15.55 Salis-Basingstoke	*D92(1)* 06.29 Basingstoke-Wloo xx.xxle to Nine Elms xx.xx to Basingstoke?	282 Basingstoke - Spare	282 Basingstoke - Spare	282 Basingstoke - Spare	*DS8?* 10.20sf Basing Up Yard-Basingstoke (*WAO to Bramley & return*) 11.15bst Basing-Up Yard 11.30le to Sailisbury
73092 (C)	**DS8** 16.30le Guildford-Southampton East Dks 20.33sp Soton East Docks-Waterloo (B5 - "Queen Mary") 23.42se Wloo-Clapham Jcn xx.xxle to Guildfd(00.40)	**DS8** 07.25le Guildfd-*Eastleigh* 14.25 Soton. West Docks-Waterloo (B12 - "Fairsky?") (*Poss. c. 2hrs shunting in Woking up yard on the way*)	*Nine Elms - No Diagram*	**Spl(22)** 08.54 Waterloo-Southampton East Dks (B17 - "Fairsky") 13.27 Soton East Dks - Waterloo ("Flavia")	**395/146** 02.45 Waterloo-Bournemouth 07.08 Bo'mouth-Weymth/ 14.45v Weymth-Westbury 17.30le to Weymouth	**396** 12.12 Weymth-Bo'mouth 21.20 Bo'mouth-Eastleigh	**395(1)** 00.54 Eleigh-Weymouth 15.00sf Weymth-Westbury 18.00le to Weymouth
73093 (C)	**281** 07.18 Wloo-Salisbury 15.55 Salis-Basingstoke	162 09.02sf Basingstoke-Feltham 12.45sf Feltham-Eastleigh 17.20sf Soton East Docks-Basingstoke	**162** 09.02sf Basing-Feltham 12.45sf Feltham-Eastleigh 17.20sf Soton East Docks-Basingstoke	**162** 09.02sf Basing-Feltham 12.45sf Feltham-Eastleigh 17.30le (or a/o) to Basing	**162** As Thursday	163 Basingstoke - Spare	**CS72** 12.50le Basing-Salisbury (with 80139) (ran in morning)
73118 (C)	**CS3/175** 09.55le Guildford- Soton East Docks(via Woking). 14.00sf Soton East Dks-Feltham 17.00le to Guildfd(18.30) Then: As Tuesday(D/H 76067)	**Spl/175** dep Guild 09.45 (work unknown) arr Guild 14.45/ 175 - As Wednesday but: (WAO at Chessington South) (D/H76067-arr Guild.09.30)	**175** 21.05le Guildford-Shalford 21.58bst Shalford-Sunbury (WAO at Sunbury) 05.15bst to Woking Up Yard 07.50le to Guildfd(09.40) (D/H 76067)	**176** As 175 Wednesday (arr Guild 08.50)	**CS3(2)/175** 14.15le Guildford-Shalford (CCE Shunt 14.30-15.30) 15.30le to Guildford Then as Wednesday but single loco (arr Guild 09.00)	**CS12** 22.35ebv Guild Yd-Liphook 00.05bst Liphook-Haslemere (WAO Haslemere-Petersfield) 06.45bst Haslemere-Liphook 07.20ebv to Guildford Yard. (arr Guild 08.30)	**CSpl.** 12.30le Guildford-Salisbury (with 73155) Poss. ran c. half hr. early

	Monday	Tuesday	Wednesday	Thursday	Friday	Saturday	Sunday
73155 (C)	**171** 20.35le Guildford-Shalford 21.28bst Shalford-Farnborough) (WAO at Farnborough) 05.30bst Farm-Shalford 06.40le to Guildford (arr 10.00)	**171** As Monday until: 06.40?le to Woking Up Yard	**CS1(1)/171** 07.18bst Woking-Shalford xx.xxle to Walton-on-Thames xx.xx(condemned stock) Walton-Clapham Jcn. xx.xxle to Guildford (arr 14.50)/ As Monday (Arr Guildford 10.05)	**171** As Monday (arr Guild 10.30)	**176** 22.00le Guildford-Woking up Yard 22.38bst Woking Up Yd-Wimbledon 00.25bst Wimbledon-Motspur Park (WAO to Epsom) 05.10bst Epsom-Woking 06.45le to Guildfd(08.20)	**CS11** 21.10le Guildford-Woking Up Yd 23.23bst Wok Up Yd-North Camp (WAO at North Camp 00.30-07.00) 07.20bst North Camp-Ascot	**CS11 Sat(cont)** 08.05bst Ascot-Farnham 09.20le to Guildford SUN: **Spl** 12.30le Guildford-Salisbury (with 73118)
75074 (D)	**113** 04.40 Wloo-Woking 06.30 Woking-Salisbury 18.38 Salisbury-Wloo 21.15le Waterloo-Clapham Jcn.	**113** As Monday	*Nine Elms - No Diagram*	**113(1)/281(2)** 04.40 Wloo-Woking 06.30 Woking-Salisbury/ 15.55 Salis-Basingstoke	**283(1)** 11.29v Basingstoke-Southampton West Dks xx.xxle to Eastleigh	Spl. c07.30le Eleigh-Salisbury	*OUT OF USE?*
75075 (D)	**280(2)** 19.04f Northam-Eastleigh 20.40v Eastleigh-Clapham Jcn 23.15le to Nine Elms (Turn) xx.xxle to Eastleigh	**290** Local freights & vans Eastleigh and Soton area 08.00 - 14.00 16.22 Eleigh-Soton Cent. 17.16 Soton-Bomo & ecs 20.45le to Eastleigh Local freights 23.25 - 02.00	**290(mon)cont/290** 04.40f Eleigh-Winchester 05.30le to Eastleigh/ As Tuesday	**290** As Tuesday	**166** 10.15e Eleigh-Soton Cent 10.43 Soton C.-Bo'mouth 13.08 Bo'mouth-Weymth 16.46 Weymth-Bo'mouth 18.51 Bo'mouth-Woking 22.10e Woking-Clap Jcn.	*Nine Elms - Spare* *(On standby for*	*Nine Elms - Spare* *Breakdown Crane?)*
75077 (D)	**343** xx.xxle Eleigh-Fratton *Carriage Shunting at* *Fratton Yd 06.30-23.00*	**343** As Monday	**343** As Monday	**343** As Monday	**343** As Monday xx.xxle to Eastleigh	Spl. c.05.00 Eastleigh-Salisbury	*OUT OF USE?*
76005 (F)	**404** 07.52le Bo'mouth-Poole 08.30f Poole-Ringwood 12.10f Ringwood-Poole 15.35f Poole-Weymouth 22.13 Weymth-Bo'mouth (D/H D65xx)	**404(1)** 07.52le Bo'mouth-Poole 08.30f Poole-Ringwood 12.10f Ringwood-Poole c15.00le to Bomo	**404** As Monday	**404** As Monday	**412** 09.20 Bournemouth-Weymouth (05.30 Ex Wloo) 12.12 Weymth-Bo'mouth 13.52 Bo'mouth-Soton Central 18.30 Soton C.-Bo'mouth 20.15e Bomo-Branksome	**412(1)/308(2)** As Thursday to Sothampton/ 17.20 Eastleigh-Fratton 19.10v Fratton-Ports Harb 20.23v Ports Harb-Fratton 23.32 Ports &S'sea-Eleigh	**308** 01.57 Eastleigh-Ports & S'sea 04.05v Ports & S.-Havant 04.55v Havant-Fratton 10.15le to Micheldever 12.56bst M'dever-Salisbury (D/H 80152)

	MONDAY 3/7	TUESDAY 4/7	WEDNESDAY 5/7	THURSDAY 6/7	FRIDAY 7/7	SATURDAY 8/7	SUNDAY 9/7
76006 (F)	149(1)/**411**(2) *Freight Shunting at Weymouth 08.00-c.10.30* 11.18 Weymth-Bo'mouth	**411/404**(2) 07.51 Bournemouth-Weymouth 11.18 Weymth-Bo'mouth/ c14.40le to Poole 15.35f Poole-Weymouth 22.13 Weymth-Bo'mouth (D/H D65xx)	**411** 07.51 Bo'mouth-Weymth 11.18 Weymth-Bo'mouth	**411/396**(2) As Tuesday/ 14.32le Bo'mouth-Brockenhurst 16.03 Brockhst-Christ'ch 16.59le to Brockenhurst C.S. 18.45 - 19.45 19.45le to Bournemouth	**411** As Wednesday	**FS23** 10.40bst Bomo Cent Gds-Eastleigh Eastleigh-Cosham 12.32bst Eastleigh 13.35le to Salisbury	*OUT OF USE?*
76007 (F)	**463** 08.31v Salisbury-Basing 10.45v Basing-Port & S'sea C.S. 13.20 - 15.00 16.00v Ports & S.-Fratton 19.06v Ports & S-Salisbury	*467/462* *10.00le Salis-Warminster* *F.S. 11.00 - 12.00* *12.00le Warminster-Salis/* *21.00f Salis-Basingstoke* *00.35f Basing-Salisbury*	*467/462* *As Tuesday*	*467/462* *As Tuesday*	*OUT OF USE?*		
76009 (F)	**411(1)**/149 *(mid)* 07.51 Bo'mouth-Weymth/ *Freight Shunting at Weymouth c.10.30-13.00* *(poss worked by 34037 or 204 drewry)*	*Weymth/* *OUT OF USE?*					
76011 (F)	**166** 10.15e Eleigh-Soton Cent 10.43 Soton C.-Bo'mouth 13.08 Bo'mouth-Weymth 16.46 Weymth-Bo'mouth 18.51 Bo'mouth-Woking 22.45le to Guildford	**165(1)/166** 03.18v Woking-Fratton *xx.xxle to Eleigh (repairs?)/* 10.43 Soton C.-Bo'mouth 13.08 Bo'mouth-Weymth 16.46 Weymth-Bo'mouth 18.51 Bo'mouth-Woking	**165** 02.28le Guildford-Woking 03.18v Woking-Fratton 10.15v Fratton-Basing 16.51 Basing-Salisbury *19.20v Salisbury-Northam* *21.22f Soton W Dks-Eleigh*	**113(2)** *xx.xxle or spl Eastleigh-Salisbury* *18.38 Salisbury-Waterloo*	**113(1)/467** 04.40 Wloo-Woking 06.30 Woking-Salisbury/ *10.00le Salis-Warminster* *F.S. 11.00 - 12.00* *12.00le Warminster-Salis/*	*OUT OF USE?*	
76026 (F)	**412** 09.20 Bo'mouth-Weymth (05.30 Ex Wloo) 12.12 Weymth-Bo'mouth 13.52 Bo'mouth-Soton C. 18.30 Soton C.-Bo'mouth 20.15e Bomo-Branksome	**412** As Monday *(May have rescued 34095-returned to shed together at 20.30)*	**412(1)/283(2)** 09.20 Bo'mouth-Weymth 12.12 Weymth-Bo'mouth 13.52 Bo'mouth- Soton Cent/ 16.20 Soton C.-Bo'mouth E.C.S. Bo'mouth Area 17.30 - 23.00	**404** 07.52le Bo'mouth-Poole 08.30f Poole-Ringwood 12.10f Ringwood-Poole 15.35f Poole-Weymouth 22.13 Weymth-Bo'mouth (D/H D65xx)	**404** As Thursday	*Bournemouth -* *No Diagram*	**DS12** 04.00le Bo'mouth-Brockhst 05.10bst Brockenhurst-Hamworthy Jcn (WAO to Dorchester South and return) 14.45bst Ham'thy Jcn-Brockenhurst 16.45le to Weymouth (finish c. 2hrs early)

Loco						
76031 (C)	**283** 11.29v Basingstoke-Southampton West Dks 16.20 Soton C.-Bo'mouth E. C. S. Bo'mouth Area 17.30 - 23.00	**280** 05.15v Bournemouth-Weymouth 10.13 Weymth-Bo'mouth 15.00le to Brockenhurst 16.15e Brockhst-Eastleigh 19.04f Northam-Eastleigh 20.40v Eastleigh-Clapham Jcn	**281** 07.18 Wloo-Salisbury 15.55 Salis-Basingstoke	*282/113(Mid)/Spl* Basingstoke - Spare/ 07.33 Basing-Salisbury/ 20.42f Salisbury-Northam Yard 22.10le to Salisbury	*ES13/ES14* 07.50le Salisbury-Andover (WAO) 16.30bst And'r-Salis 17.30bst Salis-Eleigh 19.30le to Salisbury 22.30se Salis-Clapham Jcn (via East Putney) 00.35le to Salisbury	*OUT OF USE?*
76066 (D)	**176** 21.05le Guildford-Shalford 21.58bst Shalford-Sunbury (WAO at Chessington Sth) 05.15le to Woking Up Yd. 07.50le to Guildfd(09.10) (D/H 73118)	*Spl/283(1)* 09.40le Guildford-Basingstoke/ 11.29v Basingstoke-Southampton West Dks xx.xxle to Eastleigh xx.xxle to Basingstoke	**283** 11.29v Basingstoke-Southampton West Dks 16.20 Soton Central-Bournemouth E. C. S. Bo'mouth Area 17.30 - 23.00	**280** 05.15v Bo'mouth-Weymth 10.13 Weymth-Bo'mouth 15.00le to Brockenhurst 16.15e Brockhst-Eastleigh 19.04f Northam-Eastleigh 20.40v Eastleigh-Clapham Jcn	**113** 04.40 Wloo-Woking 06.30 Woking-Salisbury C. S. 08.40 - 10.10	*OUT OF USE?*
76067 (F)	**CS12/176** As CS3 Fri to 09.10 then: 11.53bst Woking Up Yd-Twickenham 13.05le Twickenham-Shalford (Shunting 14.30-15.30) 15.30le to Guildford/ 176 - see 73118 above	**Spl/176** 10.35crane Guildford-Petersfield (re-rail empty wagons) c.16.55crane to Guildford loco(arr 17.40)/ 176 - See 73118 above	*Guildford - No Diagram*	**CS3(1)/Spl** 06.35le Guild-Woking 07.18bst Woking Up Yd-Shalford (Shunting 07.45-08.45) 08.55le to Guildford/ 12.10le Guildford-Aldershot (Shunting) c.14.35le to Guildford	**165(1)/136(2)** 02.28le Guildford-Woking 03.18v Woking-Fratton/ 18.10v Fratton-Basing 22.07v Basingstoke-Wloo	AS1?
77014 (C)	**CS1(2)** 06.30le to Shalford (cce/s) 09.50le to Guildford loco. 14.15le to Shalford (cce/s) 16.20le to Guildford loco.	**Spl** 14.15le to Shalford (cce/s) 16.05le to Guildford loco.	*Guildford - No Diagram*	**Spl./165(2)** xx.xxle to Basingstoke c.11.30le to Salisbury/ 19.20v Salisbury-Northam 21.22f Sot W. Dks-Eleigh 23.10v Northam-Ports & S'sea 02.10le to Eastleigh	**280(2)** 10.29 Eastleigh-Bo'mouth 12.28e Bournemouth-Branksome ECS Bo'mouth area to 18.45 Bank 18.15 Weymth-Waterloo from Poole to Parkstone	**FS14** 21.20v Bournemouth-Weymouth (15.00 Ex Wloo)

	MONDAY 3/7	TUESDAY 4/7	WEDNESDAY 5/7	THURSDAY 6/7	FRIDAY 7/7	SATURDAY 8/7	SUNDAY 9/7
80011 (F)	*Bournemouth -* *No Diagram*	400(1) *Or possibly all 400*	*Bournemouth -* *No Diagram*	*Bournemouth -* *No Diagram*	**407** 06.48 Bo'mouth-Brockhst 07.56 Brockhst-Bo'mouth 08.35e Bomo-Branksome 09.17le to Weymouth 17.00v Weymth- Bo'mouth	FS25? 16.10le Bo'mouth- Weymouth *(ran in morning)*	*OUT OF USE?*
80016 (D)	**308** 01.57 Eleigh-Port & S'sea 06.30 Fareham-Eastleigh 17.20 Eastleigh-Fratton 23.32 Port & S'sea-Eleigh Also freights & Vans in Portsmouth & Eastleigh areas	308 As Monday	308 As Monday Also Weds only 07.00le Eastleigh- Brockenhurst 09.00e Brockhst-Eastleigh 15.06e Eastleigh- Brockhst 16.15e Brockhst-Eastleigh	308 As Monday	**308(1)/29O(2)** As Mon to Eleigh at 14.00/ 16.22 Eleigh-Soton Cent. 17.16 Soton-Bomo & ecs 20.45le to Eastleigh Local freights 23.25 - 02.00	**290(Fri)cont/DS14?** 04.40F Eleigh-Winchester 05.30le to Eastleigh/ SAT - DS14? 13.15le Eleigh - Salisbury (with 80133?-see below)	*OUT OF USE?*
80133 (D)		DS6 09.13le Eleigh-Soton Cent 10.13 Central-West Docks (Statendam?) 10.45le to Swanwick 12.50 mats Swanwick- Eastleigh P.A.D. (via Fareham)	DS3 05.50bst Eastleigh Portsea Island Sdgs (WAO) 14.10bst Portsea Isle Sdgs- Havant xx.xxle to Eastleigh	DS?/DS13 06.30bst Eleigh ballast sidings-Salisbury 07.55bst Salisbury- Andover (WAO 08.45-16.20) 16.30bst Andover- Salisbury 17.20bst Salis-Eleigh/ 23.05le Eleigh-Fareham	DS13(Thurs)cont 00.05bst Fareham- St. Denys (WAO) 02.34bst St Denys-Soton C. 03.10bst Soton C.-St Denys (WAO to Fareham) 06.35le to Eastleigh FRI: Eastleigh No Diagram	DS15? 13.15le Eastleigh- Salisbury (with 80016?) conflicting reports - together or singly.	*OUT OF USE?*
80134 (F)	400 07.13e Bomo West-Central 08.15f Cent Goods.- Branksome Branks & Bomo West ecs 09.15 - 13.20 13.23e Branksome- Bournemouth Central	400 As Monday (but see 80011)	400 As Monday	400 As Monday	400/FS12 As Monday, then: *Bank relief Channel* *Islands Boat train - 17.27* *from Poole to Branksome*	FS27? *17.30le Bo'mouth-Weymth* *(left Bo'mouth 18.10)*	*OUT OF USE?*
80139 (D)	314(MO) P.A.D Pilot 08.00 - 16.00 18.57v Soton W Dks- Central 20.45v W. Dks-Bevoir Pk C. S. 21.05 - 21.45 22.00v Bevois Pk- Northam 22.10le to Eastleigh	314(Tu-Fri) 00.25v Eleigh-Soton Cent 01.34 Soton C.-Eastleigh 04.10f Eleigh-Sot W. Dks 06.00le to Eastleigh Then as Monday	314 As Tuesday	314 As Tuesday	314 As Tues (to 16.00?)	314 00.25v Eleigh-Soton Cent 01.34 Soton C.-Eastleigh Local freights and P. A. D. pilot until 11.30 14.50le to Basingstoke	DS10? 12.50le Basing-Salisbury (with 73093) (ran in morning)

80146 (F)	**407** 06.48 Bo'mouth-Brockhst 07.56 Brockhst-Bo'mouth 08.35e Bomo-Branksome 09.17le to Weymouth 17.00v Weymth-Bo'mouth	**407** As Monday	**407** As Monday	**407(1)/137(2)** As Monday to Branksome/ 09.08f Poole-Broadstone-Poole-Wareham-Furzebrook-Poole 17.42 Bo'mouth-Eastleigh 20.50f Eastleigh-Southampton East Dks	**290(1)/314(2)** 08.00v Eleigh-Bevoir Park 09.07f Eleigh-Soton E Dks 11.05f Eleigh-Redbridge 13.15f Soton W Dks-Eleigh/ 18.57v Sot W Dks-Cent 20.45v W. Dks-Bevois Pk 22.00v Bev Pk-Northam 22.10le to Eastleigh	**Spl.** 15.10le Eastleigh-Salisbury	OUT OF USE?
80152 (D)	**313** 06.20f Basing-Andover 09.00f Andover-Ludgershall 10.30f Ludgershall-Andover F. S. at Ludgers & Andover 15.05f Andover-Basing C. S. 19.30 - 01.05	313 As Monday	**313** As Monday	313 As Monday	**313** As Monday	**313** 09.50le Basingstoke-Southampton Central 10.57 Soton Central-East Docks (Prins der Nederlanden) 11.30le to Micheldever 12.56bst M'dever-Salisbury (D/H 76005)	OUT OF USE?
	The following light pacifics classified as under repair but never worked again.	34047 (at Feltham) *(TENDER WHEELS)* Last worked 11th May Towed? light engine to Nine Elms on 27th June Withdrawn w/e 25th June	34098 (at Salisbury) (BOILER TUBES) Last worked 19th May Withdrawn w/e 25th June	34104 (at Salisbury) (BOILER TUBES AND STEAM BRAKE) Last worked 21st May Withdrawn w/e 25th June	34040 (at Basingstoke) (BOILER TUBES) Last worked 2nd June Towed light engine to Eastleigh on Thurs 8th June. Withdrawn w/e 2nd July		

Locomotives to Trains

Down, June 5 – 11

Diag.		MON	TUES	WEDS	THUR	FRI	SAT	SUN
462	00.35F Basingstoke – Salisbury	M. X.	34100	34089	*73065*	*73065*	*73065*	
137	00.54 Eastleigh – Weymouth	*34093*	*34024*	*34021*	*34036*	*76066*	34004	D1922*
308	01.57PV Eastleigh – Ports. & Southsea	*80016*	*80016*	*80133*	*80139*	*80139*	*80139*	*80139*
136	02.30 Waterloo – Ports. Harbour	34021	**34095**	**34024**	**34090**	**34025**	**34037**	**34013**
395	02.45PV Waterloo – Bournemouth	34034	**35007**	34023	34037	35003	**73093**	
165	03.18V Woking – Fratton	**76031**	**76007**	**76066**	**75076**	**76007**	**75076**	
161	04.32V Woking – Basingstoke	M. X.	**76031**	**76031**	**76011**	**76011**	**76011**	
113	04.40 Waterloo – Woking	**34004**	35030	73037	**76026**	**76026**	34023	
280	05.15V Bournemouth – Weymouth	M. X.	*76005*	34060	35003	*75075*	34008*	
113	06.30 Woking – Salisbury	34004	35030	73037	76026	76026	34023	
161	06.50F Basingstoke – Eastleigh	*76064*	76031	76031	76011	76011		
395	07.08 Bournemouth – Weymouth	34034	35007	34023	34037	35003	**73093**	
281	07.18 Waterloo – Salisbury	35003	**73093**	**73065**	**73092**	**76009**	**80145**	
411	07.50 Bournemouth – Weymouth	*76026*	*76026*	*76009*	**34008**	**34008**	*75074*	
400	07.56 Brockenhurst – Bournemouth	*80134*	*80134*	*80146*	*80134*	*80134*		
134	07.58 Waterloo – Weymouth Quay						**34095**	
135	08.10 Waterloo – Weymouth Quay	35013	**35008**	**35008**	35008	35008	**35028**	
407	08.29 Eastleigh – Bournemouth	*76066*	34001	*76005*	*76005*	*75068*	**35007**	

Up, June 5 – 11

Diag.		MON	TUES	WEDS	THUR	FRI	SAT	SUN
314	01.34PV Southampton – Eastleigh	M. X.	*80139*	*80139*	*80016*	*80016*	*80133*	
137	05.30F Weymouth – Poole – Furzebrook	34087	34021	34036	76066	34004		
407	05.44 Bournemouth – Eastleigh	*76009*	34001	*76005*	*76005*	*75068*	**35007**	
308	06.30 Fareham – Eastleigh	*80016*	*80016*	*80133*	*80139*	*80139*		
138	06.43 Weymouth – Bournemouth	34090	34013	34021	**34025**	**76066**	**34004**	
394	06.45 Poole – Bournemouth	*34025*	34025	34037	*80011*	*80011*	75074	
400	06.48 Bournemouth – Brockenhurst	*80134*	*80134*	*80146*	*80134*	*80134*		
461	06.49 Salisbury – Waterloo	34089	34004	35030	34013	34013		
148	07.05 Basingstoke – Waterloo	*73037*	34037	34093	**73093**	34024		
136	07.30 Ports. & Southsea – Eastleigh	34021	*76007*	34024	34090	34025	75076	
461	07.35 Salisbury – Waterloo						**34013**	
280so	07.37 Bournemouth – Eastleigh	*80146*	*80146*	*75075*	**80146**	*80146*	**80146**	
147	07.49 Weymouth – Bournemouth	35028	34093	**34008**	35028	35013		
394	08.08 Christchurch – Brockenhurst	*34025*	34025	34037	*80011*	*80011*		
396	08.27 Weymouth – Bournemouth	35007	*73037*	35007	*75068*	*73093*		
463	08.31V Salisbury – Basingstoke	34108	34108	34108	34108	34108		
138	08.46 Bournemouth – Waterloo	**34090**	**34013**	**34021**	**34025**	**76066**	**34004**	

Down, June 5 – 11 continued

Diag.		MON	TUES	WEDS	THUR	FRI	SAT	SUN
145	08.35 Waterloo – Weymouth	**34013**	34008	**35028**	**35013**	**34100**	**D1922**	
254fo	09.20 W'loo-Southampton West Docks					34034		
412	09.20 Bournemouth – Weymouth	76005	75074	*75074*	75074	35007	*75068*	
AS2	09.24 Waterloo – Weymouth						**35023**	
AS4	10.24 Waterloo – Weymouth						**35030**	
166	10.43 Southampton – Bournemouth	76007	*76009*	75076	76031	75076	**76007**	
407	10.51 Bournemouth – Weymouth	*76066*	34001	*76005*	*76005*	*75068*		
463	10.45V Basingstoke – Fratton	34108	34108	34108	34108	34108		
283	11.29V Basing – Southampton	*75075*	34060	35003	*35007*	*73029*	**76009**	
148	11.05V Waterloo – Basingstoke	*73037*	**34037**	**34093**	**73093**	**34024**		
282	12.39 Waterloo – Basingstoke						73037	
166	13.08 Bournemouth – Weymouth	76007	76066	75076	**76031**	75076	76007	
394	15.01 Bournemouth – Weymouth	35007	73037	34037	35003	**73093**		
404	15.35F Poole – Weymouth	*76011*	*75075*	*75068*	*75075*	*75074*		
Spls.	Waterloo – Southampton Docks	*34024*	73020	**34090**	*34034*	*34021*		34024
	(Various departure times)					34034		
396	16.03 Brockenhurst – Christchurch	*34025*	*34025*	*76009*	*80011*	*80011*		
283	16.20 Southampton – Bournemouth	*75075*	34060	35003	**35007**	**73029**	**34025**	
165	16.51 Basingstoke – Salisbury	*76064*	**34095**	34024	75076	**76007**		
461	17.09 Waterloo – Basingstoke	**34089**	**34004**	**34013**	**34013**	**34013**		
290	17.16 Southampton – Bournemouth	**75077**	*75077*	*75077*	**75077**	*75077*		

Up, June 5 – 11 continued

Diag.		MON	TUES	WEDS	THUR	FRI	SAT	SUN
Spl.17	09.00 Weymouth – Waterloo						34008	
280	10.13 Weymouth – Bournemouth	*73065*	*76005*	34060	35003	*75075*	**73093**	
165	10.15V Fratton – Basingstoke	76031	34095	34024	75076	76007		
161	10.32V Bevoir Park. – Basingstoke	*76064*	76031	76031	76011	76011		
411	11.18 Weymouth – Bournemouth	*76026*	*76026*	*76009*	34008	34008	**75074**	
254mo	11.28 Southampton West Docks-W'loo	**34037**						
Spls.	Southampton Docks – Waterloo	**34095**	**73092**	**34095**		*34021*		34013
	(Various departure times)					34025		34060
FS19	12.05 Poole – Waterloo						**34093**	
412	12.12 Weymouth – Bournemouth	76005	75074	*75074*	**75074**	35007	75068	
147	12.34 Bournemouth – Waterloo	35028	34093	35007	**35028**	35013		
Dsl.	12.36 Salisbury – Waterloo						**34108**	
412	13.52 Bournemouth – Southampton	76005	75074	*75074*	75074	35007	**75068**	
163	14.05V Basingstoke – Surbiton	**76031**	**76031**	**73118**	**76011**	**76011**		
146	14.45V Weymouth – Westbury	M. X.	**34036**	*34025*	34037	*35003*		
281	15.55 Salisbury – Basingstoke	35003	**73093**	*73037*	73092	*76009*		
397	15.55 Weymouth Quay – Waterloo						**35028**	
135	16.00 Weymouth Quay – Waterloo	**35013**	**35008**	**35008**	**35008**	**35008**		
134	16.15 Weymouth Quay – Waterloo						**34024**	
166	16.46 Weymouth – Bournemouth	**76007**	**76066**	75076	**76007**	75076	76007	
407	17.00V Weymouth – Bournemouth	*80011*	**34001**	*76005*	*75068*	*75068*	**35008**	

Down, June 5 – 11 continued

Diag.		MON	TUES	WEDS	THUR	FRI	SAT	SUN
308	17.20 Eastleigh – Fratton	*80016*	*80016*	**80133**	**80139**	*80139*		
134fo	17.23 Waterloo – Bournemouth					**34093**		
138fo	18.22 Waterloo – Bournemouth					**34025**		
412	18.30 Southampton – Bournemouth	76005	**75074**	*75074*	75074	35007	*75068*	
147	18.54 Waterloo – Basingstoke	**34037**	**34093**	**35007**	34024	*76064*		
148	19.06PV Basingstoke – Southampton	**73037**	**34037**	**34093**	*73093*	**34024**		
461	19.11 Basingstoke – Salisbury	34089	34004	34013	34013	34013		
165	19.20V Salisbury – Northam Yard	*76064*	34095	34024	75076	*76007*		
136	19.50 Eastleigh – Bournemouth	34021	*76007*	**76066**	*34004*	**34102**	73029	
145	21.00 Bournemouth – Weymouth	34013	**34008**	35028	35013	34100	*73093*	
165	23.10V Northam Yd – Ports & Southsea	*76064*	34095	34024	75076	*76007*		
313	Andover Pilot	*80152*	*80152*	*80152*	*80152*	*80152*		

Down, June 12 – 18

Diag.		MON	TUES	WEDS	THUR	FRI	SAT	SUN
462	00.35F Basingstoke – Salisbury	M. X.	34052	34052	34052	34052	34108	
138	00.54 Eastleigh – Weymouth	*35007*	*73029*	*34024*	*34013*	*34021*	S. X.	
308	01.57PV Eastleigh – Ports. & Southsea	*80139*	*80139*	80139	80139	*80139*		
D91	02.15V Waterloo – Bournemouth				34023		*D1903*	
136	02.30 Waterloo – Ports. Harbour	**34090**	**35007**	**34025**	73043	**34060**	**34087**	
395	02.45PV Waterloo – Bournemouth	34023	35023	**34037**	35023	**34037**	35023	

Up, June 5 – 11 continued

Diag.		MON	TUES	WEDS	THUR	FRI	SAT	SUN
149	17.30 Weymouth – Waterloo	35023	**34034**	**34023**	**34093**	**34037**	D1922	
145	17.41 Weymouth – Bournemouth	34013	**34008**	35028	35013	34100		
137	17.42 Bournemouth – Eastleigh	34087	**34021**	34036	*76066*	**34004**	75074	
394	18.15 Weymouth – Waterloo	35007	**73037**	**34037**	35003	73093	**34100**	
113	18.38 Salisbury – Waterloo	**73093**	**34023**	**34100**	76026	76026	**34021**	
166	18.51 Bournemouth – Woking	**76007**	**76066**	**75076**	**76007**	**75076**	**76007**	
463	19.06V Ports. & Southsea – Salisbury	34108	34108	34108	34108	34108		
394	19.36 Bournemouth – Waterloo							**35008**
280	20.40V Eastleigh – Clapham Junction.	*73065*	*73065*	*76026*	*76009*	*75075*		
462	21.00F Salisbury – Basingstoke	34100	34089	*73065*	*73065*	*73065*		
404	22.13 Weymouth – Bournemouth	*75074*	*75075*	*Dsl only*	*75075*	*75074*		*73093*
308	23.32 Ports. & Southsea – Eastleigh	*80016*	*80016*	*80133*	*80139*	*80139*	*80139*	

Up, June 12 – 18

Diag.		MON	TUES	WEDS	THUR	FRI	SAT	SUN
314	01.34PV Southampton – Eastleigh	M. X.	*80152*	*80152*	*80152*	*80152*	*80152*	
137	05.30F Weymouth – Poole – Furzebrook	34004	34024	34013	34021	*76007*		
D91	06.22 Bournemouth – Waterloo				34023		D1903	
308	06.30 Fareham – Eastleigh	*80139*	*80139*	80139	**80139**	*80139*		
138	06.43 Weymouth – Bournemouth	*76031*	*73029*	34036	**34024**	**34013**		
394	06.45 Poole – Bournemouth	M. X.	*80011*	*34004*	*34004*	*34004*	*73093*	
407	06.48 Bournemouth – Brockenhurst	*80146*	80146	80146	*80011*	75076		

Down, June 12 – 18 continued

Diag.		MON	TUES	WEDS	THUR	FRI	SAT	SUN
165	03.18V Woking – Fratton	**76007**	**76011**	**35007**	**73020**	73043	**73155**	
161	04.32V Woking – Basingstoke	M. X.	**73020**	**76011**	**76011**	**76011**		
113	04.40 Waterloo – Woking	**76026**	**76066**	**76066**	73029	73029	**34024**	
280	05.15V Bournemouth – Weymouth	M. X.	*76009*	76064	*34087*	80145		
113	06.30 Woking – Salisbury	76026	76066	76066	73029	73029		
161	06.50F Basingstoke – Eastleigh	*76064*	73020	76011	76011	76011		
395	07.08 Bournemouth – Weymouth	34023	35023	34037	35023	34037	**35023**	
281	07.18 Waterloo – Salisbury	*73085*	35008	**34102**	**76064**	73037		
411	07.50 Bournemouth – Weymouth	34102	34102	76005	**76005**	**76005**	73093	
407	07.56 Brockenhurst – Bournemouth	*80146*	80146	**80146**	*80011*	*75076*	**D6506**	
135	08.10 Waterloo – Weymouth Quay	**35028**	35030	**35030**	D1923	**34087**	**D6515**	
397	08.30 Waterloo – Weymouth						**35007**	
145	08.35 Waterloo – Weymouth	**34021**	**35028**	**35013**	35030	**34036**	**D6540**	
254 fo	09.20 W'loo-Southampton West Docks					34025		
412	09.20 Bournemouth – Weymouth	*75074*	75074	*75074*	75076	73093	**D1926**	
166	10.43 Southampton – Bournemouth	76064	*35007*	73020	73043	*75074*	**76064**	
463	10.45V Basingstoke – Fratton	34108	34089	34089	34089	34089		
283	11.29V Basing – Southampton	*76009*	*76064*	75076	80145	76064		
148	11.38V Waterloo – Basingstoke	**34060***	**34013**	34021	Dsl or Tank	**34102**		
D91	12.30 Waterloo – Bournemouth				34023	34024	**D1903**	
166	13.08 Bournemouth – Weymouth	**76064**	*35007*	**73020**	**73043**	75074		
Spl 24	14.24 Waterloo – Weymouth						**34013**	

Up, June 12 – 18 continued

Diag.		MON	TUES	WEDS	THUR	FRI	SAT	SUN
148	06.49 Salisbury – Waterloo	**34060**	34013	34021	35028	34102		
136	07.30 Ports. & Southsea – Eastleigh	34090	35007	35007	73043	34060		
280so	07.37 Bournemouth – Eastleigh						**76064**	
147	07.49 Weymouth – Bournemouth	35013	34021	**35028**	35013	**34021**		
394	08.08 Christchurch – Brockenhurst	*35003*	*73093*	*34004*	*34004*	*34004*		
396	08.27 Weymouth – Bournemouth	*73029*	34023	35023	*34037*	35023	D6521	
463	08.31V Salisbury – Basingstoke	34108	34089	**34089**	34089	34089		
138	08.46 Bournemouth – Waterloo	*76031**	**73029**	**34036**	**34024**	**34013**	**34013**	
280	10.13 Weymouth – Bournemouth	35023	*76009*	76064	*34087*	**80145**	35023	
165	10.15V Fratton – Basingstoke	*76007*	76011	34025	73020	73043		
161	10.32V Bevoir Park. – Basingstoke	*75076*	73020	76011	76011	76011		
Spl.4	10.32 Southampton – Waterloo							34037
411	11.18 Weymouth – Bournemouth	34102	**34102**	**76005**	76005	76005	D1926	
254mo	11.28 Southampton West Docks-W'loo	**34018**						
Spls.	Southampton Docks – Waterloo		**34025**	34090		*34018*		34060
	(Various departure times)		34037			**34060**		
						34090		
412	12.12 Weymouth – Bournemouth	*75074*	*75074*	*75074*	**75076**	73093	**73093**	
147	12.34 Bournemouth – Waterloo	**35013**	34021	**35028**	35013	**34021**	D1926	
412	13.52 Bournemouth – Southampton	75074	75074	*75074*	75076	73093		
163	14.05V Basingstoke – Surbiton	**76011**	**76011**	**76011**	**76011**	**76011**		

Down, June 12 – 18 continued

Diag.		MON	TUES	WEDS	THUR	FRI	SAT	SUN
394	15.01 Bournemouth – Weymouth	35023	*34023*	35023	34037	35023		
404	15.35F Poole – Weymouth	*75068*	*75068*	*75068*	**75068**	*75068*		
Spls	Waterloo – Southampton Docks		**34025**	**34018**	**35028**	**34090**	*34060*	
	(Various departure times)		**73043**	**34090**	**73037**			
396	16.03 Brockenhurst – Christchurch	*76005*	*73093*	34004	*34004*	34004		
283	16.20 Southampton – Bournemouth	*76009*	*76064*	**75076**	80145	76064		
165	16.51 Basingstoke – Salisbury	*76007*	**73020**	**34025**	**73020**	**73043**		
Spl.1	17.00 Waterloo – Salisbury					**34018**		
290	17.16 Southampton – Bournemouth	**75077**	**75077**	**75077**	**75077**	**75077**		
308	17.20 Eastleigh – Fratton	*80139*	*80139*	80139	80139	*80139*		
254 fo	17.23 Waterloo – Bournemouth					**34013**		
138 fo	18.22 Waterloo – Bournemouth					**34021**		
412	18.30 Southampton – Bournemouth	**75074**	**75074**	*34087*	75076	F. X.		
147	18.54 Waterloo – Salisbury	**34013**	34021	**35028**	**34102**	**35013**		
148	19.06PV Basingstoke – Southampton	**34060**	34013	34021	**76007**	**34102**		
165	19.20V Salisbury – Northam Yard	*76007*	73020	*34025*	*73020*	73043		
136	19.50 Eastleigh – Bournemouth	*34024*	**35003**	*35007*	**35028**	**73093**		
145	21.00 Bournemouth – Weymouth	34021	35028	35013	*35023*	34036		
165	23.10V Northam Yd – Ports & Southsea	*76007*	*73020*	*34025*	*73020*	73043		
313	Andover Pilot	*80133*	*80133*	80133	80133	**80133**		

Up, June 12 – 18 continued

Diag.		MON	TUES	WEDS	THUR	FRI	SAT	SUN
146	14.45V Weymouth – Westbury	M. X.	**34036**	*34024*	34013	*34093*		
281	15.55 Salisbury – Basingstoke	*73085*	35008	**80145**	76064	*Dsl?*		
397	15.55 Weymouth Quay – Waterloo						**35007**	
135	16.00 Weymouth Quay – Waterloo	**35028**	**35030**	**35030**	D1923	**34087**		
D91	16.37 Bournemouth – Waterloo				**34023**	34024	D1903	
166	16.46 Weymouth – Bournemouth	76064	*35007*	73020	73043	**75074**		
407	17.00V Weymouth – Bournemouth	*80146*	**80146**	**80146**	*80011*	*75076*	D1921	
149	17.30 Weymouth – Waterloo	**35007**	**34060**	**35003**	**35007**	**35030**	D6512	
145	17.41 Weymouth – Bournemouth	**34021**	**35028**	*35013*	**35023**	34036		
137	17.42 Bournemouth – Eastleigh	*73029*	**34024**	**34013**	34021	**76007**	E6037	
394	18.15 Weymouth – Waterloo	**35023**	**34023**	**35023**	**34037**	**35023**	D6543	
113	18.38 Salisbury – Waterloo	**76026**	76066	**34102**	**73029**	73029		
166	18.51 Bournemouth – Woking	**76064***	**35007**	**73020**	**73043**	75074		
463	19.06V Ports. & Southsea – Salisbury	34108	**34089**	34089	34089	34089		
394	19.36 Bournemouth – Waterloo							*34013*
280	20.40V Eastleigh – Clapham Junction	*75075*	*34102*	76064	*34087*	80145		
462	21.00F Salisbury – Basingstoke	34052	34052	34052	34052	34108		
404	22.13 Weymouth – Bournemouth	*75068*	*75068*	*75068*	*75068*	*75068*	*Dsl only*	*34093*
308	23.32 Ports. & Southsea – Eastleigh	*80139*	*80139*	*80139*	*80139*	*80139*		

Weymouth – Westbury Tomatoes(Sun): 34102 (piloted by D6544 to Dorchester West)

Down, June 19 – 25

Diag.		MON	TUES	WEDS	THUR	FRI	SAT	SUN
462	00.35F Basingstoke – Salisbury	M. X.	34108	34108	34108	34108	34108	
138	00.54 Eastleigh – Weymouth	*73037*	34095	34013	*75076*	34036	S. X.	*34087*
308	01.57PV Eastleigh – Ports. & Southsea	*76007*	*76007*	*80139*	*80139*	*76031*	*80016*	*80016*
136	02.30 Waterloo – Ports. Harbour	*73043*	34023	34036	**34095**	**34093**	**34023**	
395	02.45PV Waterloo – Bournemouth	**34013**	**34093**	**34102**	**34060**	**34102**	34021	
165	03.18V Woking – Fratton	**75074**	**76067**	75076	*76031*	**76067**	**73085**	
161	04.32V Woking – Basingstoke	M. X.	**76011**	**76011**	**73018**	**76011**	**76011**	
113	04.40 Waterloo – Woking	34034	35030	**76064**	**76026**	34023	**76026**	
280	05.15V Bournemouth – Weymouth	M. X.	35008	*73043*	*34087*	34090		
D93	05.30 Waterloo – Bournemouth							
113	06.30 Woking – Salisbury	34034	35030	76064	76026	34023	76026	
161	06.50F Basingstoke – Eastleigh	*76011*	76011	76011	73018	76011		
395	07.08 Bournemouth – Weymouth	34013	34093	34102	34060	34102	34021	
281	07.18 Waterloo – Salisbury	**34087**	35003	35030	**34024**	*73043*		
411	07.50 Bournemouth – Weymouth	**73093**	*34102*	76005	**76005**	**76005**	*73093*	
407	07.56 Brockenhurst – Bournemouth	*80146*	*80134*	*80146*	*80146*	*80146*		
135	08.10 Waterloo – Weymouth Quay	**34023**	35013	35013	35008	35008		
Spl.	08.30 Waterloo – Weymouth							
145	08.35 Waterloo – Weymouth	**35007**	**35023**	**35028**	**35003**	**35013**		
254fo	09.20 W'loo-Southampton. West Docks			**34021**		**34087**		
412	09.20 Bournemouth – Weymouth	75076	73037	73037	73037	73037		
Spl. 2	10.06 Willesden Jcn – Soton. W. Docks			34023				
166	10.43 Southampton – Bournemouth	76067	*75074*	*73018*	*76067*	73020	**35030**	

Up, June 19 – 25

Diag.		MON	TUES	WEDS	THUR	FRI	SAT	SUN
314	01.34PV Southampton – Eastleigh	M. X.	80139	80016	80016	80016	80139	
137	05.30F Weymouth – Poole – Furzebrook	34095	73043	75075	34036	75075		
308	06.30 Fareham – Eastleigh	76007	76007	80139	80139	76013		
138	06.43 Weymouth – Bournemouth	34021	34036	**34013**	34093	34036		
394	06.45 Poole – Bournemouth	M. X.	73093	34004	73093	73093	73093	
407	06.48 Bournemouth – Brockenhurst	80146	80134	80146	80146	80146		
148	06.49 Salisbury – Waterloo	**34024**	34018	**35007**	34021	35028		
136	07.30 Ports. & Southsea – Eastleigh	73043	34023	34036	34095	34093		
280so	07.37 Bournemouth – Eastleigh						**35030**	
147	07.49 Weymouth – Bournemouth	**35023**	**35007**	35023	35028	35003		
394	08.08 Christchurch – Brockenhurst	76064	73093	34004	73093	73093		
396	08.27 Weymouth – Bournemouth	34102	34013	34095	34102	34060		
463	08.31V Salisbury – Basingstoke	34089	34089	34089	34089	34089		
138	08.46 Bournemouth – Waterloo	**34021**	34036	**34013***	34093	**34036**		
280	10.13 Weymouth – Bournemouth	34004	35008	73043	34087	34090	**34021**	
165	10.15V Fratton – Basingstoke	75074	76067	**75076**	76031*	76067		
161	10.32V Bevoir Park. – Basingstoke	76011	76011	76011	73018	76011		
411	11.18 Weymouth – Bournemouth	73093	34102	76005	76005	76005		
254mo	11.28 Southampton West Docks-Wloo	**34090**						
Spls.	Southampton Docks – Waterloo		34037	**34090**	34001	34018	**34001**	
	(Various departure times)		34090	**73020**		**34093**		
412	12.12 Weymouth – Bournemouth	**75076**	73037	**73037**	73037	**73037**	73093	

Down, June 19 – 25 continued

Diag.		MON	TUES	WEDS	THUR	FRI	SAT	SUN
463	10.45V Basingstoke – Fratton	34089	34089	34089	34089	34089		
283	11.29V Basingstoke – Southampton	35008	34025	*34087*	34090	35030		
148	11.38V Waterloo – Basingstoke	**34024**	34018	35007	**34021**	35028		
166	13.08 Bournemouth – Weymouth	**76067**	75076	*73018*	**76067**	**73020**		
394	15.01 Bournemouth – Weymouth	34093	*34102*	*34060*	*34102*	34060		
404	15.35F Poole – Weymouth	**75068**	*76009*	*76009*	*76009*	*76009*		
Spls.	Waterloo – Southampton Docks		34037		34018		**34001**	
	(Various departure times)		34090		34023			
396	16.03 Brockenhurst – Christchurch	**73093**	73093	**34004**	*73093*	*73093*		
283	16.20 Southampton – Bournemouth	**35008**	**34025**	*34087*	34090	**35030**		
165	16.51 Basingstoke – Salisbury	75074	**76067**	**75076**	*76031*	76067		
290	17.16 Southampton – Bournemouth	*80152*	**80152**	**80152**	*80152*	*80152*		
308	17.20 Eastleigh – Fratton	*76007*	*76007*	*80139*	*76031*	*76031*		
254fo	17.23 Waterloo – Bournemouth					**34004**		
138fo	18.22 Waterloo – Bournemouth					**35003**		
412	18.30 Southampton – Bournemouth	75076	**73037**	**73037**	**73037**	F. X.		
147	18.54 Waterloo – Salisbury	D N R	35007	**34021**	35028	**35023**		
148	19.06PV Basingstoke – Southampton	**34024**	**34018**	35007	**34021**	*34024*		
165	19.20V Salisbury – Northam Yard	75074	76067	*75076*	*75076*	76067		
136	19.50 Eastleigh – Bournemouth	**73043**	**75075**	**34036**	**75075**	**73037**		
145	21.00 Bournemouth – Weymouth	35007	**35023**	35028	**35003**	35013	*34018*	
165	23.10V Northam Yd – Ports & Southsea	75074	76067	*75076*	*76031*	76067		
313	Andover Pilot	80133	80133	80133	80133	80133		

Up, June 19 – 25 continued

Diag.		MON	TUES	WEDS	THUR	FRI	SAT	SUN
147	12.34 Bournemouth – Waterloo	**35023**	**35007**	**35023**	**35028**	**35003**		
412	13.52 Bournemouth – Southampton	75076	73037	73037	73037	73037		
163	14.05V Basingstoke – Surbiton	**76011**	**76011**	**76011**	**73085**	**76011**		
146	14.45V Weymouth – Westbury	M. X.	*75068*	*75068*	**34060**	*75076*		
281	15.55 Salisbury – Basingstoke	34087	35003	35030	34024	73043		
135	16.00 Weymouth Quay – Waterloo	**34023**	**35013**	**35013**	**35008**	**35008**		
166	16.46 Weymouth – Bournemouth	**76067**	75076	*73018*	**76067**	73020		
407	17.00V Weymouth – Bournemouth	*80146*	*80134*	**80146**	*80146*	*80146*		
149	17.30 Weymouth – Waterloo	**35028**	**34024**	**34018**	**35007**	**34021**		
Spl. 2	17.41 Soton E. Docks – Willesden Jcn			34023				
145	17.41 Weymouth – Bournemouth	35007	**35023**	35028	35003	35013		
137	17.42 Bournemouth – Eastleigh	**34095**	**34095**	73043	34036	**75075**		
394	18.15 Weymouth – Waterloo	34093	34102	**34060**	34102	34060		
113	18.38 Salisbury – Waterloo	**34034**	**35030**	76064	76026	**34023**		
166	18.51 Bournemouth – Woking	**76067**	**75076**	**73018**	**76067**	73020		
463	19.06V Ports. & Southsea – Salisbury	34089	34089	34089	34089	34089		
394	19.36 Bournemouth – Waterloo							35030
280	20.40V Eastleigh – Clapham Junction	*76064*	35008	*73043*	34087	34090		
462	21.00F Salisbury – Basingstoke	34108	34108	34108	34108	34108		
404	22.13 Weymouth – Bournemouth	*73037*	76009	76009	76009	76009		34102
308	23.32 Ports. & S'sea – Eastleigh	*76007*	*76007*	*80139*	*76031*	*76031*	80016	80016

Weymouth – Westbury Tomatoes(Sun): 34102(d. 12.10), *35003 or 34018(d. 15.00)*
*76031 replaced by 75076 at Eastleigh

Down, June 26 – July 2

Diag.		MON	TUES	WEDS	THUR	FRI	SAT	SUN
462	00.35F Basingstoke – Salisbury	M. X.	34108	34108	34052	34052	34052	
138	00.54 Eastleigh – Weymouth	34013	*75068*	34095	**75075**	*34018*	S. X.	*D1921*
308	01.57PV Eastleigh – Ports. & Southsea	*80133*	*80133*	*80133*	*80133*	*80133*	*80133*	
136	02.30 Waterloo – Ports. Harbour	**34095**	34036	34018	**34095**	**34087**	**73065**	
395	02.45PV Waterloo – Bournemouth	35030	**35003**	34060	34025	**34001**	**34021**	
165	03.18V Woking – Fratton	**73085**	**76007**	**76011**	**76067**	**76011**	**76066**	
161	04.32V Woking – Basingstoke	M. X.	**76067**	**76066**	**73029**	**76066**	**73018**	
113	04.40 Waterloo – Woking	**76026**	35007	**76064**	75074	*73065*	*76007*	
280	05.15V Bournemouth – Weymouth	M. X.	34025	*76031*	*76026*	*76007*		
D93	05.30 Waterloo – Bournemouth							
113	06.30 Woking – Salisbury	76026	35007	76064	75074	*73065*	76007	
161	06.50F Basingstoke – Eastleigh	*73018*	76067	76066	73029	76066		
395	07.08 Bournemouth – Weymouth	35030	35003	**34060**	**34025**	**34001**	34021	
281	07.18 Waterloo – Salisbury	34001	**76026**	**34037**	**76031**	76026*		
411	07.50 Bournemouth – Weymouth	**73037**	34004	**34004**	34004	34004	**76005**	
407	07.56 Brockenhurst – Bournemouth	*80146*	**80146**	80146	*80146*	*80146*		
135	08.10 Waterloo – Weymouth Quay	**34060**	**34060**	35030*	**34087**	**35003**		
Spl. 4	08.30 Waterloo – Weymouth						35003	
145	08.35 Waterloo – Weymouth	**34090***	**34087**	**35007**	**34024**	**35023**		
254fo	09.20 W'loo–Southampton West Docks		34093	**34013**		**34060**	**76064**	

Up, June 26 – July 2

Diag.		MON	TUES	WEDS	THUR	FRI	SAT	SUN
314	01.34PV Southampton – Eastleigh	*80139*	*80139*	*80139*	*80139*	*80139*	*80139*	
137	05.30F Weymouth – Poole – Furzebrook	*75068*	34095	*75075*	34018	**34025**		
308	06.30 Fareham – Eastleigh	*80133*	*80133*	*80133*	*80133*	*80133*		
138	06.43 Weymouth – Bournemouth	**34013**	34018	**34095**	75075	**34093**		
394	06.45 Poole – Bournemouth	M. X.	34102	**34001**	34021	34021	76005	
407	06.48 Bournemouth – Brockenhurst	*80146*	80146	**80146**	*80146*	*80146*		
148	06.49 Salisbury – Waterloo	35023	35013	**35023**	34093	*34089*		
136	07.30 Ports. & Southsea – Eastleigh	34095	34036	34018	34095	34087		
280so	07.37 Bournemouth – Eastleigh						**34037**	
147	07.49 Weymouth – Bournemouth	35013	**35023**	*34025*	*35007*	34024		
394	08.08 Christchurch – Brockenhurst	**34102**	34102	**34001**	34021	34021		
396	08.27 Weymouth – Bournemouth	35003	35030	35003	**73037**	*73020*		
463	08.31V Salisbury – Basingstoke	34089	34089	**34089**	*34089*	*75075*		
138	08.46 Bournemouth – Waterloo	34013*	**34018**	**34095**	**75075**	**34093**		
EMU	09.24 Bournemouth – Waterloo						**34025**	
280	10.13 Weymouth – Bournemouth	*75074*	34025	**76031**	**76026**	**76007**	34021	
165	10.15V Fratton – Basingstoke	*73085*	*76007*	**76011**	76067	**76011**		
161	10.32V Bevoir Park. – Basingstoke	*76067*	76067	**76066**	73029	76066		
411	11.18 Weymouth – Bournemouth	73037	**34004**	**34004**	34004	**34004**		
254mo	11.28 Southampton West Docks-W'loo	**34013**		34093		34087		

Down, June 26 – July 2 continued

Diag.		MON	TUES	WEDS	THUR	FRI	SAT	SUN
Spl. 5	09.15 Waterloo – Bournemouth						35030	
412	09.20 Bournemouth – Weymouth	76009	**76009**	*76009*	**34036**	**80011**		
Spl. 3	09.33 Waterloo – Bournemouth							**34025**
Spl. 1	09.55 Waterloo – Weymouth							**35008**
Spl.	10.40 Waterloo – Salisbury			**34090**	34090			
166	10.43 Southampton – Bournemouth	**76007**	76011	**76067**	76011	76067	**34037**	
463	10.45V Basingstoke – Fratton	34089	34089	**34089**	*34089*	75075		
283	11.29V Basingstoke – Southampton	35028	34001	**76026**	76007	**34037**		
148	11.38V Waterloo – Basingstoke	35023	**35013**	35023	**34093**	**34089**		
Spl. 2	12.20 Waterloo – Bournemouth							**35028**
166	13.08 Bournemouth – Weymouth	**76007**	**76011**	**76067**	**76011**	**76067**		
394	15.01 Bournemouth – Weymouth	35003	35028	35003	34001	**34021**		
404	15.35F Poole – Weymouth	*73093*	**73037**	*73037*	*76005*	**76005**		
Spls.	Waterloo – Southampton Docks		34093	34013	**73020**	34102		
	(Various departure times)			73093		**34013**		
396	16.03 Brockenhurst – Christchurch	*80011*	*34025*	*80011*	73037	*73020*		
283	16.20 Southampton – Bournemouth	**35028**	34001	76026	**76007**	**34037**		
165	16.51 Basingstoke – Salisbury	**76011**	**76067**	**76011**	76067	**76011**		
290	17.16 Southampton – Bournemouth	**80016**	**80016**	**80016**	**80016**	73037		
308	17.20 Eastleigh – Fratton	*80133*	*80133*	*80133*	**80133**	80133		
254fo	17.23 Waterloo – Bournemouth					**34087**		

Up, June 26 – July 2 continued

Diag.		MON	TUES	WEDS	THUR	FRI	SAT	SUN
Spls.	Southampton Docks – Waterloo		**34013**	34036		**34036**		
	(Various departure times)		**34090**	**34093**		34095		
			73093			**34102**		
412	12.12 Weymouth – Bournemouth	**76009**	76009	**76009**	34036	**80011**	**76005**	
147	12.34 Bournemouth – Waterloo	**35013**	**35023**	**35030**	**34060**	**34024**		
412	13.52 Bournemouth – Southampton	76009	**76009**	*76009*	34036	80011		
163	14.05V Basingstoke – Surbiton	**76067**	**76066**	**73018**	**76066**	**76066**		
146	14.45V Weymouth – Westbury	M. X.	*35003*	*34060*	*35007*	*35007*		34021
Spl. 1	15.00 Weymouth – Waterloo							35008
281	15.55 Salisbury – Basingstoke	34001	**76026**	**34037**	76031	**76031**		
Spl. 4	15.55 Weymouth Quay – Waterloo						**34018**	
135	16.00 Weymouth Quay – Waterloo	**34060**	**34060**	**34025**	**34087**	**35003**		
Spl. 3	16.15 Weymouth Quay – Waterloo					**73093**		
Spl. 2	16.30 Bournemouth – Waterloo							35028
166	16.46 Weymouth – Bournemouth	**76007**	**76011**	76067	76011	**76067**		
407	17.00V Weymouth – Bournemouth	**80146**	**80146**	**80146**	*80146*	**80146**		
149	17.30 Weymouth – Waterloo	**34087**	**34087**	**35013**	**35023**	**34001**		
Spl.	17.35 Salisbury – Waterloo			**34090**	*Dsl?*			
145	17.41 Weymouth – Bournemouth	**34018**	**76031**	**35007**	**34024**	**35023**		
137	17.42 Bournemouth – Eastleigh	**75068**	34095	*75075*	34018	**34025**		
394	18.15 Weymouth – Waterloo	**35003**	**35028**	**35003**	**34001**	**34021**		
Spl. 5	18.30 Bournemouth – Waterloo						**35030**	

Down, June 26 – July 2 continued

Diag.		MON	TUES	WEDS	THUR	FRI	SAT	SUN
138fo	18.22 Waterloo – Bournemouth					**34093**		
412	18.30 Southampton – Bournemouth	76009	76009	*34036*	**76009**	F. X.		
147	18.54 Waterloo – Salisbury	**35013**	**35023**	**34093**	*75075*	**34060**		
148	19.06PV Basingstoke – Southampton	**35023**	**35013**	**35023**	**34093**	**34089**		
165	19.20V Salisbury – Northam Yard	*76011*	76067	*76011*	76067	*76011*		
136	19.50 Eastleigh – Bournemouth	34095	**75075**	**34018**	**73020**	**80011**		
145	21.00 Bournemouth – Weymouth	*34018*	*34025*	**35007**	34024	**35023**	34021	
165	23.10V Northam Yd – Ports & Southsea	*76011*	76067	76011	76067	76011		
313	Andover Pilot	80139	80139	**80139**	**80139**	80139		

Down, July 3 – 9

Diag.		MON	TUES	WEDS	THUR	FRI	SAT	SUN
462	00.35F Basingstoke – Salisbury	M. X.	34052	*76007*	*76007*	*76007*	*34087*	
138	00.54 Eastleigh – Weymouth	34102	**34025**	34013	34024	*D6510*	S. X.	73092
308	01.57PV Eastleigh – Ports. & Southsea	**80016**	*80016*	80016	*80016*	80016	*76005*	
D91	02.15V Waterloo – Bournemouth	**34025**	*D1925*	34024	*D1925*	*D1922*		
136	02.30 Waterloo – Ports. Harbour	**34013**	**73020**	34060	**34036**	34004	**34037**	
395	02.45PV Waterloo – Bournemouth	**34037**	**34001**	35030	**73029**	**73092**	**34095**	
165	03.18V Woking – Fratton	34095	**76011**	**76011**	**73043**	**73029**	**76067**	
161	04.32V Woking – Basingstoke	M. X.	**73043**	**73043**	**34060**	**34060**	**34060**	
113	04.40 Waterloo – Woking	75074	75074	35008	**75074**	76011	**76066**	

Up, June 26 – July 2 continued

Diag.		MON	TUES	WEDS	THUR	FRI	SAT	SUN
113	18.38 Salisbury – Waterloo	**76026**	**35007**	**76064**	**73065**	**73065**		
166	18.51 Bournemouth – Woking	**76007**	**76011**	**76067**	**76011**	76067		
463	19.06V Ports. & Southsea – Salisbury	34089	34089	34089	*34089*	*75077*		
394	19.36 Bournemouth – Waterloo							**34037**
Spl. 3	19.59 Bournemouth – Waterloo							**34025**
280	20.40V Eastleigh – Clapham Junction	*75074*	*35030*	*76031**	*76026*	*76007*		
462	21.00F Salisbury – Basingstoke	*34108*	*34108*	*34052*	*34052*	*34052*		
404	22.13 Weymouth – Bournemouth	*73093*	*73037*	*34060*	*76005*	*76005*	DSL	
308	23.32 Ports. & Southsea – Eastleigh	*80133*	*80133*	*80133*	*80133*	**80133**		

Up July 3 – 9

Diag.		MON	TUES	WEDS	THUR	FRI	SAT	SUN
314	01.34PV Southampton – Eastleigh	M. X.	*80139*	*80139*	*80139*	*80139*	*80139*	
137	05.30F Weymouth – Poole – Furzebrook	**34093**	34013	34036	**80146***	**34021**		
D91	06.22 Bournemouth – Waterloo	**34025**	D1925	**34024**	*D1925*	*D1922*		
308	06.30 Fareham – Eastleigh	**80016**	*80016*	80016	*80016*	**80016**		
138	06.43 Weymouth – Bournemouth	**34102**	**34025**	34013	34024	**D6510**		
394	06.45 Poole – Bournemouth	**34004**	34004	34037	34004	**73020**	*34004*	
407	06.48 Bournemouth – Brockenhurst	80146	80146	80146	**80146**	**80011**		
148	06.49 Salisbury – Waterloo	**34060**	**35023**	**34102**	**34013**	**34052**		
136	07.30 Ports. & Southsea – Eastleigh	34013	**73020**	34060	**34036**	34004		
280so	07.37 Bournemouth – Eastleigh						**73043**	

Down, July 3 – 9 continued

Diag.		MON	TUES	WEDS	THUR	FRI	SAT	SUN
280	05.15V Bournemouth – Weymouth	M. X.	76031	73029	34093	76066		
D93	05.30 Waterloo – Bournemouth		**34024**					
113	06.30 Woking – Salisbury	**75074**	75074	35008	**75074**	76011	**76066**	
161	06.50F Basingstoke – Eastleigh	*73018*	**73043**	**73043**	34060	34060		
395	07.08 Bournemouth – Weymouth	**34037**	D65xx	35030	73029	**73092**	**34095**	
281	07.18 Waterloo – Salisbury	**73093**	73065	**76031**	*Dsl?*	**34024**	**82029**	
411	07.50 Bournemouth – Weymouth	**76009**	**76006**	**76006**	**76006**	**76006**	*34004*	
407	07.56 Brockenhurst – Bournemouth	80146	80146	80146	*80146*	**80011**		
135	08.10 Waterloo – Weymouth Quay	**34001**	**34087**	**34087**	**35030**	**35023**		
Spl.	08.20 Wloo -Southampton. East Docks				**34021**	**34089**		
Spl. 1	08.30 Waterloo – Weymouth						**35023**	
145	08.35 Waterloo – Weymouth	**35030***	**35028**	**35007**	**35008**	**35003**		
254 fo	09.20 W'loo-Southampton West Docks			**34025**	**73092**	**34025**		
412	09.20 Bournemouth – Weymouth	76026	**76026**	**76026**	**76005**	**76005**		
166	10.43 Southampton – Bournemouth	76011	**76011**	**34060**	**34036**	**75075**	**77014**	
463	10.45V Basingstoke – Fratton	**76007**	34052	34052	**34052**	*D6500*		
Spl. 3	11.20 Wloo-Southampton West Docks				**34037**			
283	11.29V Basingstoke – Southampton	**76031**	73029	*76066*	76066	*75074*		
148	11.38V Waterloo – Basingstoke	**34060**	**35023**	**34102**	34013	**34052**		

Up July 3 – 9 continued

Diag.		MON	TUES	WEDS	THUR	FRI	SAT	SUN
147	07.49 Weymouth – Bournemouth	35023	**34021**	**35028**	*35007*	**35008**		
394	08.08 Christchurch – Brockenhurst	*34004*	34004	34037	34004	73020		
396	08.27 Weymouth – Bournemouth	**34021**	34037	34001	34087	**73018**		
463	08.31V Salisbury – Basingstoke	**76007**	34052	34052	34052	*D6500*		
138	08.46 Bournemouth – Waterloo	**34102**	**34060**	**34013**	**34024**	**D6510**		
D90	09.40 Poole – Reading*		**34095**					
280	10.13 Weymouth – Bournemouth	**73020**	**76031**	**73029**	**34093**	**76066**	**34095**	
165	10.15V Fratton – Basingstoke	34095	73020	*76031*	73043	73029		
161	10.32V Bevoir Park. – Basingstoke	*73018*	**73043**	**73043**	34060	**34060**		
D93	11.07 Bournemouth – Waterloo		34024					
411	11.18 Weymouth – Bournemouth	76006	**76006**	76006	**76006**	**76006**		
254mo	11.28 Southampton West Docks-W'loo	**34087**			34089			
Spls.	Southampton Docks – Waterloo	**73092**	**34093**	34037	**73092**			**34021**
	(Various departure times)		*73092*		34025			
412	12.12 Weymouth – Bournemouth	**76026**	**76026**	**76026**	**76005**	**76005**	**73092**	
147	12.34 Bournemouth – Waterloo	**35023**	**34021**	**35028**	**34087**	**35008**		
412	13.52 Bournemouth – Southampton	76026	76026	76026	**76005**	**76005**		
163	14.05V Basingstoke – Surbiton	**73043**	**73043**	**73043**	**34060**	**34060**		
147	14.07 Weymouth – Waterloo							**35030**
146	14.45V Weymouth – Westbury	M. X.	**34001**	**35003**	**73018**	*73092*		

Down, July 3 – 9 continued

Diag.		MON	TUES	WEDS	THUR	FRI	SAT	SUN
D91	12.30 Waterloo – Bournemouth	**34025**	*D1925*	**34024**	**D1925**	*D1922*	**D1924**	**D1924**
166	13.08 Bournemouth – Weymouth	**76011**	**76011**	**34060**	**34036**	**75075**		
394	15.01 Bournemouth – Weymouth	**73020**	**35030**	**34001**	**34004**	**34095**		
404	15.35F Poole – Weymouth	**76005**	*76006*	**76005**	**76026**	*76026*		
D90	16.03 Reading – Poole*		**34095**					
396	16.03 Brockenhurst – Christchurch	**35030**	34037	34004	*76006*	**73020**		
283	16.20 Southampton – Bournemouth	76031	**73029**	76026	76066	73043		
165	16.51 Basingstoke – Salisbury	**34095**	**73020**	**76011**	**73043**	**73029**		
290	17.16 Southampton – Bournemouth	**73037**	**75075**	**75075**	**75075**	**80016**		
308	17.20 Eastleigh – Fratton	**80016**	*80016*	**80016**	*80016*	**76005**		
254 fo	17.23 Waterloo – Bournemouth					**34093**		
Spl.33	18.20 Wloo – Southampton East Docks						**34037**	
138 fo	18.22 Waterloo – Bournemouth					**D6538**		
412	18.30 Southampton – Bournemouth	**76026**	**76026**	**34093**	**76005**	**34004**		
147	18.54 Waterloo – Salisbury	**35023**	**34102**	**34013**	**34087**	**34025**		
148	19.06PV Basingstoke – Southampton	**34060**	**35023**	*73018*	**34013**	**34052**		
165	19.20V Salisbury – Northam Yard	34095	73020	*76011*	73043	**77014**		
136	19.50 Eastleigh – Bournemouth	34013	34036	*73020*	34021	Cl. 33.		
145	21.00 Bournemouth – Weymouth	**34021**	**35028**	**35007**	**35008**	**35003**	**34095**	
165	23.10V Northam Yd – Ports & Southsea	34095	73020	*76011*	73043	*77014*		
313	Andover Pilot	*80152*	*80152*	**80152**	*80152*	**80152**		

Up July 3 – 9 continued

Diag.		MON	TUES	WEDS	THUR	FRI	SAT	SUN
281	15.55 Salisbury – Basingstoke	73093	73065	76031	75074	34024		
Spl. 1	15.55 Weymouth Quay – Waterloo						35023	
135	16.00 Weymouth Quay – Waterloo	34001	34087	35030	35003	35023		
Spl. 3	16.15 Weymouth Quay – Waterloo					34037		
D91	16.37 Bournemouth – Waterloo	34025	D1925	34036	*D1925*	D1922	**D1924**	D1924
166	16.46 Weymouth – Bournemouth	76011	76011	34060	73029	75075		
407	17.00V Weymouth – Bournemouth	80146	80146	80146	73020	80011		
149	17.30 Weymouth – Waterloo	35007	34025	35023	35007	34013		
145	17.41 Weymouth – Bournemouth	34021*	35028	35007	35008	35003		
137	17.42 Bournemouth – Eastleigh	34093	34013	34024	80146	34021		
394	18.15 Weymouth – Waterloo	73020	35030	34001	34004	34095		
113	18.38 Salisbury – Waterloo	75074	75074	35008	76011	73029		
166	18.51 Bournemouth – Woking	76011	76011	34060	73029	75075		
463	19.06V Ports. & Southsea – Salisbury	76007	34052	**34052**	34052	**D6500**		
280	20.40V Eastleigh – Clapham Jcn.	*75075*	76031	73029	34093	**76066**		
462	21.00F Salisbury – Basingstoke	34052	*76007*	*76007*	*76007*	*34087*		
396	21.20 Bournemouth – Eastleigh						73092	
404	22.13 Weymouth – Bournemouth	76005	*76006*	76005	*76026*	76026	**D6517**	*Dsl**
308	23.32 Ports. & Southsea – Eastleigh	**80016**	*80016*	80016	*80016*	76005		
Weymouth – Westbury Tomatoes(Sun): **34095**(d. 10.20), **34052**(d. 14.20), **73092**(d15.00)								

KEY and NOTES

General

Locomotive <u>underlined</u> indicates last known working
BOLD – known working(text or photo evidence)
NORMAL – booked working.
ITALICS – probable or possible working.

Dn -	00.54 Eastleigh – Weymouth	395 diag. on Sundays	
	07.50 Bournemouth – Weymouth	412 diag. on Saturdays.	
	10.43 Southampton – Bournemouth	280 diag. on Saturdays.	
	19.50 Eastleigh – Bournemouth	412 diag. on Fridays.	
	21.00 Bournemouth – Weymouth	395 diag. on Saturdays	

Up -	08.08 Christchurch – Brockenhurst	280 diag. on Mondays	
	10.13 Weymouth – Bournemouth	394 diag. on Mondays,	395 diag. on Saturdays
	12.12 Weymouth – Bournemouth	396 diag. on Saturdays	
	22.13 Weymouth – Bournemouth	D/H D65xx Mon. – Fri.	395 diag. on Sundays

	Daily*:	
8/6	16.46 Weymouth – Bournemouth	76007 assist D.m.m.u. (16.17 Wey – Bristol?) to Bincombe?
10/6	00.54 Eastleigh – Weymouth	Terminated at Brockenhurst (P Way works). D1922 from Wloo
10/6	05.15v Bournemouth – Weymouth	34008 Diagram is FS17
10/6	19.50 Eastleigh – Bournemouth	73029 start Southampton at 20.15
12/6	08.46 Bournemouth – Waterloo	76031 replaced by 73037 at Eastleigh?

12/6	11.38v Waterloo – Basing cancelled?	34060 observed running light near Winchfield
12/6	18.51 Bournemouth – Woking	76064 replaced by 73092 at Basingstoke?
21/6	08.46 Bournemouth – Waterloo	34013 replaced by 35003 at Woking?
26/6	08.35 Waterloo – Weymouth	34090 replaced by 75076 at Eastleigh
26/6	08.46 Bournemouth – Waterloo	34013 replaced by 34024 at Eastleigh (or Southampton?)
28/6	08.10 Waterloo – Weymouth Quay	35030 replaced by 34025 at Bournemouth
28/6	20.40v Eastleigh – Clapham J cancelled?	76031 observed running light at Basingstoke
30/6	07.18 Waterloo – Salisbury	76026 replaced by 76031 at Basingstoke
3/7	08.35 Waterloo – Weymouth	35030 replaced by 34021 at Bournemouth
3/7 -	17.41 Weymouth – Bournemouth	34021 assisted by D842(to Dorchester?)
4/7	09.40 Poole – Reading	Through train to Manchester.
4/7	16.03 Reading – Poole	08. 30 from Newcastle.
6/7	05.30f Wey – Poole probably cancelled	80146 commence with 09.08f from Poole
6/7	06.30 Woking – Salisbury	*73065 replaced by 76031 at Basingstoke?*
9/7	22.13 Weymouth – Bournemouth	73092 booked to work D/H but probably didn't!

Last week of local tanks July 1967

NINE ELMS	MON 3/7	TUES 4/7	WEDS 5/7	THUR 6/7	FRI 7/7	SAT 8/7	SUN 9/7
41298	102	AS1 (or see below)	108	108	108	102	111
41312	108	108			AS1 (or see below)	AS4 11.35le to Salisbury	
41319	106	106	106	106	106	106	Spl. e.c.s./ Wloo pilot
80015	101	101(incl AS1?)	101	101	101 (incl. AS1 –part 3?)	AS3? 11.20 le to Salisbury (with 82019)	
80143	111	111	111	111	111	111/AS8 18.35le to Salisbury	
82019	105	105	105	105	105 (inc. AS1 –part 1?)	AS2 11.20 le to Salisbury (with 80015)	
82029		102	102	102	102 (inc. AS1 –part 2?)	Diesel diagram(26?). 07.18 Wloo – Salisbury	

BO'MOUTH	MON 3/7	TUES 4/7	WEDS 5/7	THUR 6/7	FRI 7/7	SAT 8/7	SUN 9/7
41224	Loco Pilot	Loco Pilot	Loco Pilot	Loco Pilot	Loco Pilot	Loco Pilot	Loco Pilot/FS14 18.30le to Weymouth
41320	409	409	409	409	409	409	408/ Bank e.c.s Poole- Parkstone 20.30le to Wey
80134	400	400 (part 2 only?)	400	400	400/(FS12)	FS27 18.10le to Weymouth	

DIAGRAMS	Mon - Fri.	Mon - Fri.	Mon - Fri.	AS1(Tues)	FS12(Fri)	Sat.	Sun.
	101 - E. C. S. Including up *Bournemouth Belle*.	106 - Evening and night Waterloo carriage shunting and a. m. *Kenny Belle*.	400 - E. C. S. 06.00 - 13.45, also 08.15F Cent. Goods - Branksome.	11.20se Barnes-Clap. Jcn	Bank relief Channel Islands boat train 17.27 Poole to Branksome	102, 106 - E. C. S. and Waterloo carriage shunting	105, 106 - E.C.S. and Waterloo carriage shunting
	102 - E. C. S, also night and morning Waterloo carriage shunting.	108 - E. C. S, including down *Bournemouth Belle* and afternoon carriage shunting at Waterloo.	409 - E. C. S. and Bomo West carriage shunting 05. 15 - 22.30. (Also usual loco for banking Channel Islands boat train from Poole to Branksome)	12.05se Clapham Jcn - Strawberry Hill	(also available - 76006)	111 - Nine Elms pilot.	111 - Nine Elms pilot.
	105 - E. C. S, also early morning Waterloo carriage shunting and p.m. *Kenny Belle*.	111 - Nine Elms pilot.		13.58(dep) Wimbledon - Stewarts Lane		409 - E. C. S. to 18.15 Bournemouth West	408 - E.C.S. and Bournemouth West carriage shunting 07.40 - 20.05.
				AS1(Fri) 3 Spl. Boat Train empties Clapham Jcn. - Waterloo		Carriage shunting. 18.45 - 22.00	

USA TANKS   **3 to 9 July**

Guildford -

30072	Loco pilot & yard trips as required		Light engine via Fratton to Salisbury	Sunday 9 July

Eastleigh - Observations rare but last week probably:

30064	Works pilot and local trips as required	*DS18?*	15.10le to Salisbury (with 30071)	Saturday 8 July
30067 & 30069	Southampton Docks pilots and banana train heating as required	*DS20/21?*	16.15le to Salisbury (together)	Saturday 8 July
30071	Eastleigh loco pilot and coal shunting (325 duty)	*DS19?*	15.10le to Salisbury (with 30064)	Saturday 8 July

Boat Trains

Bno	Date	Time		Loco	Boat/Shipping Co.	Notes
13	Mon 05-06-67	14.00	Waterloo – Southampton East Docks	34024	*Andes* – Royal Mail Line	'Royal Mail Lines'
14	"	11.27	Southampton West Docks – Waterloo	**34037**	*Edinburgh Castle* – Union Castle	*The Springbok*
15	"	18.37	Southampton East Docks-Waterloo	**34095**	*United States* – United States Line	*The Statesman*
17	Tues 06-06-67	08.20	Waterloo – Southampton East Docks	73020	*Sylvania* – Cunard	
18	"	13.20	Waterloo – Southampton West Docks	*Dsl?*	*Begona* – Spanish Line	
20	"	09.24	Southampton East Docks-Waterloo	*Dsl?*	*Queen Mary* – Cunard	*The Cunarder*
21	"	11.27	Southampton West Docks – Waterloo	**73092**	*Begona* – Spanish Line	
101	Wed 07-06-67	08.34	Waterloo – Southampton East Docks	**34090**	*Nieuw Amsterdam* – Holland–America Line	Extra – not in weekly notice 47
22	"	10.27	Southampton East Docks-Waterloo	**34095**	*Aragon* – Royal Mail Line	*The South American*
23	Thurs 08-06-67	09.20	Waterloo – Soutampton West Docks	*34034*	*United States* – United States Line	*The Statesman*
24	Fri 09-06-67	08.20	Waterloo – Southampton East Docks		*Queen Mary* – Cunard	Train cancelled - not required
25	"	08.54	Waterloo – Souhtampton East Docks	**34034**	*Queen Mary* – Cunard	*The Cunarder*
26	"	18.43	Waterloo – Southampton West Docks	*34023*	*Iberia* – P&O (Cruise)	
27	"	10.51	Southampton East Docks – Waterloo	**34025**	*Chusan* – P&O (Cruise)	

Bno	Date	Time		Loco	Boat/Shipping Co.	Notes
28	Fri 09-06-67	18.40	Southampton East Docks – Waterloo	34021	*Caronia* – Cunard	
	"	18.45	Southampton East Docks – Central	**76064**	*Stella Polaris* – Clipper Line	Attach to 17.30 Weymouth– Waterloo
29	Sat 10-06-67	09.22	Waterloo – Southampton East Docks	**D6548**	*Chusan* – P & O (Cruise)	
	"	21.47	Southampton Central – East Docks	4-TC	*Flandre* – French Line CGT	Detach from 19.30 Waterloo– Weymouth
	Sun 11-06-67	11.47	Southampton Central – East Docks	4-TC	*Bremen* – Nord-Deutsche Lloyd	Detach from 09.30 Waterloo– Bournemouth
30	"	17.30	Waterloo – Southampton West Docks	**34024**	*Ellinis* – Chandris Line	
31	"	10.48	Southampton East Docks – Waterloo	**34060**	*Ellinis* – Chandris Line	
32	"	17.44	Southampton West Docks – Waterloo	**34013**	*Achille Lauro* – FlottaLauro	Extra – not in weekly notice 49
33	Mon 12-06-67	11.27	Southampton West Docks – Waterloo	**34018**	*S. A. Vaal* – Union Castle	*The Springbok*
34	Tues 13-06-67	09.20	Waterloo – Southampton East Docks	34025	*Southern Cross* – Shaw Savill	
35	"	10.00	Waterloo – Southampton East Docks	73043	*Southern Cross* – Shaw Savill	
36	"				*France* – Sailing Cancelled	Non-runners – not in weekly notice 49
37	"				*France* – Sailing Cancelled	(Westbound 3/6 cancelled – crew strike)

Bno	Date	Time		Loco	Boat/Shipping Co.	Notes
	Tues 13-06-67	19.34	Southampton Central – East Docks	4-TC	*Maasdam –* Holland-America Line	Detach from 17.30 Waterloo – Weymouth
38	"	17.41	Southampton East Docks – Waterloo	**34025**	*Queen Elizabeth –* Cunard	*The Cunarder*
39	"	18.40	Southampton East Docks – Waterloo	**34037**	*Queen Elizabeth –* Cunard	
	Wed 14-06-67	11.42	Southampton Central – East Docks	4-TC	*Golfito –* Elders-Ffyfes	Detach from 09.30 Waterloo – Bournemouth
40	"	17.23	Waterloo – Southampton East Docks	**34018**	*Statendam –* Holland-America Line	*The Holland American*
41	"	18.43	Waterloo – Southampton West Docks	**34090**	*Reina del Mar –* Union Castle cruise	
42	"	10.55	Southampton West Docks – Waterloo	**34090**	*Reina del Mar –* Union Castle cruise	
43	Thurs 15-06-67	10.00	Waterloo – Southampton East Docks	34018	*Queen Elizabeth –* Cunard	
44	"	10.43	Waterloo – Southampton East Docks	**73037**	*Queen Elizabeth –* Cunard	*The Cunarder*
45	"	11.20	Waterloo – Southampton Docks	**35028**	*Achille Lauro –* Flotta Lauro	
46	Fri 16-06-67	09.20	Waterloo – Southampton West Docks	**34025**	*Edinburgh Castle –* Union Castle	*The Springbok*
47	"	16.00	Waterloo – Southampton West Docks		*France –* French Line CGT	In weekly notice 49 but not required?
48	"	16.40	Waterloo – Southampton West Docks	**34090**	*France –* French Line CGT	
49	"	10.07	Southampton East? Docks-Waterloo	**34090**	*Rotterdam –* Holland-America Line	*The Holland American*
50	"	10.59	Southampton East Docks – Waterloo	**73020**	*Capetown Castle –* Union Castle	*The Springbok*

Bno	Date	Time		Loco	Boat/Shipping Co.	Notes
51	Fri 16-06-67	19.07	Southampton East Docks – Waterloo	**34060**	*Carmania* – Cunard	
102	Sun 18-06-67	10.48	Southampton East Docks – Waterloo	**34060**	*Aurelia* – Cogedar Line	
52	Mon 19-06-67	10.55	Southampton West Docks – Waterloo	**34090**	*Pendennis Castle* – Union Castle	*The Springbok*
53	Tues 20-06-67	07.00	Waterloo – Southampton West Docks	**34037**	*Aurelia* – Cogedar Line	
54	"	08.20	Waterloo – Southampton East Docks	**D6551**	*Carmania* – Cunard	
55	"	08.54	Waterloo – Southampton East Docks	**34090**	*Caronia* – Cunard	
56	"	17.23	Waterloo – Southampton East Docks	73020	*Rotterdam* – Holland-America Line	*The Holland American*
57	"	16.52	Southampton West Docks – Waterloo	34090	*United States* – United States Line	*The Statesman*
58	"	17.38	Southampton West Docks – Waterloo	**34037**	*United States* – United States Line	
59	"	18.19	Southampton West Docks – Waterloo		*United States* – United States Line	3rd train in weekly notice 51 – not required?
60	Wed 21-06-67	08.54	Waterloo – Southampton West Docks	**34021**	*United States* – United States Line	*The Statesman*
61	"	09.00	Southampton East Docks – Waterloo	**73020**	*Queen Mary* – Cunard	*The Cunarder*
62	"	09.38	Southampton East Docks – Waterloo	**34090**	*Queen Mary* – Cunard	
63	Thurs 22-06-67	07.45	Waterloo – Southampton East Docks	**73020**	*Queen Mary* – Cunard	
64	"	08.20	Waterloo – Southampton East Docks	**34018**	*Queen Mary* – Cunard	*The Cunarder*
65	"	10.43	Waterloo – Southampton East Docks	**34023**	*Capetown Castle* – Union Castle	*The Springbok*

Bno	Date	Time		Loco	Boat/Shipping Co.	Notes
66	Thurs 22-06-67	17.41	Southampton East Docks – Waterloo		*Sylvania –* Cunard (Cancelled)	Cunard t/t – Ran aground leaving Montreal
67	Fri 23-06-67	09.20	Waterloo – Southampton West Docks	**34087**	*S. A. Vaal –* Union Castle	*The Springbok*
	"	11.45	Southampton Central – West Docks	4-TC	*Europa –* Nord-Deutsche Lloyd	Detach from 09.30 Waterloo-Bournemouth
68	"	16.55	Southampton East Docks – Waterloo	**34093**	*Ellinis –* Chandris Line	
69	"	*xx.xx*	*Southampton East Docks – Waterloo*		*Castel Felice –* Sitmar Line	Non-runner. Ship diverted – Suez crisis
70	Sat 24-06-67	07.45	Waterloo – Southampton East Docks	**34001**	*Ellinis –* Chandris Line	
	"	10.42	Southampton Central – East Docks	*Dsl?*	*Oranje Nassau –* Royal Netherlands	Detach from 08.35 Waterloo–Weymouth
71	"					Missing from SN. Non-runner?
72	"	10.09	Southampton East Docks – Waterloo	*Dsl?*	*Nieuw Amsterdam-* Holland-America Line	
73	"	10.57	Southampton West Docks – Waterloo	**34001**	*Chusan –* P&O (Cruise)	
74	Sun 25-06-67	*xx.xx*	*Waterloo – Southampton East Docks*		*Castel Felice –* Sitmar Line	Original dep date – Nat arch Australia
75	"	*xx.xx*	*Waterloo – Southampton East Docks*		*Castel Felice –* Sitmar Line	Non-runners – r/t 07/07 (Suez crisis)
76	Mon 26-06-67	11.27	Southampton East Docks – Waterloo	**34013**	*Reina del Mar –* Union Castle cruise	
77	Tues 27-06-67	08.54	Waterloo – Southampton East Docks	**34093**	*Reina del Mar –* Union Castle cruise	

Bno	Date	Time		Loco	Boat/Shipping Co.	Notes
78	Tues 27-06-67	09.24	Southampton East Docks – Waterloo	D1925	*Queen Elizabeth* – Cunard	*The Cunarder*
79	"	10.00	Southampton East Docks – Waterloo	**34013**	*Queen Elizabeth* – Cunard	
80	"	09.00	Southampton East Docks – Waterloo	D1921	*France* – French Line CGT	Special notice, poss loco(09.00 retimed)
81	"	10.27	Southampton East Docks – Waterloo	**73093**	*France* – French Line CGT	Special notice, probable loco, Tyler
82	"	10.55	Southampton West Docks – Waterloo	**34090**	*Andes* – Royal Mail Line	Royal Mail Lines
83	Wed 28-06-67	08.54	Waterloo – Southampton East Docks	**34013**	*Nieuw Amsterdam-* Holland-America Line	*The Holland American*
84	"	13.20	Waterloo – Southampton East Docks	*34036*	*Montserrat* – Spanish Line	
85	"	14.00	Waterloo – Southampton East Docks	**73093**	*Andes* – Royal Mail Line	'Royal Mail Lines'
86	"					Missing from SN. Non-runner.
87	"	15.09	Southampton East Docks – Waterloo	*Dsl?*	*Arlanza* – Royal Mail Line	*The South American*
88	"	11.28	Southampton East Docks – Waterloo	**34093**	*Montserrat* – Spanish Line	
	Thurs 29-06-67	10.42	Southampton Central – East Docks	34095	*Bremen* – Nord-Deutsche Lloyd	Detach from 08.35 Waterloo-Weymouth
89	"	12.43	Waterloo – Southampton East Docks	**D6572**	*Queen Elizabeth* – Cunard	
90	"	13.20	Waterloo – Southampton East Docks	**73020**	*Queen Elizabeth* – Cunard	*The Cunarder*
91	Fri 30-06-67	09.20	Waterloo – Southampton West Docks	**34060**	*Pendennis Castle* – Union Castle	*The Springbok*

Bno	Date	Time		Loco	Boat/Shipping Co.	Notes
92	Fri 30-06-67	16.00	Waterloo – Southampton East Docks	**34102**	*France* – French Line CGT	
93	"	16.40	Waterloo – Southampton East Docks	**34013**	*France* – French Line CGT	
94	"	10.00	Southampton East Docks – Waterloo	**34036**	*Statendam* – Holland-America Line	*The Holland American*
95	"	10.24	Southampton West Docks – Waterloo	**34095**	*Himalaya* – P & O (Cruise)	
96	"	10.59	Southampton East Docks – Waterloo	**34102**	*Iberia* – P & O (Cruise)	
97	"	11.27	Southampton West Docks – Waterloo	**34087**	*Himalaya* – P & O (Cruise)	
1	Sat 01-07-67	08.54	Waterloo – Southampton East Docks	**76064**	*Iberia* – P & O (Cruise)	
2	"	09.22	Waterloo – Southampton West Docks	**E6036**	*Chusan* – P & O (Cruise)	
3	"	09.42	Waterloo – Southampton West Docks	**D6523**	*Himalaya* – P & O (Cruise)	
4	Mon 03-07-67	11.27	Southampton West Docks – Waterloo	**34087**	*S. A. Oranje* – Union Castle	*The Springbok*
5	"	20.33	Southampton East Docks – Waterloo	**73092**	*Queen Mary* – Cunard	*The Cunarder*
6	"	21.14	Southampton East Docks – Waterloo	Dsl?	*Queen Mary* – Cunard	
7	Tues 04-07-67	08.20	Waterloo – Southampton West Docks	*DNR?*	*Statendam* – Holland-America Line	*The Holland American*
	"	10.13	Southampton Central – West Docks	*80133*	*Statendam* – Holland-America Line	Detach from 08.30 Waterloo– Weymouth
8	"	10.07	Southampton East Docks – Waterloo	34093	*Rotterdam* – Holland-America Line	*The Holland American*

Bno	Date	Time		Loco	Boat/Shipping Co.	Notes
9	Tues 04-07-67	16.52	Southampton West Docks – Waterloo	D1926	*United States* – United States Line	*The Statesman*
10	"	17.38	Southampton West Docks – Waterloo	*73037*	*United States* – United States Line	
11	Wed 05-07-67	08.54	Waterloo – Southampton West Docks	34025	*United States* – United States Line	*The Statesman*
12	Tues 04-07-67	14.25	Southampton West Docks – Waterloo	*73092*	*Fairsky* – Sitmar Line	Late extra on daily alterations
13	Wed 05-07-67	xx.xx			*Caribia* – Siosa Line	Missing from notices. Non-runner.
14	"	13.31	Southampton East Docks – Waterloo	*34037*	*Castel Felice* – Sitmar Line	Late extra on daily alterations
15	Thurs 06-07-67	07.45	Waterloo – Southampton East Docks	*Dsl?*	*Queen Mary* – Cunard	
16	"	08.20	Waterloo – Southampton East Docks	34021	*Queen Mary* – Cunard	*The Cunarder*
17	"	08.54	Waterloo – Southampton West Docks	73092	*Fairsky* – Sitmar Line	
18	"	11.20	Waterloo – Southampton West Docks	34037	*Fairsky* – Sitmar Line	Sitmar Line– Australia
19	"	10.59	Southampton Docks – Waterloo	34089	*Caribia* – French Line CGT	Late extra.
	"	13.27	Southampton East Docks – Waterloo	73092	*Flavia* – Siosa Line	
20	"	17.41	Southampton East Docks – Waterloo	34025	*Carmania* – Cunard	
21	Fri 07-07-67	08.20	Waterloo – Southampton East Docks	34089	*Caribia* – Siosa Line	
22	"	08.54	Waterloo – Southampton East Docks	34025	*Castel Felice* – Sitmar Line	

Bno	Date	Time		Loco	Boat/Shipping Co.	Notes
23	Fri 07-07-67	11.20	Waterloo – Southampton East Docks	**E6002**	*Castel Felice* – Sitmar Line	Sitmar Line– Australia
	"	15.33	Southampton Central – East Docks	4-TC	*Caribia* – Siosa Line	Detach from 13.30 Waterloo– Weymouth
24	"	16.00	Waterloo – Southampton East Docks	**D6510**	*Carmania* – Cunard	
	Sat 08-07-67	10.57	Southampton Central – East Docks	**80152**	*Prins der Nederlanden* – Royal Netherlands	Detach from 08.35 Waterloo– Weymouth
25	"	18.20	Waterloo – Southampton East Docks	34037	*Rotterdam* – Holland-America Line	*The Holland American*
26	"	10.29	Southampton West Docks – Waterloo	*Dsl?**	*Aurelia* – Cogedar Line	
27	Sun 09-07-67	11.07	Southampton East Docks – Waterloo	34021	*Ellinis* – Chandris Line	
					** Cancelled as steam special. May have been re booked to diesel or not run.	

KEY

Bold Type - Loco known to have worked or booked to work this train.
Normal Type - Loco probably worked this train.
Italics- Loco possibly worked train or possible ship where unknown.
Bno- Boat train running number

Withdrawal of rebuilt 'Light Pacifics' January to May 1967

In order of being taken out of service:

34088 – Withdrawn week ending 19 March, *213 Squadron* is last recorded as working a boat train from Waterloo to Southampton Docks on 16 March. As it ended its days at Nine Elms it presumably worked back to London with another boat train or empty stock, either the same or the following day. It was withdrawn straight away.

34077 – Withdrawn week ending 26 March, the last duty for *603 Squadron* was a probably a ballast train out of Guildford on the night of Monday 20 March. It then ran light to Eastleigh for repairs but was withdrawn straight away.

34071 – Withdrawn week ending 30 April, the last day's work for *601 Squadron* was on the 26th of that month. It worked Guildford 165 duty, mainly van trains, starting with the 03.18 from Woking to Fratton, including the 16.51 passenger from Basingstoke to Salisbury and ending at Eastleigh in the early hours of the following morning.

34056 – Withdrawn week ending 7 May, the last train for *Croydon* was the 07.18 from Waterloo to Salisbury on Thursday 27 April. It was taken out of service due to valve gear problems and broken piston rings.

34044 – Withdrawn week ending 21 May, *Woolacombe* had not worked since the first of the month. It hauled the 12.20 special passenger train from Waterloo to Weymouth, the 18.05 special back as far as Southampton Central and then retired to Eastleigh shed.

The following locomotive were theoretically in service during the last weeks but stopped for repairs:

Withdrawn week ending 25 June, in order of last day in traffic:
34047 – The last work for *Callington* was possibly the 14.00 special freight from Southampton Docks to Feltham on Thursday 11 May. It was stopped at Feltham with Tender bearing problems and was towed light engine to Nine Elms for disposal on 27 June.

34098 – *Templecombe* is last recorded as working the first part of Guildford 165 diagram on Friday 19 May. This started with the 03.18 vans from Woking to Fratton, then the 10.15 vans from there to Basingstoke and finally the 16.51 passenger train from Basingstoke to Salisbury. It was stopped for repairs to boiler tubes but did not work again.

34104 – The last known work for *Bere Alston* is the first part of Nine Elms 136 duty on Sunday 21 May: 03.35 vans from Waterloo to Portsmouth and Southsea and empties to Fratton, then light engine to Eastleigh. After that it worked to Salisbury somehow, but faults with boiler tubes and steam brake caused its demise.

Withdrawn week ending 2 July:

34040 – Another locomotive with Boiler tube problems, *Crewkerne* last worked on Friday 2 June. It had started Nine Elms 148 diagram, the 07.05 Basingstoke to Waterloo and the 11.05 vans back to Basingstoke. It was towed light engine from there to Eastleigh on 8 or 9 June for further repairs but did not work again.

Acknowledgements

I would like to thank the following people for providing help and/or contributing information to this book:

Graham Aitken, Don Benn, John H. Bird, Jim Boudreau, John Braybrook, Steve Brentnall, John Clifford, Paul Cooper, Martin Elms and the Bluebell Railway Archive, The late Barry Fletcher, Dave Postle and The Kidderminster Railway Museum photo archive, Peter King, Bjorn Larsson (Maritime Timetable Images), Tony Leaver, Paul Little, John McIvor and the Nine Elms website, Roger Merry-Price, Chris and Richard Norris, The late Ray Ruffell, Ian Simpson, Colin Stone, John Tyler and Peter Underwood. Also Geoff Burch, Alex McClymont & Lew Wooldridge, formerly footplate crew of Guildford steam shed. Thanks also to Richard Peirce for being my Devil's advocate and to his son Christopher for teaching us oldies how to buy photographs from Ebay!

The following provided information and photographs:

Jim Blake, Alan Hayes, Keith Lawrence and Keith Widdowson.

Thanks also to the others who have allowed me to use their photographs (FlickR photo sharing pages in brackets, if any):

The Rail-Online website, Ernie Brack (Ernie's Railway Archive), Professor Stefan Buczacki (Professor S B), Jonathan Greenwood (Tiptree Jon), Dave Harvey (Unfathomable), Derek Jones (Glawster Oldspot), Al Kennett (D1015), Jon Knight (jonL1049H), Dave Lennon (Dallam Dave), Dave Mant (Dave58282), Dick Manton (Gricer1946), Gerald T. Robinson (Gerald T Robinson), G. W. Sharpe, Mike Sheridan, Andrew Southwell (4486Merlin), George Woods (George of Dufton), Bill Wright (Barking Bill) and Christopher Yapp (yappchristopher) .

Bibliography

The following publications have been used for research:

Southern Steam Surrender – John H. Bird, Kingfisher Railway Publications 1987
Southern Steam Sunset – John H. Bird, Runpast Publishing 1992
'Waterloo Sunset' supplement in *Steam Railway Magazine* – John H. Bird 1992
Southern Steam Finale – Barry Eagles, Waterfront Publishing 2002
Decline of Southern Steam – Michael Welch, Capital Transport Publishing 2007
Ramblings of a Railwayman – Geoff Burch, Self Published 2011
Further Ramblings of a Railwayman – Geoff Burch, Self Published 2013
The Great Steam Chase – Keith Widdowson, The History Press 2013
Round the Horne Scripts – Barry Took and Marty Feldman, Futura Publications 1975
Southern Steam Operaions 1966-67 – Ian Simpson, Crecy Publishing Ltd 2017

Permanent locomotive diagrams.
Daily alterations to locomotive diagrams.
Weekly special notices.

Railway Observer, Railway World, Railway Magazine
Steam Railway, in particular issues 328 & 329 Southern Rover articles – Marsh and Bobrowski and Issue 337 – End of Southern Steam commemorative issue.
Steam Days, in particular April 1995 Sunset of Southern Steam – John Heaton
January 1998 Dorset at the End of Steam – Colin Stone
July 2017 Southern Steam Swansong – John H. Bird

The following internet sites were also used:

Blood and Custard
National Archives of Australia
Solent Maritime Society magazine 'The Scanner'
Timetable Images (Maritime)
Six Day War
ESPN cricket info
Tennis Archives

BBC On This Day
That Was the Tear That Was 1967 (on FlickR)
Other FlickR pages
Photographs on Ebay
Online Encyclopaedias
BFI Screen Online